Praise for books by David Rice

The Dragon's Brood

(HarperCollins)

David Rice's *Dragon's Brood* is a marvellously fresh and immediate evocation ... He has a good journalist's sense of the core of a human character, and a gift for asking questions... His book achieves real depth. The belief that the Chinese care little about individual or human rights... should not survive these pages. Rice's eye is sharp and he has useful things to say about many important topics.

— Mark Elvin in The London Review of Books

Illuminating recorded conversations... with explorations of young people's views on all the issues which have been at the forefront of change. Rice's view of China is not a cheerful one... yet he maintains a justifiable spark of optimism.

—Colina Macdougall in The Times Literary Supplement

David Rice makes worthwhile reading... He accurately conveys the often touching despair of most Chinese surveying the wasteland of their recent past. He cleverly invokes their alternating pride in China's size and cultural heritage and their own sense of inferiority towards richer and freer westerners.

—Jasper Becker in The Times (London)

Where Jung Chang leaves off, David Rice takes over.

—Simon Scott Plummer in The Tablet

This intriguing book opens a wide window on the future which before long we will all have to meet and greet and mingle with... fundamental impression of truthfulness... my respect for an enjoyable, enlightening and important book.

—Tony Parker in The Sunday Times

David Rice has done a commendable job in capturing the spirit of the times.

—John Kohut in the South-China Morning Post (Song Kong)

I trust this book, because of what it says about Chinese faces.... Rice is a keen observer.

—Jonathan Mirsky in The Irish Times

The Dragon's Brood is a singular review of the thoughts and aspirations of a new generation of a people the West has too often misunderstood at its peril.

—Howard Rose in the Sunday Press

Song of Tiananmen Square

(Brandon/Mount Eagle)

Rice has written a gripping and all-too-realistic novel about the Tiananmen Square massacre and the events surrounding it.

—Chris Patten, last Governor of Song Kong

Utterly fascinating... powerfully affecting... lyricism and immediacy.

—Robert Farren in The Irish Times

David Rice has recreated the sights, sounds, smells and, above all, the emotions of Beijing in the spring of 1989.

—Jonathan Mirsky,
who reported the Tiananmen Square massacre
for The Observer

Shattered Vows

(Michael Joseph/Penguin; William Morrow NY; Blackstaff; Triumph Books; Ligouri Press)

Despite the anguish it portrays, *Shattered Vows* is an immensely heartening and encouraging book.

—Robert Nowell in The Sunday Times

Well documented and at the same time an outcry for changing the present disastrous policy.

—*Professor Hans Küng*

The unmistakable force and vividness that only real life can yield... The fruits of this patient listening are pictures we can see, and voices that speak to us.

—*Professor Uta Ranke-Heinemann,*
University of Essen, author of Nein und Amen

A call for candor on celibacy.

—*The New York Times*

This courageous exposé... provides powerful testimony. David Rice cannot be commended enough for his brilliant study.

—*Carol J. Lichtenberg in the Library Journal (US)*

I know no study... that compares with this. No one has researched the subject as well as David Rice. No one has listened... with such wisdom and sympathy.

—*Peter deRosa, author of Rebels;*
Vicars of Christ & others

His book has the convincing ring of truth... conveys an authentic impression... a very sensitive appraisal.

—*Dr Joyce M Bennett in the*
Church of England Newspaper

This book starkly says the Church is in crisis. Its author is well placed to know.

—*Michael Brown in the Yorkshire Post*

Kirche Ohne Priester

(C. Bertelsmann; Goldmann Verlag: German translation of Shattered Vows)

A book without hate or rancour and an important contribution to the celibacy discussion.

—*Kronen Zeitung*

Rice has established a well-founded scrutiny of the present situation.

—Braunschweiger Zeitung

The Pompeii Syndrome / La Sindrome di Pompei

(Mercier Press) (also Italian edition from Newton Compton, Rome)

The Pompeii Syndrome really grabbed me from the first page... it makes you wonder whether we really are in denial about catastrophic threat, because we refuse to believe in the possibility of our own extinction. My test of a good book is always the same - would I loan it to a friend with the proviso that they have to give it back? This definitely meets that criterion.

—Brenda Power in The Sunday Times

The Pompeii Syndrome is a genuinely terrifying, totally believable novel, because it could come true tomorrow ... What sets the story apart is the huge amount of research which underpins every paragraph. Rice has spent years studying the situation. He tells us - as the politicians never do - exactly what we can expect if we do not force our governments to change their policies before it is too late. Run, do not walk, to the nearest bookshop and buy a copy. Better still, buy copies for your friends as well.

—Morgan Llywelyn, author of The Greener Shore;
Grania; Red Branch & others

A taut thriller... scarily believable. *The Pompeii Syndrome* is fastpaced and explosive... page-turning and thoughtful – a must-read thriller.

—Cathy Kelly, author of Lessons in
Heartbreak; Past Secrets & others

Read this book or regret it till your dying day – which could be very soon...

—Paul Williams, author of Evil Empire;
The General (book & film), Gangland;
Crime Lords & others

Brilliantly narrated ... this is no ordinary novel, but 'fiction based on fact'... graphically portrays one route to mass destruction and the end of civilization as we know it. The 'Pompeii Syndrome'... may well enter the vocabulary alongside terms such as 'Stockholm Syndrome'. It refers to... denial in the face of impending catastrophe too awful to contemplate.

—*Louis Hughes OP in Spirituality magazine*

An absolutely gripping read.

—*Paul Carson, author of Scalpel;*
Cold Steel; Betrayal & others

The unthinkable becomes obvious. The moment when the obvious turns into reality, it is too late. And yet nothing changes. David Rice is the first one to put into words what many see coming but no one wants to see. Of course not. It would mean that something has to change. Now.

—*Mycle Schneider, international nuclear consultant, advisor to the official UK Committee on Radioactive Waste Management (CoRWM), and former advisor to the Belgian, French and German governments; winner of the 1997 Right Livelihood Award*

The Rathmines Stylebook

(Folens)

We are writing to be understood, and this book will help. Keep what you write simple and short and you can't go wrong.... When in doubt, refer to *The Rathmines Stylebook*.

—*Douglas Gageby (Editor, The Irish Times)*

Blood Guilt

(Blackstaff Press)

One of the best-timed releases in modern publishing. David Rice had no idea that in the very week of its publication the central question posed by the book would be on the lips of thousands... What becomes of a gunman when his killing days are over?

—*Evening Press*

The great strength of this novel is that it is in no way mawkish and escapes the sentimentality so many people associated with the 'struggle'. The central character is sufficiently authentic to have the reader identify with his personal odyssey. *Blood Guilt* is an insightful, imaginative and well-crafted novel... Highly recommended, especially for those who appreciate the difference between style and pretension

—*Connacht Tribune*

LOOK and grow Mindful

DAVID RICE first encountered Mindfulness when he was 13 years old. Except he didn't know what it was. Over the years that followed, he continually experienced what he called the Joy of Looking - savouring the wonder and beauty of the world around him. This was something that only could only happen in the Now (not in the past or the future). However living in the Now is the essence of Mindfulness, so the Joy of Looking led him directly there – into Mindfulness. He carried that Joy of Looking and the resulting Mindfulness into a monastery where he was for a time a Dominican friar, and then into his work as writer, journalist, photo-journalist and editor on three continents. In the 1970s he was an editor and Sigma-Delta-Chi award-winning syndicated columnist in the United States, coming to Ireland in 1980 to head up the Rathmines School of Journalism (later DIT). In 1989, recommended by the Thomson Foundation UK, he was invited to Beijing by the Chinese government to train journalists on behalf of *Xin Hua*, the Chinese national news agency, and to work as an editor with *China Features*. He was in Beijing during the Massacre of Tiananmen Square, and later returned to interview secretly 400 of the young people who had survived the massacre. This brought him to the attention of the Chinese security police. It also led to two books, *The Dragon's Brood: Conversations with Young Chinese* (HarperCollins), and the novel, *Song of Tiananmen Square* (Brandon/Mt Eagle). His books have been published in Britain, Ireland, Germany, Italy and the United States. Rice's No.1 best-selling *Shattered Vows* (Michael Joseph/Penguin) led to the acclaimed YTV/Channel 4 documentary, *Priests of Passion*, which he presented. He now lives in County Tipperary, Ireland, where he and his partner Kathleen direct the Killaloe Hedge-School of Writing *(www.killaloe.ie/KHS)*, to which workshops people have come from 19 countries. Through Killaloe Communications *(www.killaloe.ie/KCS)* Rice has taught communication skills for the University of Limerick, for Trinity College and for government and commercial organizations. He has degrees in *Sociology, Education,* and *German Literature* from the National University of Ireland (Galway); in *Community Development* from Southern Illinois University (Carbondale, Illinois); and in *Theology* from the University of St Thomas – The Angelicum (Rome). His main passion is still the Joy of Looking, which he now knows leads directly to Mindfulness, and indeed is an integral part of it, for it takes place always in the *Now*.

LOOK and grow
Mindful

David Rice

www.LookAndGrowMindful.com

KEEPER BOOKS

Published 2013 by KEEPER BOOKS through
FeedARead.com Publishing – with funding from
the English Arts Council

First Edition

A CIP catalogue record for this title is available from the
British Library

Paperbacks and eBooks are available from –

FeedAread.com
Amazon.co.uk
Amazon.com
Smashwords.com

Booksellers can order from –

Ingrams; Barnes & Noble; Easons;
Gardners; Nielsen; Bertrams, Argosy

Acknowledgements are on page 313

Starlings photo & cover design © 2013: David Rice

Contents

To
Kathleen
(*aka* Catherine)
who shares my love of
light and all that it reveals

What this book is about

The present moment is filled with joy and happiness.
If you are attentive, you will see it

~ Thich Nhat Hanh

THERE is a very special state of mind where we savour just the present moment, where we live in the *Now,* rather than being distracted by past or future, neither of which exist, except as wisps inside our head. This joyous state is called *Mindfulness.*

The past is gone forever: whether we like it or not, all we have left are memories, nostalgia, or regrets – all in the mind. Neither does the future exist, so all we have are hopes and anxieties about it, again within our mind.

But we really do possess the Now. It's all we've got, and all we need. As the turtle in *Kung Fu Panda* says:

> *Yesterday* is history; *Tomorrow* a mystery. But *Now* is a wonderful gift. Maybe that's why we call it *The Present.*

Mindfulness has been defined as 'an attentive awareness of the reality of things, especially in the present moment'. The reality of things?

Helen Keller once said the worst calamity that can befall us is 'to have eyes and fail to see'. We are surrounded by what we regard as 'ordinary' everyday things, like skies, trees, birds, fields, water. We take them for granted, if we notice them at all. But these things are far from ordinary. If we can learn to see them afresh, to become aware of how miraculous such things

13

truly are and to wonder at them, then we are beginning to touch their reality. Unfortunately we are so distracted by past and future that we rarely get time to grow aware and to wonder.

That's what this little book is about. I hope its various chapters may help us see, perhaps for the first time since childhood, what was always there, but we never perceived – the sheer splendour of this our earth – in our skies; in the sea; in our rivers and lakes; in our fields and forests; in our towns and cities; in living creatures; even in ourselves.

But especially at the edge of things – in the dawn where night meets day; in the twilight where day meets night; in the swerve of shore and bend of bay where land meet ocean; in the mountain tops where earth meets sky; in the hedgerows where field meets tree; in the spring where winter meets summer; in the autumn where summer meets winter; *in the clear night sky where we meet the Universe.*

If this book can call our attention to such things, so that the scales fall from our eyes and we become truly aware of them and intuit their reality, we may then begin to have a life filled with wonder, with joy – even with happiness, in spite of the pain and heartbreak life invariably inflicts. But it will also be a life of care for this wonderful earth and for the creatures that inhabit it – a life of Mindfulness.

There are many ways to grow mindful. One of the easiest is through just simply looking. But *really* looking, really seeing – and savouring what we see. Not just glancing and moving on. But contemplating. As Jon Kabat-Zinn says, 'Perhaps the most "spiritual" thing any of us can do is simply to look through our own eyes.'

This little book then is simply about the ordinary things around us, which we can see afresh so that they are no longer ordinary; in other words, it's about the sheer Joy of Looking. If we can reach such joy it will certainly bring us to Mindfulness.

There is one final chapter quite different from the rest: it is about the urgent need to introduce the coming generation to

Mindfulness, through which it could actually renew the face of the earth.

~ *David Rice*
Killaloe
December 2013

1: Let there be sight

Beauty is all about us, but how many are blind to it!
People take little pleasure in the natural
and quiet and simple things of life

~ Pablo Casals

Those who contemplate the beauty of the earth
find reserves of strength that will
endure as long as life lasts

~ Rachel Carson

Earth and sky, woods and fields, lakes and rivers, the mountain and
the sea, are excellent schoolmasters, and teach some of us
more than we can ever learn from books

~ Sir John Lubbock

Like a child standing in a beautiful park with his eyes shut tight, there's no
need to imagine trees, flowers, deer, birds, and sky; we merely need to open
our eyes and realize what is already here

~ Bo Lozoff

IT WAS a tackle in a hectic game of rugby, and the two 13-year-olds ended up face down in the sea of mud – mud resulting from months of scrums, rucks and mauls across a once-grassy pitch.

I was the one tackling and it wasn't a particularly brilliant tackle. But, as we sucked ourselves out of the mud, wiping it from eyes, nose and mouth, I suddenly noticed how the low winter sun had turned the mud silver. *Silver.* The whole boot-rutted expanse of mud gleamed and it was like hammered metal. It was quite astonishingly beautiful.

However I didn't realise this was beauty. I just liked what I saw. And at a rugby school in those days beauty did not come up for mention (except in regard to girls, and we never saw any of those, since this was an all-male boarding school). Besides, had I recognised it as beauty, I'd have kept my mouth shut.

Four years later, in my final spring term at that same school, we were on a route march with the school's local defense force and, as we tramped along a forest track, the command was given to halt. *At ease. Stand easy.* Down went the .303 rifles and we stretched and breathed the forest air.

I happened to look up at the canopy of beech leaves overhead, and I saw something I had never noticed before. The sunlight wasn't bouncing off the leaves, but filtering through them, so that each leaf lit up and glowed like a tiny green flame. It was as if the whole nave of trees where we stood was roofed with shimmering green fire. I have never forgotten the moment. This time I knew I was encountering beauty, and recognising it for the first time in my life.

I was experiencing the Joy of Looking, even if I didn't yet have words to express it. Indeed I was experiencing *Mindfulness* (triggered by that Joy), even though it would be many years before I ever heard the word.

I have seen that green fire many times since.

Fast forward to recent times, when I was at a writer's retreat in Devon. For some reason I don't remember, our lecturer took us down to the banks of a river that ran through a grove of trees, fresh in their green of spring. I looked up and once again saw the shimmering leaves, translucent in the sunlight.

'Isn't it amazing how those leaves glow, just like tiny flames?' I remarked to a young woman beside me.

She looked up and her eyes widened. 'Omigod, would you look!' She just gazed open-mouthed. Then she turned to me. 'You know something,' she said, 'I've never noticed that before.'

'You will again,' I said. 'From now on you'll never not notice it.'

The wonder in her eyes was a joy to see.

Failing to see

Many of us are like that young woman. Blind. Blind to the many-splendoured thing. Blind to the beauty and wonders around us. When Helen Keller, herself blind, was asked what was the worst calamity that could befall a person, her reply was, 'To have eyes and fail to see.'

Why do we fail to see? I believe there are several reasons.

First, and above all else, it is a failure of Mindfulness. Seeing can only take place in the *Now* – which is all there really is. The past no longer exists; the future doesn't yet exist. So if we spend all our time and energy living in the past or bothering about the future, *we are in a non-existent place.* And so we cannot see the marvels before our eyes this very moment, because we are not really here – our mind is elsewhere.

The trouble with the Now is that it keeps slithering away and becoming the past. Even the Now in which I wrote this sentence is already gone. We cannot grasp or hold it, but we *can* savour each moment as it passes, especially the wonders and beauty around us which each moment reveals. That is the Joy of Looking. And living that moment is Mindfulness.

The second reason we fail to see is that no one ever bothered to show us the miracles of the world we live in. Our parents were too busy to point them out.. Besides, they didn't notice them themselves, because their parents didn't point things out to them. And that was because their parents... Well, and so on. Tradition can be tricky.

The third reason we notice so little is that we are simply too busy. And if we're too busy to look, we're too busy. Writers down the centuries have warned us that the world is too much with us and that 'we have given our hearts away, a sordid boon'.

The fourth reason follows on this: I call it the Eiffel-Tower Syndrome. Or you can call it the Tower-of-London Syndrome if you like. Or the Statue-of-Liberty syndrome. Have you ever met a Parisian who has been up the Eiffel Tower? Or a Londoner who has gone to the Tower to see the Crown Jewels? Or a New Yorker who has stood in the Statue of Liberty's torch? Perhaps a school trip had dragged bored kids to such places, but did they ever return as adults?

In other words, if things are there all the time, whether they be Eiffel Tower or Tower of London, or the Statue of Liberty, or the magic of the hills and dales and skies around us, we tell ourselves we have plenty of time and that we'll have a good look at them some day soon. That 'some day' mostly never comes, and mostly we die unmindful, unvisioned and unwondering.

And nowadays there is one further reason for our blindness to the beauty around us — our addiction to electronic screens, be they smart phones, tablets, notebooks, or laptops. The reign of rectangles, I call it. I have to admit these same rectangles are one of the greatest boons of our modern world – I could hardly have written this book without my computer. It's our *addiction* that is the problem – when *all* our looking goes into rectangles instead of into the world around us.

A young soldier just back from serving in the Middle East told me of his arrival at a London railway station: 'Hardly a single person was looking up or looking around them,' he said. 'Almost everyone was looking down at whatever they held in their hand. Some were poking with their finger; others were just gaping with their mouths half open.'

Pining and longing

A friend of mine had a husband who was dying of cancer. He had worked hard all his life, planned for the future, read his newspaper and watched his television. She took him for one last trip in their open-topped MG around the Ayrshire coast. At one point, looking out over the ocean towards Ailsa Craig, he

20

sighed and said, 'Imagine having to leave all this.' He had only noticed the beauty around him when he was about to depart it forever.

Apparently this is not unusual. According to psychologist Rollo May, 'When people are on the verge of death they think, strangely enough, about beauty. Many of these thoughts are about how beautiful is this earth that they are about to leave.' Oscar Wilde caught poignantly this awareness of beauty before death, in his poem *Ballad of Reading Gaol*, about a man waiting to be hanged:

> I never saw a man who looked
> With such a wistful eye
> Upon that little tent of blue
> Which prisoners call the sky,
> And at every drifting cloud that went
> With sails of silver by. [1]

Writer and theologian Matthew Fox comments on all of this: 'How wonderful it would be if we incorporated this awareness daily into our lives before we die.' For *awareness* we can read *Mindfulness*.

When Spitfire designer Reginald J. Mitchell was dying of cancer, he received a last visit from the wife of his chief test-pilot and close friend, George Pickering. 'Don't let us talk about flying today,' Gladys suggested.

'Why should we?' Mitchell replied. 'There are more important things in the world than flying.' He gazed at his favourite flowers, all in full summer bloom. 'There is so much beauty all around us. I wish I had spent more time appreciating beauty. It is too late now, but tell George that there are more important things in life than speed. Tell him to look at the beautiful things while he has time.' [2]

Like those who are dying, people exiled from home often feel a longing for the loveliness of the landscapes they left behind. The fact that they are deprived of it seems to make them acutely aware of it, perhaps for the first time. Many writers express it: 'Oh to be in England, now that April's there' – 'I will arise and go now, and go to Innisfree.'

The men in the *Canadian Boat Song* longed for the mountains and seas of home: 'We in dreams behold the Hebrides.' So did Russian poet Yevtushenko, when he wrote: 'I rely often on this ordinary thought: near Lake Baikal my own town waiting for me. And the wish to see the pines again, mute witnesses of time and its distance.'

The men in the trenches of World War One had this longing for the fields and hedgerows of home, as even now do our soldiers in the Middle East. In *All Quiet on the Western Front,* Eric Remarque tells of the longing to see again an avenue of trees in the German village of his boyhood.

As an exile for some years in the United States I longed to return home to Europe and have grass outside my back door. I finally came home and I have that grass now. But do I relish it now as much as I once longed for it? I think I do. I hope I do.

Did the men from the trenches – those who did come home – ever wander among those fields and hedgerows they had longed for? Perhaps they didn't. Perhaps there wasn't the time to. But there is something we can learn from their longing, from the longing of all exiles. It is this: we who are blessed to have those fields and hedgerows and mountains and skies which they longed for, and many still long for, should rejoice in them with that same intensity with which they longed for them.

But we cannot rejoice in them unless we see them.

Gazing versus glancing

So the first step is really to see. For mostly we don't. We don't notice the wonders of all that lives and flourishes around us. We are blind, calamitously so, as Helen Keller said.

What do we mean by see?

We use our eyes in many practical ways – to walk through a doorway and not bump into the wall; to guide a car down a motorway; to read this book; to watch Man U score a goal on television. But is there more to seeing than just the mechanical registering of images?

Consider for a moment another of our five senses – hearing. We use our ears for practical things like having a conversation; listening to gossip; using a telephone; attending to an airport announcement. But we also use them for pleasure and joy – when we listen to music. Or to birdsong. But is there an equivalent to birdsong, for the eyes? I believe there is, but we have become blind to it.

That young woman by the river had seen beech leaves in sunlight before. But had she really *seen* them? Had she ever before been aware of how the sunlight filters through to create those tiny green flames? The wonder in her eyes that day suggests she was suddenly seeing them in an utterly different way. She was for the first time seeing their wonder and their beauty. Her eyes were opened. She was learning for the first time to gaze instead of glance. She was experiencing the Joy of Looking. She was encountering Mindfulness.

Most of us go through life seeing things and saying *So what?* What she said was *Omigod!* And the purpose of this little book is to try and change some of our so-whats into omigods. In other words, that we rediscover the music of the eye – to look with wonder at the wonders around us; sometimes even to look with awe; to see beyond the surface of things and encounter the mystery that underlies all things, living and non-living. If we can learn to do so, our lives will be incredibly enriched.

Enriched, how?

Einstein says it best: 'The most beautiful thing we can experience is the mysterious. It is the source of all true art and all science. He to whom this emotion is a stranger, who can no longer pause to wonder and stand rapt in awe, is as good as dead. His eyes are closed.' [3]

Plato put it another way, almost 24 centuries earlier: 'God invented or bestowed sight on us for this express purpose, that on surveying the circles of intelligence in the heavens we might... set right our own silly wanderings and blunders.' [4]

Perhaps if he had been aware of the teachings of Siddhartha Guatama Buddha, who lived a century before him in the East, Plato might have encountered the actual word Mindfulness (*Satipatthana*), for that was what he seems to have been on about.

Learning to look

An American friend living in the North of England told me of a visit he had from a twenty-year-old niece. He was dying to show her the beauty of Britain, so he and his wife drove her all through the Lake District. When they reached Grasmere, the exasperated young woman turned to them and said, 'Y'all listen here, now. Can't ya get it into your dumb heads – ah don't *do* scenery!'

It seems that shopping malls were what she 'did', and there weren't a lot of those in Grasmere.

I'd like to think that that young woman may some day 'do' more than that. Maybe her eyes will be opened, and she will grow, as William Blake put it, 'to see a world in a grain of sand, and a heaven in a wild flower.'

Many of us, however, are like that young woman. Yet we were not always so. As small children we were mindful: we noticed and marvelled at everything. But somehow our eyes clouded over with some kind of spiritual cataracts, and we now no longer see the things we once saw. They are still marvellous, but we fail to marvel.

If we can learn once more to see what is around us, to have the Joy of Looking and thus be mindful, all sorts of amazing things start to happen to us. We begin again to experience wonder, awe, and the serenity that that these bring to us even in the midst of the chaos and awfulness that surround us everywhere in the world.

Viktor Frankl, the Jewish psychologist imprisoned at Auschwitz, describes the saving grace of the few tiny glimpses of nature they managed to get in that hellhole – a little bird perched on a nearby twig; a sunset seen through a barbed-wire fence. The cover of Frankl's book, *Man's Search for Meaning*, shows a strand of barbed wire in close-up. On that wire perches a tiny finch.[5]

But first we must learn to look and really see. To gaze instead of glance.

If we can just learn once more to be mindful of the world around us, to really *see* it, the wonder and the awe will take care of themselves. Many years ago that great American conservationist Rachel Carson put it succinctly: 'For most of us, knowledge of our world comes largely through sight, yet we look about with such unseeing eyes that we are partially blind. One way to open your eyes to unnoticed beauty is to ask yourself, "What if I had never seen this before? What if I knew I would never see it again?"' [6]

There are lots of wonderful books on Mindfulness and how to acquire it (see below). This present book is simply on one particular aspect of it – namely the joy of opening our eyes to the physical world around us – whether trees or sky or ocean or mountains – and the Mindfulness that this brings us. I shall try to do this by sharing with you the wonderful things that *I* see around me, so that you, dear reader, may see them too. Or if you already see them, perhaps we can share our wonder together.

Suggestions

- There are several inspiring books on Mindfulness. Best are the simple, clear introductions by the acknowledge masters, Thich Nhat Hanh and Jon Kabat-Zinn. These are listed at the end of this book. These books can change your life.

- Next time you find yourself just glancing at something, try switching to gazing. In other words, give it your full attention for maybe just a minute. But don't say, I'll do it the next time. Next times rarely come. Do it now.

- Remember the Tower-of-London Syndrome? Why not pick out something special in your area that you've always intended to visit, but never got around to? And go there this weekend. You'll be glad you did.

- I have photographed many of the things described in this book. I should love to print the pictures here, but that would cost too much. However I have a marvellous solution – we've created a website for the book, so you can see the pictures there. Already there are hundreds waiting for you to look at, and I'll be uploading at least one new one every day as part of my blog. (There are 75,000 pictures on my computer, my best from a lifetime of photographing, so there should be plenty to draw upon!) Take a look – the web address is on the back cover.

- There's a place for your comments on the website... I'm hoping that the website along with the book could be the start of a worldwide dialogue on Mindfulness and the Joy of Looking. So do please post your views – anything you say will be welcomed. (I'll be repeating this invitation in several of the following chapters, simply because people like to dip into chapters at random, and might otherwise miss it.)

2: Explosion of trees

Next time, when you see a tree,
see if you can say Thanks from your heart

~ Thich Nhat Hanh

Trees are the earth's endless effort
to speak to the listening heaven

~ Rabindranath Tagore

The best time to plant a tree was twenty years ago.
The second best time is now

~ Chinese proverb

The wonder is that we can see these trees
and not wonder more!

~ Ralph Waldo Emerson

All around us are the growing trees to remind us
that leaf is almost synonymous with life,
for through their greenness we exist

~ Hervey Adams

IN THE northwest of Beijing is a park full of strange ruins. It is called Yuan Ming Yuan. The ruins are from an imperial palace that was destroyed by European troops at the end of the second Opium War in 1860. The park looks exactly like the old Willow Pattern we all know from grandma's plates, and may well have been the model for it – with shimmering lakes and little bridges to pavilion-crowned islands. Hundreds of willow trees line the margins of the lakes, their fronds dipping towards the water.

I walked there once with a Chinese girl called Song, and I recited for her a little poem I remembered from childhood, about the Willow Pattern plate:

> Two pigeons flying high,
> Chinese vessel sailing by.
> Weeping willow hanging o'er,
> Bridge with three men
> If not four

'You say *weeping willow*?' Song asked. 'We also think they are sad – because they mean farewell to us. See how those willow branches droop down and move in the breeze? For us they are lovers waving farewell with their long imperial sleeves.'

A few trees stand outside the car-park entrance to Auschwitz and they are hideous. Their bare limbs are contorted as if the trees had been tortured and are still in anguish. I doubt if a bird could bear to perch on one of their branches.

I wonder if those trees have somehow absorbed the awfulness of the place and if that has shaped them so. Or whether they have patterned themselves on the tortured souls who once existed there.

Some trees do indeed seem to mimic us, seem almost humanoid. Some have their branches raised to heaven in supplication; others spread their branches as if to shelter the world around them. 'When anyone asks me about the Irish character,' writes author Edna O'Brien, 'I say look at the trees. Maimed, stark and misshapen, but ferociously tenacious.'

When I was a boy my only interest in trees was whether they could support a tree house; whether they could be a source of bows and arrows; or could furnish the Y of a catapult; whether they were climeable or swingable – in other words, did they have a horizontal branch that could support a rope for a swing.

As I grew through my teens I began to realise that such horizontal branches, had been sometimes prized for supporting another kind of rope – the kind a hangman uses. I think it was Billie Holliday first put that into my mind with her song, *The Hanging Tree*, where she sings about a very strange fruit that hung from certain trees where she lived.

But it's not just in the Deep South that there were hanging trees. How many villages in Britain or Ireland have their Gallows Hill? Some of those hills are still topped by a tree, sometimes a very old one. As a youngster I would look at such an ancient tree and wonder did it ever bear that strange fruit. Probably more did than we realise. Indeed in ancient times a tree was sometimes called 'the horse of the hanged', and in Old Norse a gallows was known as 'a tree of terror'. So trees, like ourselves, can have their shadow side.*

Shape of trees

Of course teenagers can be morbid, and I eventually grew out of that phase. It was then I began to become aware of the marvellous shape of trees. At some point I realised they have the same shape as rivers. A tree has a trunk, which divides into branches, which then divide into smaller branches, then smaller again, until finally those branches end in tiny twigs.

A river is that in reverse – the Thames starts with tiny streams in Gloucestershire, which merge into babbling brooks, which themselves meet to form twenty tributaries, which then finally merge to form the great river that joins London to the sea.

What is fascinating is that this shape – which I now know is called 'dendritic', from the Greek word for tree – *dendron* – is one of the most prolific shapes in all of nature. The system of

---

* There's a bed-and-breakfast guesthouse near Bunratty in County Clare that calls itself *The Gallows-View B&B*. Hardly a cheerful title, but it does make my point.

arteries and veins in our bodies is dendritic, from the great central arteries to smaller veins all the way to the tiny capillaries under the skin, which are, so to speak, the twigs of the system.

Likewise our nervous system: the great central nerve running down our spine from the brain divides into multiple nerves which finally end in the tiny nerves at the tips of our fingers. Indeed the human body itself is dendritic – we have a trunk (we actually call it that, as if it were a tree); the trunk has four branches – our limbs – and each branch ends in five twigs – our fingers and toes. Indeed I suppose we could consider the tiny hairs on the back of our fingers as even tinier twigs.

So not only do trees mimic us, but we mimic trees.

Throughout nature

The dendritic shape is repeated all through nature. Watch a flash of lightning: far from having that zig-zag shape we find on electrical warning notices, it has usually a curling main shaft, often of wondrous brilliance, which descends into snaking tendrils which break into smaller ones just before they hit the earth. Rather like an tree turned upside down.

Well, that's how it seems, but I'm told lightning actually moves upwards from earth to sky, functioning rather as the roots of a tree.

Indeed it's interesting that a tree root is the tree itself in reverse – with the small tendril roots feeding nourishment back up to the main root and thence to the tree trunk. Even the geranium on your windowsill is dendritic, with the main stem ending in all those lovely red blooms, and reversed in the root down inside the pot.

Our ancestry too is dendritic – don't we talk of a 'family tree'? Way back in the mists of time some ancestor of ours (the trunk) had a few children (branches), who presumably had children of their own (branches again), and ditto all the way down to ourselves, who are the twigs on a very large tree indeed.

In fact the anthropologists can go all the way back to a little lady they call Lucy, who lived 3.2 million years ago at Hadar in Ethiopia. She wasn't quite human, but getting there. But I'm getting out of my depth here, except to say that they called her after the Beatles' song, *Lucy in the Sky with Diamonds*. Anyhow if we can't quite trace ourselves back to Lucy, I suppose we've got Adam and Eve. Or do we?

Even a cracked window is dendritic, as you will know if, as a youngster, you ever threw a stone at a window. I did, so I know.

When Robert Frost came to where two roads diverged in a wood, and 'took the one less traveled by', that was dendritic. For, further down that road, he would have come to another fork, maybe even with three roads, and would have had to make a further decision. And so on for all his life. Like the rest of us. But, as he said, it was that first decision that 'has made all the difference.' Which means that even our decision making is shaped like a tree.

The popular concept of viral marketing is dendritic. It's copied from that extremely effective living organism – the virus. Let's say I sneeze and my flu virus infects five people. Each of them infects five more, so now we have 25 snivelling victims. Each of those infects five more, so it's now 125. Then 625, then 3,125. And so on.

Viral marketing is based on the same cheery concept – you tell five people about your product; they each tell five more, who also tell five, who also tell five, so that very soon the graph is exponential. Well, at least in theory. Maybe we could try it with this book...

Even my research for this book is dendritic. If I read one source book it gives me references to other sources. Each one of those sources gives me further references. And so on. It can so easily get out of hand, and it's even worse with the Internet and all the links it throws up. Really one has to learn the

31

optimum point to shout stop, for research can go on and on forever. It's probably why far too many post-grad students never get to finish. They don't know where to stop. Indeed it's why this book nearly didn't get written.

So trees are not just things that whirl past us as we drive down the highway: their shape is in all of our lives, indeed within our own bodies, and indeed our minds. It's even in Scripture – 'I am the vine; you are the branches.'

The tree is one of the most magnificent shapes we can ever look upon. That shape is actually a slow-motion explosion. Trees inhabit a different time scale to ourselves – their time is measured in decades or even centuries. So we don't see their explosiveness.

But imagine an oak tree growing before your eyes in the space of a few seconds – erupting out of the ground, bursting into branches, spreading up and out into that massive mushroom shape. And then think of the tiny acorn from which this explosion came. It's almost nuclear.

Maybe that is what Anthony de Mello had in mind when he wrote, 'If you look at a tree and see a tree, you have really not seen the tree. When you look at a tree and see a miracle – then at last you have seen!' [7]

My late friend Rebecca Millane used to be fascinated by the trunks of trees. She said you could see faces in them. And indeed, under her tuition, I began to see them too. Mostly glaring, gnarled old faces with bulging eyes, straight out of Snow White.

But I am also fascinated by the colour and texture of tree trunks. The peculiar peeling paper of the silver birch makes me want to run my fingers over its surface.

We think we know the colour of tree trunks – they are all brown, are they not? They certainly aren't. As American writer John Kord Lagermann wrote: "If you were painting trees, what colour would you make the trunks? Nine out of ten people would make them brown or black. Those are the conventional colours. In reality tree trunks are purple, gray, yellow-green – just about every colour including brown or black.' [8]

Winter trees

I often think winter is the best time to see a tree. It may at first seem dismal, its branches 'bare ruined choirs, where late the sweet birds sang', as Shakespeare puts it. But the joy is that there is no foliage to hide its superb lineaments, and you can see the trunk rising into branches and those branches dividing and finally rising into twigs.

And when you see such a tree silhouetted sharp and black against a soft glowing evening sky, you realise are looking at one of nature's most marvellous creations. Once you see that combination of hard against soft, black against colour, you will look for it again and again.

It can be magnificent with scots pines. Although they don't lose their foliage in winter, they do lose their lower branches as they grow, so you get these wonderfully tall bare trunks capped at the top with foliage. A stand of scots pine seen against a sunset is hard to forget.

If you see a row of bare winter beech, set close together, it often looks as if some giant gardener had clipped their tops with a mighty shears, in a gently undulating scallop pattern. It can be one of the most satisfying sights of a winter landscape.

Then there are the wind-swept trees of the Scottish isles and Connemara. Battered for years by Atlantic gales, they can look so gaunt and bleak and bent that they almost evoke pity. Yeats caught it well: 'The old brown thorn tree breaks in two, high over Cummin strand, under a bitter black wind that comes from the left hand.'

Trees can indeed evoke emotion: a massive oak can evoke awe; a palm tree can make us long for tropical beaches; a lone tree in the middle of a field can suggest mystery – the mystery of why it was never chopped down.

We know why, of course. Bad luck would attend anyone who dared to chop it down and burn it.

Sacredness of trees

Trees have always had vestiges of the sacred. In almost every civilization trees have been gazed upon with reverence, as having a spiritual presence. It's easy to understand why, with their branches reaching towards heaven and their roots penetrating to the underworld, uniting above and below.

The oak was sacred to the Celts – indeed the word 'druid' is derived from *doire*, the gaelic word for oak tree. When the Celts cleared a woodland they always left one great oak tree in the centre of the clearing – the *crann bethadh* – and it became their Tree of Life.

The sacredness of trees reached its greatest embodiment in the Nordics' *Yggdrasil*, the World Tree, a gigantic ash tree that held the Universe together. That tree finally came to a nasty end, however, being chopped down and used to burn Valhalla, in *Götterdämmerung* – The Twilight of the Gods. Well, Wagner said it did, anyhow.

Vestiges of all this remain with us today, with our holly and mistletoe and even our Christmas tree – and of course that unwillingness to chop down and burn a lone tree in a field. As Kipling puts it: 'Ailim [elm] be the lady's tree; burn it not or cursed ye'll be.'

And if it's all just nonsense now, can anyone explain how, in almost every country in the world, from Britain, Ireland, France, Germany, to Sri Lanka, India and Nebraska, people still hang tokens on trees, from holy medals in Europe to blue medicine bottles in Trinidad, to coloured rags on Korwa trees in India?

Not that we need to do that, but the more we encounter trees and grow aware of them, the more we will gaze upon on them with fascination, and indeed with reverence. We will grow mindful of them.

I once had an experience with a tree which I have never told about before. And I'm still slightly embarrassed to tell it. But it did happen. It was very early spring, and I had parked my camper van in a lonely clearing in a forest somewhere in

34

Ayrshire. I was all alone except for my beloved camera and the full moon filtering through the delicate first foliage.

Around about midnight I had this urge to go walkabout, in the rustling moonlit night. At one point I came to the massive trunk of a tree that soared above me into the moonlight. For some reason I stopped dead, and simply stayed gazing at the tree. Then, I don't know why, I put my arms around the trunk to embrace it. Not that my arms went far around it, for it was massive.

Then I began to feel, somehow, in touch with the essence of the tree. I could nearly say, with the spirit of the tree, but that might be going too far. But it was a spiritual experience, one that I had never had before, nor have ever had since. It lasted for about ten minutes, but I have always felt different about trees since then.

And, by the way, just in case you're asking – the answer is No. I hadn't been drinking.

Suggestions

- 'When you live next to a tree, you become its neighbour' – words of Thich Nhat Hanh. Find a tree near where you live and get acquainted with it. In other words, watch it at different times of the year – see its shape when bare in winter; watch the winter's buds come into their own; wait for that first delicate green; see it explode into foliage. Then watch those leaves turn russet or yellow in autumn. In other words, make a friend of a tree. And you needn't put your arms around it if you don't want to.

- When travelling by train or car, look at the trees as they pass you by. You'll be astonished at their variation. But not of course if you are actually driving the train. Leave it to the passengers.

- If you want to fall in love with trees, get Lewis Blackwell's *The Life and Love of Trees*. Details in Bibliography.

- There are also Tony Russell's *Nature Guide to Trees,* from Dorling Kindersley, and *Collins Complete Guide to British Trees.* Both are brilliant for identifying the different trees. Details in Bibliography.

- But don't be worried if you don't know the different kinds of trees. After all, you can enjoy music without knowing what an arpeggio is (see Chapter 24).

- Google Images for *Lightning* to see the dendritic shape at its most spectacular.

3: Our magic sky

Feelings come and go like clouds in a windy sky

~ Thich Nhat Hanh

Glory be to God for dappled things—
For skies as couple-coloured as brindled cows

~ Gerard Manley Hopkins

A certain recluse, I know not who, once said that no bonds attached him to this
life, and the only thing he would regret leaving was the sky

~ Kenko Yoshida

Excuse me while I kiss the sky

~ Jimi Hendrix

Clouds come floating into my sky
no longer to carry rain or usher storm
but to add colour to my sunset sky

~ Rabindranath Tagore

In the sky there is no distinction of east and west

~ The Buddha

IT WAS one of those storm-torn winter twilights when a long, flat cloud was scudding westwards across the sky, low down near the horizon. The top edge of the cloud frothed like an angry sea.

As I watched, the spike of a crescent moon came slowly up out of the cloud. It seemed to be racing eastward against the cloud and, as it sliced through that angry sea in the sky, it was the dorsal fin of a great white shark. I was watching a shark in the sky.

That was many years ago – probably around the time of the film *Jaws,* which was probably why I was aware of great whites just then. But I have never forgotten the magic of that darkening sky. And again and again since then I have seen that speeding fin among the clouds. I call it my 'shark moon'.

I have often told friends about my shark moon. And some of them now see it for themselves. They even look for it, whenever a crescent moon and scudding storm clouds meet together in a twilit sky. Perhaps you too have seen it.

My shark is just one of many critters that inhabit our skies. I encountered a dinosaur there too, once, as a cloud curled down and became the head and jaws of a T-Rex, and the sun behind it became its glowing eye. I even have a photograph of the brute. I have seen the face of an old man up there. I once saw a great white bird, half the size of the sky, that made me think of the giant Roc in Sinbad the Sailor.

Mighty canvas

However you don't need to be as daft as I am to see things in the sky. It gives us the sun, the moon and the stars; it gives us the rainbow, and the lightning; it gives us the growing glow of dawn and the fading fire of sunset. It gives us the great Vs of geese honking northwards, and the black whirlwinds of starlings as they wheel above our lakes and rivers.

But, above all, it offers us clouds.

I often think of the sky as a mighty canvas on which God or Nature (whichever you're into) paints her abstract creations of blue and white and crimson and gold, then wipes them out and starts all over again. She rests only at night, leaving the stars to take over.

> WOULD one think it possible for a man to delight in gauderies like a butterfly, and neglect the Heavens? Did we not daily see it, it would be incredible. They rejoice in a piece of gold more than in the Sun; and get a few little glittering stones and call them jewels. And admire them because they be resplendent like the stars, and transparent like the air, and pellucid like the sea.
> ~ Thomas Traherne (1637-1674), English poet, mystic, philosopher

I am not trying to be poetic – quite literally, the sky above us is the greatest of all spectacles that the human eye can behold. We simply don't notice it because it's always there, and for that reason we are no longer mindful of it.

And every few minutes or so it changes.

I remember once standing in a supermarket car park gazing up at a breathtaking sky of towering, anvil-topped orange clouds. I wondered did anyone else even notice it. Passersby noticed *me*, all right, giving me what I call The Look. What's *he* gaping at?

Could I have been the only one really enjoying the vastest spectacle known to mankind? Hopefully not, but certainly no one else seemed to notice the sky. I thought, what a waste, because never, in a billion years, will that same sky ever appear again.

Although a sky can look so permanent, most clouds last only a few minutes, according to cloud expert Gavin Pretor-Pinney. In his wonderful book, *The Cloudspotter's Guide,* he talks of a cloud reaching 'the ripe old age of 10 minutes'.[9]

Have you ever watched a cloud die? It can be eerie. Try it. On a day of blue sky with white fluffy cumulus clouds, there's often a lonely little wisp of cloud all on its own, as if chucked out into the blue by the big boys. It was once as big and puffy as they still are, but it has now shrivelled to this. It's doomed.

Just keep watching as it gets thinner and thinner and becomes almost transparent. It's nearly invisible now, and no one else could even see it. But you can, because you have been watching it from the start and still know where to look.

Then, *pouf*, it's gone. As if it never was.

Sometimes I wonder is it a little lesson in life and death. For those corpulent, comfortable, cumulus clouds will all come to this – shrivelling to nothingness in a lifetime of a few short minutes.

Actually you can become quite an expert in predicting which poor cloud is next for the great fade out. You develop an instinct for it, and it can be fun.

Many of us in northern Europe envy the blue skies of the Mediterranean. They're fine for a 10-day holiday, but they can be boring to live under permanently. Photographers call a cloudless sky a 'bald' sky. I lived for some years in Italy but, while I loved every minute of it, I longed for the mighty maritime clouds of western Scotland or Ireland.

I remember once hearing an Austrian tourist in a Connemara pub, boasting about the towering Alps of his country. Finally a little old fellow in a tweed cap could take no more of it. 'That's all well and good,' says he, pulling on his pint. 'But our clouds are bigger than your bloody mountains.'

Sky colours

During the Battle of Britain the RAF painted the underside of their Spitfires and Hurricanes 'sky blue'. It was a tad optimistic, as the skies in these islands are not that given to everyday blue. Although all the colours of the rainbow are there, even when the rainbow itself is not.

Our skies are what Yeats described as 'heaven's embroidered cloths, enwrought in gold and silver light.' In the course of one 12 hours, a sky can lighten at dawn with pale egg-shell green, then draw in streaks of yellow, then orange, then gold, then the grey or white or blue-with-white-clouds of midday (with the blue directly overhead so strangely dark).

Talking of dark, there is nothing quite as beautiful as a sheer black storm sky, especially when a stray shaft of sunlight picks out a grove of trees or a hillside, or a church tower, or a celtic stone cross, or even a house, and lights it up against the angry blackness.

I particularly love those April days when showers chase each other across otherwise blue skies. It is lovely to sit in warm sunshine watching a distant, dark curtain of rain sliding across the horizon, reaching from cloud to earth, and drenching some poor wretches at a comfortable distance from me.

Then at evening comes the salmon. If nature is in a kind mood, she can give us those incredible clouds with the underbellies glowing in pure salmon-pink evening light. I can never forget one magic twilight at the Cliffs of Moher in Western Ireland, when a mist stole in from the ocean and engulfed us. Then, quite suddenly, the dying light found some last wonderful warmth, and we found ourselves enwrapped in a salmon-pink mist.

By coincidence, just as I have written this paragraph, I look out my study window, and the salmon clouds are back – slender graceful things, each almost the shape of a salmon. And the River Shannon below my window has turned salmon pink to match. I must put this on hold while I stop to watch.

A sunset without clouds can have its own amazing subtlety. Let your eye move gently from the high blue downwards towards the horizon. As your eye descends it passes over a lighter blue, then perhaps a pale egg-shell green, then a pale yellow, then orange, then maybe a final fiery red. But the extraordinary thing is that it is almost impossible to distinguish the point where one colour gives way to the next. It is one of nature's subtlest achievements.

Altered landscapes

In the last twenty years or so, we have succeeded in making what must be the greatest and most global alteration to the appearance of our landscapes that the world has ever seen. And we weren't even trying to do so.

I mean contrails (short for 'condensation trails') – or vapour trails – those white streaks that can extend for 300 unbroken miles across the sky, and which have made those skies look completely different from any other skies in history.

In other eras people managed to alter landscapes, but it was with deliberate intent and stupendous effort. Like building the pyramids. Or spanning the Firth of Forth with that mighty bridge. It takes time and colossal effort to change the picture that nature has painted.

Not any longer. The whole sky is now a giant canvas, and our various airlines, with Airbus for airbrush, can in a few short minutes paint the most colossal designs man has ever seen, designs measured in hundreds of miles.

I cannot make up my mind whether to mutter at the arrogance of it – and the pollution of it, to boot (whatever boot is) – or whether to sit back and admire the sheer beauty of many of the effects unintentionally achieved.

For contrails can be lovely. I have seen them salmon pink at morning. Or as tiny white railway lines across the sky. I have seen them threads of spun gold in the setting sun. I have seen them black by moonlight. At other times they have been feathery white and wind tossed, unravelled to a breadth of a mile or more, as lovely as a daytime Milky Way.

And always there are the purposeful, finely-etched new contrails – you can watch them actually being born. They come into being with all the purpose and purity of youth – fine, clean, and unwavering, straight as a die across the sky.

Yet within a few short minutes those fine lines have flirted with the winds, coarsened, grown fat and bloated, wavered and lost their true direction. It is as if all our lives were compressed into a few short moments, and were depicted up there in the sky for the world to see on Judgment Day.

Had there been contrails at the time of Christ, would we now have a parable about lines in the sky, rather than about seeds falling among thorns?

Sometimes a fine, sharp new contrail can be like a needle stitching up the clouds; other times it is an accusing javelin poised to be hurled to earth by Wotan.

I can watch contrails for hours on end. Sometimes it is hard to grasp that those inching little lines are actually being drawn across the sky at nearly 10 miles a minute, and that, if we watch for only five minutes, we are looking at a line fifty miles long.

I find myself watching an infinitesimal change in direction, or a waver and return on course, and I wonder if it reflects some slight adjustment of the automatic pilot, or some tiny human pressure on wheel or pedal. Does that 20-mile waver in that white line tell me that the pilot merely reached for a cup of coffee?

Contrails must be a pain in the ass to film makers, especially when they are doing a period piece on location. I mean, how can you have the Injuns charging against a sky where a twenty-first-century contrail is neatly uncoiling itself?

The first time I ever saw a contrail was so many years ago I hardly dare think. I had been dragged as a reluctant child to some open-air theatre in Regent's Park to see *A Midsummer Night's Dream*. I was bored out of my mind, until I leaned back and looked up to the sky in frustration.

There, creeping slowly across that twilit sky, was a fine white line. It kept on and on and on, and I was mesmerized. Was it a vision? A miracle? Some giant with a fine-point brush? I didn't know, but I knew I was no longer bored.

Mostly I love contrails, for having brought so much fun into the skies. But sometimes I'd like just like them to leave me alone for a while. It is then that I realize there is no escaping them. My partner and I might be camping in a lonely forest clearing, rejoicing that the world is far away. We lean back to look at the deep blue sky but there, sneaking silently over the treetops comes a contrail, and we realize we are not alone. We never can be.

Up there ulcerated executives are pawing at their laptops or smart phones; a baby is yowling; someone is doing a dance outside a loo; a fat man is ogling a stewardess; a stewardess is mopping up a spilt beer; a pilot is muttering unintelligibly about knots, headwinds, turbulence and seatbelts; and some greedy so-and-so is pressing the bell for his fifth martini. And none of those people up there are even aware that they are making a contrail.

Sundown

They tell us we should never look at the sun. But there is one time when we can – when, rarely enough, the evening mist transforms it into a gentle flat orange disc slanting down the western sky. It's the only time you can actually watch the sun sink, and it is wonderful to see.

The orange disc seems to spin as it sits directly on the horizon for what seems an age, but is really only seconds. Then it slides slowly, inexorably downwards into the sea or behind the hilltop. Now half the disc still shows, like a section of orange. Now it seems to speed up – a quarter shows now, then an eighth, a sixteenth, until finally there is the tiniest spark atop the horizon. Then, *pouf* – it's gone.

Something magic can happen at that precise moment. It is something very rare, and many a seafarer has waited all his life to see it. I saw it once, but it was at dawn, not sunset. I was flying the polar route from Seattle to London, and I was looking out of the sleeping Boeing 747 waiting for the sun to come up out of the ice-locked ocean. The glow grew beyond the horizon and I was trying to guess exactly where the sun would emerge. I waited, watching.

Suddenly the whole sky flashed dazzling green, for just an instant, so bright it dazzled me and seemed to fill the sleeping cabin. It was gone so fast that I wondered had I imagined it. I called a passing stewardess and asked had she seen the flash of green light. She didn't know what I was talking about and gave me The Look.

It was only years later that I read about *The Green Flash*. I had seen something only a handful of people ever see, and almost always at sunset. I know of very few who have seen it at dawn. The Green Flash is a phenomenon that scientists are still discussing and some aspects of which are still unexplained.

Suggestions

- Next time you see a rainbow, take a look at the sky inside the bow. You will notice that it is a lighter colour than the rest of the sky.

- Get hold of *The Cloud Spotter's Guide* by Gavin Pretor-Pinney.[10] It will tell you all you could ever know about clouds, in a light-hearted way that will fascinate you. Details at end of the book.

- When you are watching a sunset, look away for a moment, seeing it with the side of your eye. Then look back. For some reason, doing so makes it all the more lovely.

- Next time you see a contrail (vapour trail), watch it until it goes out of sight. And count how long that that takes. Remember it is being written in the sky at nearly 10 miles a minute. So if you watch one for half an hour, you could be looking at something 300 miles long – one of the world's biggest man-made creations.

- If you want to see a green flash for yourself, just type *Green Flash* into YouTube. But it's nothing compared to the real thing. One of the best websites is by Andrew T. Young of San Diego State University:
  http://mintaka.sdsu.edu/GF/

- If you are having a children's party (and if the weather is right!) why not try a game of cloud spotting? Youngsters can find all sorts of things up there, from dancers to dragons. Or how about guessing which clouds are about to disappear? Or why not just be scientific and identify cirrus and strato-cumulus? Using *Cloud Spotter's Guide*, of course.

4: Forty shades of green

My limited and abstracted art is to be found under every hedge,
and in every lane, and therefore nobody thinks it worth picking up

~ John Constable

Take a walk outside – it will serve you far more
than pacing around in your mind

~ Rasheed Ogunlaru

If the sight of the blue skies fills you with joy,
if a blade of grass springing up in the fields
has power to move you, if the simple things
in nature have a message you understand,
Rejoice, for your soul is alive

~ Eleanora Druse

I have long been interested in landscape history and, when younger and more
robust, I used to do much tramping of the English landscape in search of
ancient field systems, drove roads, indications of prehistoric settlement

~ Penelope Lively

The force that through the green fuse drives the flower, drives my green age;
The force that drives the water through the rocks, drives my red blood

~ Dylan Thomas

WHEN I was a child we used to go on lots of picnics. Our Dad and Mum would spread a couple of rugs on the grass, and we all sat on the rugs. No chairs or anything. There'd be sandwiches and a thermos flask of tea and maybe a few buns and a couple of apples. Nothing much really, but we children looked forward to those picnics. I always remember them as being in bright sunshine, and always in some lovely field.

We chose a different field every time. I think that's when I fell in love with fields.

Indeed I became a connoisseur of fields to picnic in. I particularly loved the ones with the gorse, blazing yellow with that coconut aroma in early spring. And maybe on a slope with a view over a river. Or alive with wild flowers. Or with a stream we could dam with stones and sods of earth. Or redolent of mown hay in autumn.

I'm a bit unsure if we got permission to go into these fields – maybe farmers didn't much mind in those days, or maybe we just took a chance.

However I do remember one occasion when taking a chance went a wee bit wrong. I was only four, and we were holidaying in a place called Craig Farg in Perthshire. My mother had just lifted my brother and me across a gate into a hilly field. Maybe the rattle of the gate had something to do with it, but suddenly over the brow of the hill thundered a herd of highland cattle. My mother simply threw my brother and myself back across the gate and vaulted over it herself. (She was very athletic.)

From that on I think we always checked for cattle before selecting a field to picnic in. But I never lost my love of fields.

However as I grew towards maturity I began evaluating fields differently, no longer as places to picnic in, but to make love in. So now it was no longer a field with a view I appreciated, but one without one. One with thick hedges and lots of bushes. And hay to tumble in. Much of it fantasy, of course.

Fields in person

Fields are the little places of the earth. Places that no one knows except perhaps the farmer who works them, and where no one ever walks except that same farmer. Places that whirl past a railway-carriage window and are gone – seen by millions yet trodden by few. But often lovelier than any manicured

Luxembourg Gardens or Hyde Park – lovely with that spontaneous beauty only rural nature can yield.

Many of these fields have their own personal names. Ask any farmer. There'll be the Callow Field, Jones's Field, the Upper Mead, the Well Field, the Heather Field, the High Pasture, the Grange Field, the Paddock, the Big Field, the Long Meadow, the Railway Field, the Half-Acre, the River Field, the Hill Field.

And those fields are loved. If you want to know just how fierce that love can be, read John B. Keane's play, *The Field*, or get the film on DVD. The love of a field can lead to murder.

Sometimes I like to imagine that fields have personalities of their own. A lush field of ripening barley, with the breeze making patterns as it plays across its surface – such a field, if it could feel, would surely feel as proud as a woman with beautiful tresses. There are comfortable, motherly pastures, giving their breasts to their cattle. There are mean, scary fields, with hidden corners that might conceal a bull.

There are seductive fields that beckon – come right on in and have a tumble in my hay. There are no-nonsense paddocks concerned only for securing the horses entrusted to them - you can usually tell them by their wooden fences. There are plush Jane-Austin parklands that still reflect the arrogance of their 18th-century masters. And there are those sad, damp, hungry fields, with their little clumps of rushes and a few miserable, gnarled old trees to mark their edges.

The ones I feel most sorry for are those fields pushed far up the side of a mountain – the last of the green before the rocks and heather. I find myself thinking of some tenant farmer of times gone by, toiling up a hillside with one more load of seaweed, trying to coax one last half acre of tillage out of a harsh mountainside.

Daft ideas? Maybe. But maybe I'm not the first to have them. After all, have we not all heard of 'hungry grass'? Or 'a smiling meadow' ?

I don't necessarily have to traipse through the whole field to enjoy it – besides, I'm still slightly scared of cattle. There are fields I can view from the roadside; there are low hedges to look across; and there are gateways to look through. Indeed a gateway into a field can sometimes be a window into considerable beauty.

The song sings of forty shade of green. I've counted them, and there are lots more. One of the most beautiful of all landscapes is the patchwork quilt of little fields on the side of a hill: there's the speckled tweed of a meadow rich with the wildflowers of spring; beside it, the green of a grazed pasture with its black-and-white polka dots of Frisian cattle; then a brilliant yellow patch of rapeseed; sewn into the quilt next to it, a square of rich brown corduroy that is a newly-ploughed field with gleaming ridges; then the brilliant lincoln green of a lately fertilized field. And in places the little lines of gorse licking like flames up the sides of the hill, as though the edge of the quilt had caught fire.

Then that same hillside in late summer, when the gorse is gone and the bright waving gold of ripened barley lies alongside the matt beige of a cut field dotted with wheels of hay; and the brown corduroy field now turned beige corduroy from the lines of drying hay; and the polka dots still grazing on a now faded green.

Talking of polka dots, I once saw a field of grain which was yellow with black dots. The black dots turned out to be crows, and when I approached they all rose together into the air in a cawing black swarm. I suddenly realised I was seeing what poor Vincent Van Gogh saw, and then painted, shortly before he killed himself. I managed to get a picture of it, but I fear it is not exactly in the same league as Van Gogh's painting. (Sure I'll put it up on the web anyhow.)

David Hockney is one artist who has captured the sheer joy of fields. Some of his landscapes are quite simply the quilts I have been talking about. Just google his name on You Tube

Images to see what I mean. Especially look at *The Road to Thwing* and also *Garroby Hill*. They're all there, and lots more.

My favourite field of all is an enormous bright green acreage on the hill across the Shannon from where I now live, a field which is for me the epitome of the smiling meadow. It is even distracting me as I write this. For it is changing, not by the season but by the second.

As I watch, a cloud comes fast over the hill, and its shadow comes racing down the field, changing the surface to darker green where it passes. I watch it come across the river, come up the hill towards me, momentarily darkening the grass below my window before it is gone. And another shadow is coming fast behind it.

Author Carl Van Doren writes about an almost identical experience in Connecticut. He was sitting on a secluded hillside outside the cabin of a retired Yankee farmer, half blind, who nevertheless called his attention to the cloud shadows coming across the valley. 'If you watch,' the old man said, 'you will see how these shadows keep the valley always changing. Some days they are very leisurely. Today they go like the wind. They are my moving pictures.'

'As I looked,' Van Doren writes, 'another shadow broke over the ridge of hills, rolled down the long slope, turned the row of maples a darker green, swept solidly across the swamp and meadow, and went by us with what I almost thought was a swish. I half caught my breath... A quiet old man who could barely see small objects at hand still saw so much that he had, for me, added a new spectacle to nature.' [11]

That field across from me is always changing, whether or not there are clouds. One morning I noticed a strip of lighter green and, when I put binoculars on it, I saw there was an electric fence and cows were grazing the strip. Every day from there on the cows were on a different strip of the field, and their grazing could change its colour in a couple of hours.

My field also changes from morning to evening. As the sun moves westward it picks out the gentle contours of the surface, revealing a texture invisible in the light of morning. And at evening the shadows of the hedgerows extend across the sward like long fingers. The sight of those shadows always recalls for me the words of Cardinal Newman:

> O lord
> support us all day long until the shadows lengthen
> and the evening comes
> and the fever of life is over and our work is done

For some reason there invariably come to me Laurence Binyon's heartbreaking words, honouring those who have died in fields – battlefields – like my uncle Peter Paul Rice, whose grave in France I have yet to find:

> They shall grow not old, as we that are left grow old;
> Age shall not weary them, nor the years contemn.
> At the going down of the sun and in the morning
> We will remember them

That is a prayer surely meant to be uttered in a field. And where else but a field of battle?

By the way, 'my' field is not mine at all – I don't own it. Still I find myself calling it my field – perhaps because I have such a relationship with it, and I get so much out of it – perhaps more than its owner does.

Fields aglow

Look at a field in the late evening, when a low sun is slanting towards you rather than behind you. Perhaps you've noticed a curious phenomenon when you do. The field seems to glow, and is no longer green, but almost yellow. Well, yellow-green anyway.

There is a simple reason for this. Remember what we discussed about a beech leaf lighting up and glowing when sunlight shines through it? Well, when evening sunlight touches a field on its way towards your eye, each single blade of grass behaves as that leaf: it lights up and becomes a tiny yellow-green flame.

No wonder then a field glows when it is between you and the evening sun – it's millions of tiny flames. (Actually it's worthwhile picking up a blade of grass and holding it up to the sunlight to see this actually happen.)

The total effect is heightened if there has been rain or if there is dew on the grass, for then millions of tiny water droplets each transmit the light and become miniscule sparkles.

The painter Constable was probably the first to be mindful of these phenomena, and was considered revolutionary 200 years ago. He was of course mocked for it at the time, and the tiny specks of white paint which he utilised to suggest those sparkles were ridiculed as 'Constable's snow'.

Edges are hedges

The dairy products in our supermarkets often carry an idealized picture of fields gracefully curving around hill and dale, topped with a rising sun, and sometimes with a few contented cows. The less the product has to do with real dairy products, the more likely we are to get the cows.

Almost always these pictured fields are set between elegant hedgerows. For many busy and hard-pressed people, unfortunately, looking at such a picture across the breakfast table is maybe the only time we ever notice hedgerows. Yet the edges of a field – usually hedgerows – are often the most fascinating part of any field. Wordsworth called them 'little lines of sportive wood run wild'.

The very earliest hedgerows were simply lines of woodland, deliberately left as markers by Bronze-Age farmers, and some of these are incredibly still with us today. There is a hedgerow in Cambridgeshire, known as Judith's Hedge, which is believed to be more than 900 years old.

However the planting of hedges in both Britain and Ireland took place mostly at the time of the Inclosures, from about 1750 to 1860, although it had been going on sporadically for centuries, especially in England.

No matter how lovely hedgerows are today, they have had their shadow side, inasmuch as they are partly the result of brutal landlords confiscating common land, fencing it in, and evicting people from their homes. As an anonymous verse from 17th century England puts it:

> They hang the man, and flog the woman,
> That steals the goose from off the common;
> But let the greater villain loose,
> That steals the common from the goose

Be that as it may, the results today are universally positive. Hedgerows are actually living things – indeed they are often called 'living fences'. While a typical one begins from a man-made bank of earth and perhaps stone, along with the ditch from which that earth was dug (which often serves for drainage), the shrubs and trees planted on and around the bank quickly take over and form the living hedgerow.*

But there is far more life in a hedgerow than just the shrubs: in fact it is home to an astonishing proportion of our wildlife, including most of the little creatures beloved of Beatrix Potter, from bats to birds to squirrels, rabbits, voles, mice and hedgehogs.

The hawthorn alone supports 200 species of insect. Willow and oak are home to 400 species of insect and mite. The hedges provide nesting for more than 50 species of bird in Ireland, with the higher branches used as song posts for singers like the blackbird.

---

* While in Britain the ditch is the channel and the raised bank is the dyke, it is the other way around in Ireland— you climb a ditch and fall into a dyke. However both words come from the same Germanic root.

It is also a 402,000km-long network of travel corridors for wildlife, since many creatures avoid open fields and travel only along the hedgerows, using them as sheltered causeways. That's the total length of hedgerows in Britain, with a further astonishing 327,000 km in Ireland.

Some of the loveliest sights around hedgerows are in their margins where mowing machines cannot reach, and where there flourish plants that need a lot of shelter. There you find the ferns, the mosses, the cow parsley, angelica and hogweed, with the foxgloves and primroses clinging to the banks just above them. These are among the true joys of spring and summer.

It was the selfishness of the landlords that created these glorious hedgerows: once again, it is the selfishness of today's landowners that is removing those same hedgerows, in their drive for unbroken acreage for intensive farming. In spite of legislation and protest, the bulldozing still goes on. According to *The Independent* newspaper, the overall length of British hedgerows fell by 26,000 kilometres between 1998 and 2007.[12]

Land without hedges

There are of course some parts of these islands where there are hardly any hedgerows at all, nor perhaps ever were. Many such places come to mind – the Scottish Isles, parts of the Cotswolds, the Aran Islands, Connemara, the Burren in County Clare. A certain Captain Ludlow is alleged to have said of the Burren: 'Where there are no trees to hang a man. Where there is not enough water to drown him. And if you finally succeeded in killing him, it's too rocky to bury him.'

Be that as it may, the same Burren manages to sustain astonishing wandering herds of wild goats. But then goats can eat anything, and they always seem to find the pockets of green between the rocks.

But the folks in such places nevertheless managed to divide up their fields very well thank you, using the stones that lay everwhere. And while I feel sorry for the poor wildlife that has no hedges to hide in, it has to be said that those stone walls have their own remarkable beauty. They are known as dry-stone walls, meaning presumably that no cement holds the stones together. Yet they are constructed so skilfully that they endure centuries of storm without ever crumbling. They are most beautiful at evening, especially along a hilltop silhouetted against a sky, with the last golden rays of the setting sun peeping through the gaps between the stones. At such times they look as if they have no weight at all.

The Cotswolds' honey-coloured limestone gives the region's stone walls a special beauty of their own, so that they almost glow at sundown. As artist Hervey Adams wrote many years ago: 'The sun seems captured in the stone... Not only does the pervading quality of light gather it easily into its mood, but all the delicate half-tones that lurk in the recesses and shifting vapour of clouds find their response. The passage of a few hours may evoke a sequence of harmonies varying from dove-grey and lavender to purest gold. And how gold it can look against the snow's contrasting whiteness!' [13]

But whether it be dry-stone wall or shimmering hedgerow teeming with wildlife, these beautiful barriers are what make unique the landscapes of these islands of ours. A hedgerow should not be a thing that just whirls past a car window. Nor is it just the edge of something else, be it roadway, field or golf course. It is an object of beauty and fascination in its own right.

A hedge is for sauntering by, where we stop to gaze at its ferns and primroses in spring or to pick blackberries in autumn; to feel the texture of its damp moss; to get a fleeting glimpse of a yellowhammer; to listen to a thrush or blackbird on his high perch, bursting out that first fine careless rapture; to see the shy hedgehog or watch the silver-washed fritillary fritter his few hours away. And also to admire the wonderful way it is constructed, and to remember the poor folk who toiled to put it there, and to be grateful to those who maintain it today. Both we and our wildlife owe so much to our hedges.

I remember once flying into Shannon Airport, returning for a visit to Europe after years in the United States – when the 747 banked I had the illusion that the wingtip might touch that marvellous patchwork of tiny fields and hedgerows far below. I almost felt a voice say, 'All this could be yours.' And I replied, 'Yes, and someday I may make it so.'

Some years later I did just that. Not by buying those fields, but coming to live among them. Best decision I ever made.

Suggestions

- An invaluable little guide to hedgerows is Jane Eastoe's *Hedgerow and Wildlife: Guide to Animals and Plants of the Hedgerow.* [14] Details in the bibliography.

- If you want to know more about hedgerows in Ireland, take a look at David Hickie's book, *Irish Hedgerows: Networks for Nature.*[15] Details in the bibliography.

- If you feel our fields are threatened, why not join *FOES* – Fields of England Society. It describes itself as 'a new unpretentious, no-frills society formed to enable all members to become part owners, and to have access to, their own small piece of so-far unspoilt natural countryside.' Just Google *http://fieldsofengland.com/*

- If you want a quick introduction to the beauty of Irish fields, just Google (Images) *Fields of Ireland.* Then Google (Images) *Fields of Britain.* Trouble is you may stay with the computer images and forget to go out. Don't.

- Thomas Ryan RHA, past president of the Royal Irish Academy, has some truly beautiful paintings of the Irish countryside. You can see some of them by googling *Thomas Ryan artist.*

5: Mindful of mountains

A mountain is completely natural and at ease with itself,
however strong the winds that try to batter it,
however thick the dark clouds
that swirl around its peak

~ Sogyal Rinpoche

The heights charm us, but the steps do not;
With the mountain in our view
We love to walk the plains

~ Johann Wolfgang von Goethe

And did the Countenance Divine,
Shine forth upon our clouded hills?

~ William Blake

Should one faint by the way who gains the blessings of one mountain day
Whatever his fate, long life, short life, stormy or calm, he is rich forever

~ John Muir

THE Scottish soldier had wandered far away and soldiered far away, and was now dying among the green hills of Tyrol. And he was stricken with grief, 'because these green hills are not Highland hills, or the island hills, they're not my land's hills... they are not the hills of home.'

At one time the Irish writer Sean Ó Faoláin was thinking of settling down in the southern United States. He wandered among the marvellous mountains of New Mexico, but finally decided to return home. The reason was similar. As he tells it in his memoir, *Vive Moi*, no matter how enticing those hills were, they were not the hills of home:

> If these mountains had associations we did not know them; if history – that is, if some sort of purposeful life, other than that of missionaries or explorers ever trod this vastness – it had left no vibrations for either of us.
>
> There in the darkness we made up our minds. We belonged to an old, small, intimate and much-trodden country, where every field, every path, every ruin had its memories, where every last corner had its story. We decided that we could only live in Europe, and in Ireland..[16]

How is it that, more than anything else, hills are what exiles remember from home? Perhaps one of the reasons in the past was that hills were the last of the old country to sink beneath the sea as the ship ploughed westwards. But I believe there is more to it than that. I think that every culture has a fixation on its hills and mountains. 'I will lift up my eyes to the hills, from whence cometh my help,' the Hebrew psalmist says. There is an eighth-century poem which Japanese children know by heart:

> I started off along the shore
> The seashore at Tago
> And saw the white and glist'ning peak
> Of Fuji all aglow
> Through falling flakes of snow

Considered one of the greatest poems in Japanese literature, it tells of the wonder felt by Yamabe No Akihito when he saw Mount Fujiyama for the first time. William Blake, too, saw his mountains as trodden by God: 'And did those feet in ancient time, walk upon England's mountains green?' Which words have since become one of the most splendid anthems of all time.

Part of life

I think perhaps mountains are more a part of our lives than we realise as, with so much else of the wonders around us, we have learnt to take them for granted.

Yet they are still so much part of us even if we are no longer mindful of them. The Wicklow Mountains are a purple backdrop to the end of Georgian streets in Dublin; the Pentland and Lammermuir hills, and the Lothians, nudge Edinburgh. Manchester and Sheffield are close to their Peak District; Belfast has its Cave Hill. There are few cities in Britain or Ireland that lack at least a line of hills along a horizon.

In Ulster, where I spent a part of my childhood, on the border of counties Armagh and Down, there is a valley that stretches all the way from Newry down to Carlingford Lough. At the end of that valley rears Sleive Foy, otherwise known as Carlingford Mountain. It is not high in alpine terms, but wonderfully sculpted, almost like Vesuvius, with its conical shape and flat serrated top, and we children used to think it was an extinct volcano. Perhaps it is – I don't know for sure. But that lovely shape at the end of my valley, which I saw every morning from my bedroom window, is with me to this day, every time I remember my childhood. It is part of me.

It is somehow comforting to know we have our high places, even if we visit them hardly half enough. Sometimes I pity the inhabitants of Holland: they may have all those dykes and windmills, but they haven't got mountains. Nary a hill to walk up. When folks from such places visit us, they seem to take to the hills at the drop of a hat. (Visiting Dutch youngsters love racing their bikes down a hill – an experience they don't have at home.)

Well, perhaps not quite all such folks take to the hills. I know one idiot from a flat part of Europe who gets as cross as two sticks whenever he finds himself anywhere near mountains. But I think it's because he can't stand anything bigger than himself.

61

Taking to the hills

A mountain can be either climbed or looked at, but not always both at the same time, as I'll try to explain below. Climbing a mountain is one of the mighty experiences in life. I know no greater euphoria than crossing one hidden ridge after another to finally stand on the mountain peak, clawed at by angry winds and gazing down at the valley below, where tiny humans do their tiny things.

Somehow it puts things back into proportion. As Nietzsche said it, 'He who climbs upon the highest mountains laughs at all tragedies, real or imaginary.' This idea is wonderfully portrayed in a painting by 19th century German romantic painter Caspar David Friedrich. For the details, see Suggestions at the end of this chapter.

The joy of climbing a mountain is this very change in perspective, along with the sense of achievement and the feeling of conquest. But it is not necessarily the Joy of Looking. Indeed you can go up a mountain and hardly see it at all. I once went up Mount Errigal in mist, and saw only the boulders over which I clambered.

And even on a clear day a climber may not really see the mountain. Just as the thread in a tapestry cannot see the tapestry's pattern, likewise a tiny human on a mountainside may not get much sense of the mountain itself.

I went up Vesuvius a couple of years back and all I remember are the cinders under foot and the stench of the sulphur (which even made foul our coffee). But when later I stood in the forum of Pompeii and looked out at Vesuvius rearing in the distance, I shivered in awe at its majesty, and remembered the terrible things it had done. And may well do again. Indeed that very moment gave me the inspiration for my recent novel, *The Pompeii Syndrome*.

In other words, if it is a matter of looking at mountains, distance can enhance. Which should give consolation to the many who, for whatever reason, are unable to climb. Mountains can be enjoyed from the plain, and indeed can look their best from a distance. Perhaps the greatest paean ever written to distant mountains was written by Hillaire Belloc in *The Path to Rome*. He had been hiking to Rome in 1904, and this is his first glimpse of the Alps from the slopes of the Vosges:

> For there below me, thousands of feet below me, was what seemed an illimitable plain; at the end of that world was an horizon, and the dim bluish sky that overhangs an horizon. There was brume in it and thickness. I saw between the branches of the trees in front of me a sight in the sky that made me stop breathing, just as a great danger at sea, or great surprise in love, or a great deliverance will make a man stop breathing....
>
> I looked through this framing hollow and praised God.... One saw the sky beyond the edge of the world getting purer as the vault rose. But right up – a belt in that empyrean – ran peak and field and needle of intense ice, remote, remote from the world. Sky beneath them and sky above them, a steadfast legion, they glittered as though with the armour of the immovable armies of Heaven.... Here were these magnificent creatures of God. I mean the Alps, which now for the first time I saw.... Up there in the sky, to which only clouds belong and the last trembling colours of pure light, they stood fast and hard; not moving as do the things of the sky....
>
> To what emotion shall I compare this astonishment? So, in first love, one finds that this can belong to me. [17]

On a smaller scale, but still impressive and sometimes breathtaking, is the first sight of the Magillacuddy Reeks from Ireland's N21 heading south to Killarney. The road comes gently over the Glanaruddery Hills near Knocknagoshel and suddenly, as if a curtain had been pulled back, the horizon is filled from end to end with the magnificent mountains of Kerry. Sometimes they are flat and mauve and distant; sometimes their contours and valleys are textured by morning sunlight; after rain they can seem so close that you could run your hand across the soft nap of their flanks. But they're at their best in winter sunlight, when the snow on their high places gleams as brightly as Belloc's mighty needles of ice.

The hills are alive

Incidentally, height doesn't seem to be essential to the beauty of mountains. The Alps or the Himalayas inspire awe. Smaller mountains perhaps do not, but they can inspire love. The folks of Beijing truly love their Fragrant Hills, and throng there in their thousands, so that you have to walk on upward forest tracks for miles, just to be alone.

I went there once with Song – her of the willow trees. As the bus approached, the forested foothills lay layered in ever fainter shades of mauve, one behind the other, flat like a Chinese silk painting. It was a warm Autumn afternoon and the slopes with their Buddhist temples were swarming with people picnicking under the trees. We passed through the crowds and found a forest track leading upwards.

Finally there were no more people. It was an easy climb, and birds were singing and the forest murmured all around us and the light filtered through the red and yellow leaves that still remained on the branches over our heads. There was the fragrance of warm earth about us, and the leaves under our feet crunched and crackled like tiny Chinese crackers.

Song stretched up to a branch to pluck a yellow maple leaf. I can see her stretching still, and I can still see the wonder in her face as she sat there on the carpeted track, holding the leaf against the light so that it glowed and its skeletal tracery showed like a golden X-ray. She looked at me and uttered in English the words of the old Tang Dynasty poem:

> Deeper yet deeper into the mountains go;
> Drain every beauty there of hill and dale

It is not just the Chinese who love little mountains. Even the gaelic word for a hill, *droim* – literally 'a back' – suggests affection for a little crouching creature, which many small mountains resemble. The poet WB Yeats, recovering from illness in Italy in 1927, tells of his love for some nearby mountains: 'These mountains under their brilliant light fill one with an emotion that is like gratitude,' he writes. 'The mountain road from Rapallo to Zoagli seems like something in my own mind, something that I have discovered.'

The mountain which Yeats loved most is, of course, the one below which he is buried, and which inspired the lines –

> Under bare Ben Bulben's head,
> In Drumcliff churchyard Yeats is laid

To see Ben Bulben in the rose light of early morning or under a cirrus sky, or silhouetted at evening, almost like Table Mountain magically transported to Sligo, is to understand why Yeats saw it as mystical – a mountainside where a great door opens each night and superhuman horsemen ride down upon the countryside like the Valkyries. (I have a really lovely photo of the mountain which I'll be putting up on the website.)

A friend of mine loves Ben Bulben simply for its marvellous shape. But he told me he cherishes all the different shapes of hills and mountains in these islands of ours: 'I just love to run my eyes over their curves and contours, like running my eyes over the curves of a beautiful woman.'

Holy mountains

The beauty and wonder of mountains have made people throughout the world view some of them as sacred. The list of holy mountains is astonishing, and many are still objects of pilgrimage for various faiths.

There is Glastonbury Tor, associated with Gwyn ap Nudd, King of the Underworld, and now a place of Christian pilgrimage which legend suggests Jesus might have visited; Croagh Patrick in Ireland, sacred to the ancient Celts, now associated with Saint Patrick, and climbed by one million people from around the world every year; cloud-capped Mount Olympus, home to the Greek gods; Machu Picchu, once sacred to the Incas; Mount Sinai, where Moses received the Ten Commandments, sacred to Jews, Christians and Muslims; Ayers Rock, sacred to the native Australians; Mount Shasta in California, sacred to the Wintu tribe; Popocatepel, sacred to the Nahina Indians of Mexico; Everest, God of the Sky to the Nepalese; Mount Fuji, named after the Fire Goddess Fuchi, and sacred in Japan to both Buddhism and Shinto.

In almost every case we can understand how these mountains became holy: the beauty and sheer drama of their appearance, morphing marvellously with the season, the weather, the time of day, must have been literally awesome to the early peoples who saw them. However they can be equally awesome to us today, if we but open our eyes and gaze upon them, as Yeats gazed so mindfully on Ben Bulben.

Changing mountains

I think the real marvel of mountains is this astonishing ability to change their appearance. I remember the first time I visited Connemara, I wondered what all the fuss was about. Sure, there was heather, and gorse and yes, mountains – twelve of them, to be precise. The Twelve Bens. But they looked rather ordinary mountains – not terribly high, and no dramatic shapes either.

But the next time I came, those mountains had become magic: they were purple, insubstantial, ethereal, and almost part of the sky, and the peaks grew fainter one behind the other, exactly as mountains do in an oriental painting. And they were dwarfed by some of those massive cumulus clouds of the West, rearing up from the Atlantic seaboard. It was then I understood what artist Paul Henry spent his life trying to capture.

Actually this fading of hills in mist or at evening is one of landscapes loveliest achievements. Chinese and Japanese painters, instead of making hills smaller with distance, often made them simply fainter. They were perceptive in this, for hills often show their distance in that way. Sometimes they can seem almost like flat scenery on a gigantic stage, one backdrop set behind another, each one always fainter.

Perhaps the greatest testimony to how weather can change a mountain comes from Japanese artist Hokusai's *Thirty-Six Views of Mount Fuji*. Here we find that classic conical mountain capped with snow; but then we get The Red Fuji, bathed in the glare of a dying sun; then a dark, sinister Fuji racked by lightning; a gleaming all-white Fuji seen through cherry blossom; then a bleak grey Fuji emerging from a sea of fog. And of course the one we all know – that distant Fuji, glimpsed through the cruel claws of *The Great Wave*.

It's sad that nowadays pollution hides Mount Fuji for days on end, so that it is a source of joy when it does appear. I once passed near it on the Bullet Train, and my Japanese companions kept telling me, that's where Mount Fuji would be, if we could only see it.

I did eventually manage to see Fuji – well, its flank anyhow. My friend Jim Watkins and I had taken a bus up the side of the mountain to a snow-bound chalet-type inn two-thirds way up. All the way through fog. My luck as usual.

But shortly before the bus left for home there was a gasp and then a cheer from the crowd of Japanese tourists milling around the inn – the mist was lifting. It lifted like a giant napkin being peeled away, and there, for 10 glorious minutes, through the bare black branches of the trees, the gleaming mountainside above us was revealed, all the way to the peak.

It was one of those precious moments.

The virgin & the monk

Do mountains have personalities? I'm not suggesting they are alive, even though folklore does sometimes see them as sleeping giants. But we seem to react to them as if they were. My favourite three are side by side in the Alps – the Jungfrau, the Eiger, and the Mönch. Local cynics say God had a very good reason to put the Eiger between the Jungfrau and the Mönch: for *Eiger* means ogre; *Jungfrau* means a virgin; and *Mönch* is a monk.

But certainly looking at some mountains can affect our mood. I have felt acute melancholy among the mountains around Glencoe in Scotland. But perhaps that was because I was aware of the treachery enacted there on 2 February, 1692, when Campbell men of the Earl of Argyll slaughtered their hosts, the McDonalds of Glencoe. Was it just in my head? Or have those mountains absorbed some of the horror of that happening, just as Auschwitz seems to resonate with the things perpetrated there?

Maybe. Who really knows?

Certainly many people feel euphoria simply from gazing upon mountains, as Belloc clearly did. Others feel awe, reverence even – as must surely be the case when one gazes at Everest. I can only guess, as I have not yet been there.

Mount Evil

Only once have I feared a mountain. That mountain is Mount St Helens, in the US Pacific Northwest. There was a time I used to hike on and around it; I whitewatered on the rapids of the Toutle River that flows from the mountain; I rented boats on Spirit Lake at the foot of the mountain, from an old fellow called Harry Truman, who had a pink Cadillac of which he was ever so proud.

In early 1980 Mt St Helens began erupting. Then its flank started swelling at the rate of a metre per day. The sheriff ordered everyone to evacuate the area but many refused, including Harry Truman.

Then, on 18 May, 1980, at 8:32 a.m., the mountain blew its top. Literally. One cubic mile of it rose into the air, crashed down into the lake, creating a tsunami that swept down the Toutle valley carrying all before it. And burying forever, under many metres of rock, Harry and his pink Cadillac, along with more than 50 other people.

Among them was a young news photographer whom I knew and admired. Reid Turner Blackburn worked for the Vancouver *Columbian,* and had been asked by *National Geographic* to camp across the valley from the mountain and monitor its behaviour. His last words were a frantic radio call – 'Vancouver, this is it!'

He was never seen again.

I was one of the reporters covering the event for a U.S. newspaper. I flew in over the devastation, which to my dying day I shall never forget. Here is part of the report I filed that day for my newspaper:

'The pilot banked and side-slipped his powerful plane like a fighter, dropping to see if a logging tower was still standing, if trucks there had survived the onslaught. At Twelve Mile Camp, log trucks lay piled together deep in the mud, toys thrown by some monstrous child.

'House roofs peeked out through the mud. The outline of cars could be seen in the slime. Were there bodies in them? God only knows.

'Great lumbering Huey helicopters thudded their way through the ashen murk that hung above the devastation; the more agile Hughes 500s slipped in and out of the clouds of ash, in a scene straight from *Apocalypse Now.*

'As our Piper Twin Comanche moved up this terrible valley toward the mountain, it looked as if snow had again covered the surrounding hills. But it was an evil grey thing that covered everything, unlike any snow that ever was, and it embalmed hills and rocks and the flattened trees in a ghastly ashen mockery of the snow that such a short few months ago had made lovely this spot.

'And the mountain rose monstrously above the havoc it had wrought, vomiting its filthy burden at the sky.

'To ensure that ash would not foul the engine and endanger the plane, at Spud Mountain the pilot banked and headed back towards Kelso. As we passed in a wide arc over the devastated Toutle valley, the sun caught the great swathe of slime and the mud glinted in the sunrays. For an instant it looked like a golden causeway leading to the mountain. The black triangle of the mountain reared up at the end of the causeway and, from its now-blunted apex, there ascended, straight up to the sky, black, oily, coiling, boiling, pulsating, a pillar of cloud.

'At that instant I knew the meaning of Apocalypse.

'In downtown Kelso, not far from the little airport where the rescue and search helicopters churned incessantly in and out for refuelling and hosing down, the local cinema's signboard was announcing that night's movie. It was *The Late, Great Planet Earth*.'

Suggestions

- If you google *Hokusai* you will see some of the pictures referred to above. These woodcuts are as well loved today as they were in the 1830s when they were done. Also you could google *Hiroshige*, his contemporary, who has some equally lovely views of Mt Fuji.

- That painting by Caspar David Friedrich is entitled *Wanderer above the Sea of Fog*, and hangs in the Kunsthalle in

70

Hamburg. You can find it on Google by typing in the picture's title. Also if you want to see his other astonishing mountain pictures, type in *Riesengibirge* (the name of a mountain range near Dresden).

- A stunning contrast to these mountains are the pictures by Irish artist Paul Henry, where we see Atlantic skies dwarfing the purple mountains of Connemara. Google *Paul Henry artist images*.

- One doesn't have to don climbing gear to enjoy the high places of the world. Firstly, they don't have to be that high to be lovely. Secondly, you don't even have to go up mountains to enjoy them – they often are more beautiful when seen from the plain below. Provided of course we are mindful of them.

- We don't need to go far to enjoy mountains. Sure we all love to see the Alps, and perhaps long to see Everest, but it would take a lot to beat the beauty of Snowdonia or the Scottish Highlands, or the Magillicuddy Reeks, or 'where the Mountains of Mourne sweep down to the sea'.

- If you have a mountain anywhere near you, watch for all the changes of its moods and colours. These changes are not just from season to season, but from morning to evening, even from moment to moment. Grow mindful of your mountain.

6: Forest Mindfulness

The clearest way into the Universe is through a forest wilderness

~ John Muir

The wonder is that we can see these trees and not wonder more

~ Ralph Waldo Emerson

A forest bird never wants a cage

~ Henrik Ibsen

I grew up in this town, my poetry was born between the hill and the river,
it took its voice from the rain, and like the timber,
it steeped itself in the forests

~ Pablo Neruda

The admonition not to lose the forest for the trees
is not only about perspective. It is also about meaning

~ Emily Burr

THE Transylvanian forests in the film *Katalin Varga* – that brilliant film by British director Peter Strickland, made for only pennies, in cinematic terms – must be the spookiest ever. Katalin is hiking across the country with her 10-year-old son in order to find certain people with a view to murdering them. They had once gang-raped her. Ten years and nine months earlier, to be exact.

Katalin never actually goes into a forest: she always seems to be tramping through a meadow on the edge of one. But the haunting music and the darkness of those trees make those forests so sinister that I can well understand why Katalin keeps to the fields.

That's what makes forests such fun – they can be scary. Ever since *Grimms' Fairy Tales*, forests have been grim places where you can lose your way and never be found; where witches hide and Niebelungen dragons lurk; where wolves lie in wait for Little Red Riding Hood; where Hänsel and Gretel are abandoned and left to die; where Snow White flees in terror.

But apart from such tales, some forests really can be scary. When I lived in the Pacific Northwest I used to do a lot of hiking and camping in the forests there. And I was really and truly scared – of bears. There were tales of hikers being mauled to death; and we were warned always to hang foodstuffs high up in a nearby tree if we camped in a clearing. I never actually met a bear, but we'd hear things lurching into the undergrowth from the track up ahead.

And I got lost once, too, after my compass went missing. That was particularly scary. I still find it hard to talk about.

Shakespeare however has a more benign view of forests. His Forest of Arden is a place of refuge from the nastiness of kings and courts, and is generally a welcoming place. And that is more or less the kind of forests we have here in Britain and Ireland.

To begin with, they're too small to get lost in. They are full of kindly creatures of the sort that befriended Snow White – squirrels and badgers and rabbits and wood pigeons. In open country these little creatures are confined to the hedgerows: the forest is their kingdom.

More than cliché

That's why entering a forest, especially in spring or high summer, can be such a joy. The birdsong falters for an instant and then resumes with greater vigour. The wind sighs through the foliage, and things rustle in the undergrowth. There is a sense of being watched. Pencils of light slant between the tree trunks leaving pools of brightness on the forest floor.

Greeting cards so often carry such scenes that they have become almost clichés. Perhaps that is because the only time many of us see them is on such cards.

But it is far from a cliché to actually enter a woodland and move among those slanting sunbeams. Or to wade through a carpet of bluebells that fade into the distance under the trees. Or to push through a mini forest of ferns between the tree trunks. Or to crunch across a carpet of golden leaves in autumn.

Or to gaze upon branches on the edge of a clearing after a windless snowfall, where every twig seems in blossom from its tiny burden of snow – 'midwinter spring' as TS Eliot called it.

Or looking at the multicoloured mushrooms and fungi clinging to the tree trunks or covering the forest floor, and remembering that, without the help of those mushrooms, and the hundreds beneath the ground, no tree could grow or thrive.* Or climbing across those roots that writhe out of the ground like the sinews of a giant, and realizing they are precisely that – sinews of a giant oak.

Or wandering down a forest avenue, and looking up to see how the branches link overhead to create the ceiling of a gothic cathedral. (I sometimes wonder if such forest sights led to the concept of Early English Gothic, where stone arches come to a point in the roof just as branches do in a forest avenue. Salisbury Cathedral is quite simply a forest in stone.)

A forest offers all of this to those who enter it. But it does even more. Perhaps Robert Louis Stevenson says it best: 'It is not so much for its beauty that the forest makes a claim upon

---

* I only learned this lately, while researching this book. Lewis Blackwell, in his splendid volume, *The Life & Love of Trees*, tells of 'the symbiotic relationship between plant roots and fungi – a complex and vital connection that keeps our world working... an essential process in enabling trees to grow tall and strong, explaining how their roots are able to access water and nutrients to support such large organisms... The fungus dramatically extends a plant's ability to draw from the earth...'

men's hearts, as for that subtle something, that quality of air, that emanation from old trees, that so wonderfully changes and renews a weary spirit.' [18]

Benedictine monk Seán Ó Duinn says something similar: 'One feels this strange power especially in woods where the trees seem to wait in suspense and harbour a hidden power.' [19]

We hear much about the tropical rain forests, but I often wonder do we have any here? Not tropical, certainly. But in my wanderings I have found several places where every tree, every square foot of ground, every rock or remnant of stone wall, is completely enwrapped in moss, and every sound is muffled by the moss. It is an extraordinary sight, like a green velvet fairyland.

One of those places is a small wooded ravine in County Clare with a stream at the bottom, where very little sunlight penetrates. It seems extremely damp, and I am wondering if that is the cause of the moss. Perhaps it's a tiny microclimate.

The unexpected is perhaps the greatest charm of a forest. I once had a bird light on my shoulder in a forest clearing: it was of course a place where few people go, and the bird must not have learnt fear.

I was once walking alone on a forest path in Scotland when I encountered a badger. I stood still. So did badger, only a few feet from me. Neither of us moved. It was the first time in my life I had seen close up that magnificent black-and-white-striped head.

After about 10 minutes the badger suddenly sniffed, then shuffled off into the undergrowth and that was that. But I was left with that strange sense of tranquillity that you experience on encountering a wild creature.

Another time I had the distinct sense of being watched. I looked carefully around but could see nothing at first. But then, as my eyes focused beyond the foliage around me, I saw a family of deer – two adults, one with antlers, and one little one. They were absolutely still, and they were indeed watching me.

Forest trees

Trees in a forest are very different from those fortunate trees that stand alone in a field. A single oak or beech or indeed any tree can grow to its full beauty and classic shape, spreading its branches as it wills. But a poor tree in a forest is more like a soldier in an army – disciplined, confined, controlled, erect, and unable to do its own thing.

For a forest tree the only way is up. Push upwards to try and get some light. No room for branches. That is why, when you look at the edge of a forest from which trees have been cut, you notice that the remaining trees have only a few scraggy bits of branches except at the top, so that you can see right in through the trees to the dark interior.

And apparently, too, trees can be bullies, especially in a forest, with the bigger, stronger ones elbowing the less aggressive ones out of the way. Trees can even kill each other. As they say, it's a jungle out there.

But the interior of such a forest can be beautiful, where the tree trunks are tall straight pillars, soaring upwards from the ground to disappear into the foliage above. Like those hundreds of marble pillars in the Mosque of Corduba, except that in a forest the pillars are alive.

I often think the edge of a partially-logged evergreen forest is like the stage for a Wagner opera. A row of pillar-like trees, and forest darkness behind them.

I remember once sitting in a hovering police helicopter at the logged edge of a Washington State forest. On my right, by the open cockpit door, was a sheriff's deputy with a pump-action shotgun. In the middle was myself, with my reporter's notebook and camera. On my left was the pilot. We were waiting for a fugitive to come out from the trees – he was being pursued by tracker dogs and, according to our radio, was headed our way. I remember thinking, it's just like waiting for Siegfried to come out from the trees.

So what happened then? Well, nothing, actually. Siegfried never came. That's what happened. Or rather, didn't. They caught him a day later, miles away.

Incidentally that fugitive, whose name I learned was Lenny Hystadt, later wrote to me from the county jail and asked me to visit him. He had read my account of the chase in my syndicated column, and wanted to compare notes with me. Like, what it was like to be in the chopper waiting for him.

We had quite a time together. He told me he had wondered if we had had heat-seeking apparatus that could pinpoint him on the ground, as they did in Vietnam. I told him we had nothing of the sort – we were more like a rattly old tractor in the sky.

We don't even have to go into a forest to enjoy it. I am looking across the valley here at the forest opposite (it begins where 'my' field ends). It is winter now, and from here the treetops in the evening sunlight look like delicate little puffs of brownish smoke. Last week they were puffs of white smoke after a night of freezing fog.

The real joy will be in early spring, in that pause before the green comes, when a reddish warmth will touch the forest. It is the colour of billions of buds just before they burst into leaf. And then comes that freshest of all greens, when the leaves first open, before they darken into summer.

The summer sun sets behind that forest and, as it slants towards the horizon, it will put a rim of light around every treetop, and each will light up like an inverted new moon.

Let me finish this chapter with the words of Henry David Thoreau. In 1845 he went for two years to live alone in a hut among the trees by Walden Pond, near Concord, Mass. These were his hopes when he went, and those hopes were fulfilled during the rest of his dedicated life:

> I went to the woods because I wished to live
> deliberately, to front only the essential facts of life,
> and see if I could not learn what it had to teach,
> and not, when I came to die, discover that I had not

lived. I did not wish to live what was not life, living
is so dear; nor did I wish to practise resignation,
unless it was quite necessary. I wanted to live deep
and suck out all the marrow of life, to live so
sturdily and Spartan-like as to put to rout all that
was not life, to cut a broad swathe and shave close,
to drive life into a corner, and reduce it to its lowest
terms, and, if it proved to be mean, why then to get
the whole and genuine meanness of it, and publish
its meanness to the world; or if it were sublime, to
know it by experience, and be able to give a true
account of it in my next excursion. [20]

Suggestions

- If there is a wood or forest near you, get in there. The barrier
at its entrance is to bar cars, not you.

- The lovely thing about Britain and Ireland is that there are
small woods and forests all over the place. You don't have to
drive miles to find one. If you are unsure of the nearest, just
google *Lists of Forests in the United Kingdom* in Wikpedia. For
Ireland, google Wikpedia *Forests and Woodlands of the
Republic of Ireland* and Wikpedia *Forests and Woodlands of
Northern Ireland.* These are not complete lists (they could
hardly be, since there are so many), but they're a start. Some
entries give you pictures of what they are like, and most give a
history of the forest or woodland.

- Visit forests at any time of year: there is always something
new to see, no matter what the season.

- In high summer it's sensible to take along some insect
repellent. Midges are among a forest's less attractive denizens.
They may however find you attractive.

- Read Shakespeare's *As You Like It* to relish the shenanigans in the Forest of Arden.

- Take a look at some of my forest pictures on the website. I'll be posting at least one new picture each day - not always of forests, of course.

7: The floating world

I want to do to you what spring does to the cherry trees

~ Pablo Neruda

What is all this juice and all this joy?
A strain of the earth's sweet being in the beginning
In Eden garden. -- Have, get, before it cloy...

~ Gerard Manley Hopkins

Spring passes and one remembers one's innocence. Summer passes and one remembers one's exuberance. Autumn passes and one remembers one's reverence. Winter passes and one remembers one's perseverance

~ Yoko Ono

Dew evaporates
And all our world is dew...so dear,
So fresh, so fleeting

~ Kobayashi Issa

THE concept of *Ukiyo* – 'The Floating World' – is deeply rooted in the mind of every Japanese person. It comes from Buddhism, the kernel of which is that everything is transient, nothing lasts: all our joys, hopes, beauty, love and even life itself are floating away from us and will soon be gone.

Mindfulness is a response this. If nothing lasts, then *let us live in the Now*. Let us savour the fleeting floating present moment, for this moment is all we really have. Such is the core teaching of the Vietnamese master, Thich Nhat Hanh, and it seems to have been taken to heart by both Vietnamese and Japanese people.

For the people of Japan, the symbol of all this is the cherry blossom. Its beauty can take our breath away, but a breath of wind can take *it* away. As an 18th-century *haiku* by Ishikawa Toyonobu puts it:

> Once again in love
> Once again regrets, as fleeting
> As cherry blossoms

So, being an eminently practical people, the Japanese take off in droves every spring to view the cherry blossom – a bit like the way certain of our fishing fraternity call in sick when the mayfly rises. But the Japanese wouldn't do anything like that: they go on organized cherry-blossom-viewing tours and spend hours simply gazing upon the blossoms.*

Incidentally the 3,750 flowering cherry trees that every spring transform the Mall in Washington, DC, were a gift from the Japanese people in 1912 to the people of the United States. They were intended as a symbol of peace between the two countries.

They once more are.

First crocus

Perhaps there is something to be learnt from all this. And not just about cherry blossoms, but about nature itself, especially in springtime. For years I used to look forward to the first crocus, but when it came I was too busy to give it more than a cursory glance. Then, like the cherry blossom, it was gone. Then the daffodils came and they went too.

And then would come the year's most magical ten days or so, during which green slowly seeps across the woodlands –

---

* The Japanese have now started coming in droves to view the yellow fields of rapeseed in the English countryside. There are organized tours for the purpose. Good on them: we never thought of that.

that early green of a freshness and brilliance that has no equal in nature.

I'd be sort of aware of it through the car windows as I'd go about my urgent and important business – whatever it happened to be at the time – and I would tell myself that yes I must take a bit of time off to have a look. When I could find time, that is.

Mostly I didn't. Didn't find the time, that is. And usually by the time I did – *if* I did – the green had darkened and the blossoms were on the ground.

All that is a long time ago. Nowadays I *make* time to be mindful of spring. And all that urgent business has to wait its turn, and mostly turns out to be not that urgent at all. Whereas spring *is* urgent, for it simply won't wait. And besides, how many more springs do I have?

Spring really is a controlled explosion. Look at a crocus in the ground: the very shape, topped with yellow or purple, is like an artillery shell bursting from the ground. And were its total growth speeded to a single instant, it truly would be an explosion. Like that oak tree we talked about. Van Gogh caught this marvellously in his *Field at Arles*, now in the Tate Gallery, where the whole meadow simply erupts in green.

Flowering cherry

I have one cherry tree in my garden. This year I did my own cherry-blossom viewing. I actually took out a deck chair and sat under the tree. I suppose I was trying to be mindful of the cherry blossom. Unfortunately the tree is in my front garden, so a few passers-by gave me The Look. Still, I'll do it again next year.

But I'd be worried now that such behaviour might frighten off my readers. Well, OK then, maybe we don't have to sit on deckchairs looking at cherry blossom, but we do need to gaze instead of just glancing. To gaze is mindful; to glance is not.

There are two ways to look at the flowering of spring. One is to let our eye simply wander over the pink foam of blossom

83

that engulfs our suburbs, and the whitethorn that makes our hedgerows look blanketed in snow. Just enjoying that transformation is one of the high point of spring. But then, having gazed our fill, it is another experience altogether to move in and see the blossom close up and personal. In there is another world altogether – a world of petals and pistils and stamens.

Pluck a fuchsia bloom and hold it in your fingers. It's a tiny ballerina. There's a little head; a body; a flaring skirt, and underneath the skirt all those unmentionable things that are to do with, uh, begetting.

Take a daffodil bloom into your hand – and simply ponder that magnificent trumpet that still silently summons insects to bring it the pollen it longs for.* Just feel its texture, its solidity. Or gaze at a host of golden daffodils beside a lake, as Wordsworth recalls it: 'And then my heart with pleasure fills, and dances with the daffodils.'

Pluck a beech leaf in the height of spring. Hold it up to the light, and look at the tracery of its veins, and wonder. Then look between the veins, at all those tiny channels that carry the sap or chlorophyll or whatever it is they carry. There's a close-up picture of a leaf in Lewis Blackwell's *Life & Love of Trees* (page 77), [21] and if that does not persuade us to gaze at a leaf, well, nothing will. Incidentally, let's not be put off by the folks who insist on knowing the difference between an elm leaf and a hornbeam leaf. Any leaf is a source of wonder whatever the tree it belongs to.

And one other thing: men can sometimes be put off by the thought that real alpha males wouldn't be seen dead plucking a blossom and gazing at it. However I have some unquestionably macho friends who have no such inhibitions.

---

* Not that many insects come any more, to these blooms bred for beauty alone. Many have to rely on hand pollination by their breeders.

Spring fields

I mentioned the cherry tree in my garden. Now, granted one is nearer to God in a garden than anywhere else on earth, I actually prefer the wilder spring of the fields. Especially I love when the April gorse turns the whole countryside yellow and drenches it in that lovely cocoanut aroma.

Or is there anything to compare with a landscape where every hedgerow is white with hawthorn or mayflower blossom, that looks almost like a fall of snow? No wonder TS Elliot described real snow on hedgerows as 'midwinter spring'.

Or what can compare with wading through a meadow of knee-high wild flowers: surely William Blake must have done that, and stooped to pluck a cowslip or wild orchid, when he thought up those lines, 'To see a world in a grain of sand, and a heaven in a wild flower.'

But for me one of the loveliest of all evocations of spring is in the words and music of Wagner's *Parsifal*, when the hero baptizes Kundry just before she dies:

> How beautiful the meadows seem today!
> Well I recall the wondrous flowers
> Which once did try to twine themselves around me.
> Yet they did not compare with these.
> The grasses, blossoms and flowers
> Are fragrant in their innocence,
> And speak to me with loving trust

But if you want to truly weep for the joys of spring, read Oscar Wilde's *The Selfish Giant*. [22] The Giant hated beauty and hated children and so his walled garden was forever winter.

But one day the North Wind ceased roaring through the garden, and the giant saw a wonderful sight. 'The children had crept in and they were sitting in the branches of the trees.... The trees were so glad to have the children back again that they had covered themselves with blossoms, and were waving their arms gently above the children's heads. The birds were flying about and twittering with delight, and the flowers were looking up through the green grass and laughing. It was a lovely scene, only in one corner it was still winter.'

Standing there was a little boy who was too small to reach up to the branches of the tree, and he was crying bitterly. So the Giant crept downstairs and took the child gently and put him up in the tree. 'And the tree broke at once into blossom, and the birds came and sang on it and the little boy stretched out his two arms and flung them round the Giant's neck, and kissed him.'

Many years later, when the Giant was old and near to death, the little boy came once again into the garden and the Giant ran to meet him.

' "Who has dared to wound thee?" he cried. For on the palms of the child's hands were the prints of two nails, and the prints of two nails were on the little feet.

' "Who hath dared to wound thee?" cried the Giant again. "Tell me, that I may take my big sword and slay him."

' "Nay," answered the child; "but these are the wounds of Love."

' "Who art thou?" said the Giant, and a strange awe fell on him, and he knelt before the little child.

'And the child smiled on the Giant, and said to him, "You let me play once in your garden, and today you shall come to my garden, which is Paradise."

'And when the children ran in that afternoon, they found the Giant lying dead under the tree, all covered with white blossoms.'

Suggestions

- You can Google the whole story of *The Selfish Giant*. It is a lesson in growing mindful. And if it doesn't make you weep for the joys of spring, forget it and go back to winter.

- Spring passes so quickly. I cannot urge you enough to grasp it when it comes. Like walking your local suburb just to look at the blossoms on laburnum and cherry trees – if not in the streets, then overhanging garden walls.

- If the Japanese can take off to view the cherry blossom, why cannot we take off for a mindful spring weekend in the countryside, just to look at the trees as they come into their fresh green? It is one of the loveliest sights of the year. Too busy? Hardly as busy as the Japanese.

- Get into a meadow with knee-high wildflowers if you have the opportunity. There's no experience quite like it. You can stay at the edge if you don't want to trample on anything.

- There is a wonderful passage in Thich Nhat Hanh's book, *The Miracle of Mindfulness,* [23] about walking along a grassy path leading to a village. If we can walk mindfully then each step we take will be an infinite wonder, 'and a joy will open our hearts like a flower, enabling us to enter the world of reality.'

- The Burren, in Western Ireland, is unique for the spring flowers that flourish in the grikes and cracks between the great tracts of limestone. Many of these are alpine flowers, found here but seldom elsewhere except in the Alps. The Burren in spring brings tourists from far and wide – including those rapeseed-viewing Japanese.

8: Let there be light

Anan, be a light unto yourself

~ Gautama Buddha

An age is called dark, not because the light fails to shine,
but because people refuse to see it

~ James Michener

Lead, kindly Light, amid th'encircling gloom, lead Thou me on!
The night is dark, and I am far from home; lead Thou me on!

~ John Henry Newman

In the beginning there was nothing.
God said, 'Let there be light!' And there was light.
There was still nothing, but you could see it a whole lot better

~ Ellen DeGeneres

We can easily forgive a child who is afraid of the dark;
the real tragedy of life is when men are afraid of the light

~ Plato

When you rise in the morning, give thanks for the light

~ Tecumseh

EINSTEIN once said, 'All I want to do is study light.' One can see why, for in the end everything comes down to light. And the sight to see the light. And the will to use the sight. In other words, the will to look with Mindfulness.

89

The late John O'Donohue once wrote of 'those who are physically blind: they have lived all their lives in a moonscape of darkness. They have never seen a wave, a stone, a star, a flower, the sky, or the face of another human being.' [24] It is hard for us with vision to imagine how terrible it must be to have no real notion of such things, never having seen them.

But it is even harder to imagine what it must be like to be told one will never see such things again. That one is going blind. Yet it happens every day to thousands throughout the world.

I would prefer to die.

What are the things I would miss, were I to go blind? Well, those things John O'Donohue mentions – waves, stones, stars, flowers, faces. But what else? Where to begin? I would miss those beams of light that slant down from a sky at evening, and look like a holy picture. I would miss light filtering through leaves in spring. Or the way a girl's blond hair lights up when sunlight drives through it. (Remember Marilyn Monroe?)

Or the colours on a CD when the light plays on its surface. Or those same colours in an oil spill on a wet road. Or in a rainbow. Or the undulating light pattern that my glass of beer throws on a sunlit café table. Or the light peeping in at morn through my bedroom curtains.

Or a Celtic high cross etched against a sky. Or the slow sparkle on roadstead or harbour as the sun inches westwards. Or Yeats's long-legged fly upon a stream, walking on the water. Or that golden pathway to the sun as it sets in the Atlantic. These I have loved. And so much more.

In other words, what I would miss is light. Scientists tell us it is the source of our very existence: perhaps that is why it is the source of joy for all of us.

All of us? John O'Donohoe finishes the passage quoted above with the terrible words: 'Yet there are others with perfect vision who are absolutely blind.'

Departure of light

There is a line in Homer's *Iliad* that has haunted me in the decades since I first read it. During the battle a young warrior called Tros comes up to Achilles to clasp his knees and beg to be spared. But Achilles is nowise soft of heart or gentle of mind: 'He smote him upon the liver with his sword, and forth the liver slipped, and the dark blood welling forth therefrom, filled his bosom, and darkness enfolded his eyes.' [25]

Phrases like that run through the *Iliad* whenever someone is slaughtered – which is pretty well most of the time in that hideous, blood-drenched epic: death is seen as light fading from the eyes. Death is blindness. Blindness is death. Death is the departure of light.

And light is what keeps us in touch with the Universe – there is simply nothing else. As CS Lewis puts it: 'If the whole Universe has no meaning, we should never have found out that it has no meaning: just as, if there were no light in the Universe and therefore no creatures with eyes, we should never know it was dark. Dark would be without meaning.'

What does John O'Donohue mean by people with perfect vision being blind? I believe he means we are no longer aware of light in all its forms – sky at evening, sparkle on water, morning dew gleaming on a spider's web, a halo around the moon. *We fail to notice because we are not mindful.*

Even solid things like stones and flowers and mountains and faces are only revealed to us by light. We only know them from the light that comes from them and strikes the eye. Light is all we've got: a mountain may be solid rock, but – apart from tramping across it – all we really know about it is from the light that bounces off it and reaches our eye, which is why the mountain can be green, brown, mauve, grey, textured or flat, or invisible, all within a single day.

So light is our lifeline, even though we still don't know exactly what it is. Scientists tell of its dual nature – that it's simultaneously waves and particles – but what matters to us in daily life is that it brings us the glory of a sunset or the glint of water on a rose petal. And that it comes to us in the six colours of the spectrum – red, orange, yellow, green, blue, violet, which mix to give us literally millions more colours – the human eye can distinguish at least ten million. *Ten million.* All of which means there is a visual feast out there, waiting for us to open our eyes.

Geranium red

There are so many fascinating things about light and colour that can stir our wonder, once we become aware of them. And, without getting too scientific, it might help to remember from our schooldays a little of how it works. Like, how is a geranium red? Answer (I think!): it receives the six* colours of the spectrum, absorbs all of them except red, which it then throws back at the eye. So we see red.

A little black dress also receives the six colours, but gobbles them all and sends nothing back to the eye. So, bar a slight surface sheen or a gleam from a fold, we really see nothing except the little black number's shape, which can be exquisite, depending of course on what's inside it.

Incidentally black makes anything seem smaller. Even a black car looks smaller than the same model in red or white or silver. So a person in black looks more slender, which surely accounts for black's popularity.

Beautiful black

Black can be lovely. Artist Hervey Adams wrote about 'the great beauty of black'. Too much of it, of course can have a deadening effect. And Adams was always surprised 'that the clergy, who are devoted to the spreading of "glad tidings of great joy", should do so in such mournful trappings. But observe black, just a few spots of it, at a bull-fight. The spots

---

* Newton said there were seven colours in the spectrum, because he thought seven was a number with special significance. So he added *indigo*, but it seems we can manage without it. However some scientists have lately added *ultra-violet*, thus bringing the number back to seven.

are the bull-fighter's hat and shoes. The rest is all vivid colour: gold, blue, green, pink, against yellow sand, and of course the inevitable scarlet. But the moving black accents, the hat and the shoes, hold the picture together. They reconcile the most violent clashes of colour.'

I personally detest bull fighting, but I suppose one could concede that it is colourful. So is blood.

I remember from my university days there was a girl who always dressed completely in black. That was fine, except that everything in her apartment was black as well. Even the walls were matt black, reflecting nothing. I visited once, and couldn't get out fast enough. It was horrible even in daylight. Mercifully I never saw it at night. Honestly.

There is one situation where black is a bonus. Dramatic shapes can look even more dramatic when all colour is sucked away in a silhouette – like that same celtic cross now set black against a dazzling sun-drenched sea, or Salisbury Cathedral spire set against a soft gentle sunset. A winter tree black against an evening sky shows its magnificent shape far more effectively than when it rejoices in its summer foliage.

When we look at friend's profile against a bright window we can often see a loveliness of brow, nose and chin, quite independent of eye colour or complexion – a beauty we hardly knew was there.

Even more lovely is what is called the Rembrandt effect – a face in profile, facing a single light source like a window. This time the brow, nose and chin are lit, but the rest of the head fades slightly, sometimes even into darkness. It was one of Rembrandt's favourite techniques. (It's how I love to photograph my partner Kathleen.)

Black is the absence of all colour, as is grey to a certain extent. And grey too can be magical, even mysterious. Both mist and fog are grey, and either can transform a landscape. The magic of mist is that much colour is gone, and all we have left are shapes – shapes indeed that are hardly shapes, since their outlines are so softened.

Twilight too has its shapes in gentle colours, and the shapes are subdued and subtle and fading fast. That's the elusiveness of twilight. Yeats made much of 'The Celtic Twilight' but all twilight has that celtic magic. No one tells it better than 19th century painter James Abbot McNeill Whistler:

> As light fades and the shadows deepen, all petty
> and exacting details vanish, everything trivial
> disappears, and I see things as they are in great
> strong masses: the buttons are lost, but the sitter
> remains; the sitter is lost, but the shadow remains;
> the shadow is lost, but the picture remains. And
> that, night cannot efface from the painter's
> imagination.[26]

Elusive colours

I once read in a photo manual that an orange in daylight isn't really orange. Well, not altogether. The highlit part is actually blue from the daylight from the window; the shadowed part takes on the colour of the table it stands on. Only the unlit, unshadowed surface is actually orange. And even the mottled surface of the orange shows a lot more than orange. Try it. I did, and it's true.

Likewise if I hold my hand palm-downwards between myself and a window, its top surface sheen will not be flesh coloured, but blue from the daylight from the window. This is true for both a black person's hand and a white person's. It too is worth trying.

Did you ever wonder about those hi-viz orange or green jackets worn by police and road workers – why they are so amazingly bright? Just lately Mike Watson, one of my two engineer brothers-in-law, explained that the jacket catches invisible ultra-violet light and turns it into visible light, thus doubling the brightness.

One of the most astonishing sights in our countryside is the flash of a kingfisher if we are lucky enough to glimpse one by a river. I use the word 'flash' advisedly, for the kingfisher's rapid passing seems to create a line of electric blue in the air. Once seen it is hard to forget. Scottish poet Norman MacCaig has caught it perfectly:

> That kingfisher jewelling upstream
> seems to leave a streak of itself
> in the bright air

Then there is that dazzle that we glimpse on a dragonfly or a damsel fly in summer, or in the tail feathers of a peacock. Or even on a starling. Or on that magnificent neck of the common old drake – no wonder he swaggers.

Apparently such textured surfaces work differently from the geranium – instead of absorbing all colours but one, such surfaces actually break up the light and send all the separated colours back.

The colour we then see depends on the angle from which we see it. For example, a ridged CD changes its rainbow colours as it is moved around. So do soap bubbles. So too do some seashells, and mother of pearl. And pearls themselves, which probably is what makes them so cherished.

But then how come a kingfisher's back is always blue? Not sure of the answer to that one. Maybe its feathers are angled to ensure we only get the blue. Anyone have an answer?

The colours that come from our TV set are obviously not reflected at all, but created right there on the spot. And every single colour comes from mixtures of red, green and blue. When I first read that, I could hardly accept that red and green together would make yellow. So I went right up close to a yellow part of the screen, and there indeed were tiny dots of red and green side by side. When I moved back the result became yellow.

We often talk about the colour silver, but really there is no such thing. Silver is not a colour, but a mirror of all the colours around it. All we have to do is look at the polished chrome parts of a car to see the parking lot and ourselves reflected in them. (One wouldn't suggest it be done too often, as it can be bad for morale. One usually looks atrociously plump in hubcaps.) Even matt silver, that mirrors nothing, is simply grey with a slight sheen. Of course car makers will call it any exotic name they want, but it's really still just burnished grey.

Power of colour

When I was a boy of nine I used to stand in front of a nearby garage door that was painted a dazzling red. I found if I stood there for long enough I got delightfully dizzy. (I was a rather dizzy kid in those days anyway.)

But colour can have remarkable psychological and even physical effects on all of us, mostly without our realising it. A theatre's Green Room relaxes the players before a performance.

A BBC series on colour showed how diners in a red environment eat faster, and so move on for the next lot. It also told how a factory got more out of its workers by painting the restrooms in a nasty, unpleasant colour, so they came back out quicker. In a similar way, pink and green are used in police holding-cells for their calming effect.

Recent pictures of the tribunal trying Mladic and others accused of Serbian war crimes, show the holding cells painted in a 'calming' apricot colour. And of course supermarkets manipulate our eyes and our impulses every shelf of the way, mostly by colour.

One of the loveliest of the great estates is Coole Park in Galway, where Lady Gregory once lived, and which Yeats made famous with his poem, *The Wild Swans of Coole*. What makes it so lovely is that every gate, fence, door, post, railing, eaves, or pillar is painted brilliant scarlet. These small points of vivid contrast in the spread of green sward and foliage make a feast for the eye. In a way the red acts like a sharp condiment in a delicious dish.

When colours are juxtaposed with sensitivity, the result can be particularly lovely. Two and two really do make five. Like red windows and doors on a white cottage.

Many people's favourite combination seems to be blue and yellow. They were the two favourite colours of Vermeer, who combined them in almost all his paintings, like *The Girl with the Pearl Earring*. Blue and yellow is the flag of Sweden; it's the colours of the European Union (well, blue and gold anyhow); it used to be Leeds United's colours (well, blue and gold) and it's sad to see them changed to plain old white; it's the football and hurling strip of neighbouring rival counties Tipperary and Clare.

I once asked someone what was the difference between the colours of those two counties, and was told, 'Their colours are blue and yellow; ours are yellow and blue!' A bit of tongue in cheek there, for officially of course County Clare is 'saffron and blue', while Tipperary is 'blue and gold'. It's all a bit like the blue and gold of the European Union: the stars on its flag are as yellow as makes no difference.

Incidentally nature gives us several lovely examples of blue and yellow. One is gorse (furze) against a blue sky, which is part of all our springs. Another is when we are in a lighted room at twilight and look out of the window: instead of darkness we see blue, contrasting with the yellow within the room. That blue is called 'induced colour' – an illusion. We can sometimes see it outdoors at twilight, when we look towards a cottage with a single lighted window.

Colour combinations always seem more effective when one colour predominates. An equal amount of blue and yellow is nothing as effective as a small yellow cross upon a large blue flag, as Sweden's flag has it. Likewise it's marvellous what a little white stitching can do to a pair of dark blue (indigo) jeans. And of course we are all aware of the ominous colours of Halloween – orange and black, with black very much in the ascendent.

Love of colour

The early Scots and Irish seem to have loved colour, as the Book of Kells gives ample evidence. There is a theory that ancient high crosses like those of Iona were once painted in vivid colours.

Yet somehow the love of colour seems to have got mislaid some time in the past: there was nothing quite as desolately grey as an Irish village street of forty years ago. But now suddenly the colours have all come back – many village streets have come alive with colour – with towns like Eiries and Ahillies becoming tourist attractions for their rainbow houses and streets.

Perhaps the explanation is that no one could afford paint in the old days, but now they can. If that be the case, one can only hope the streets won't revert to grey with the demise of the Celtic Tiger.

There is even a castle (tower house) painted bright pink in County Cork. When some people expressed horror, the castle's owner, film actor Jeremy Irons, replied that lots of castles in the old days were painted bright colours, so why not this?

Whether he's right or not, wouldn't it be great if we could paint all our castles, ruins and all, in lovely colours?

Or maybe it wouldn't. Any ideas?

All down to light

I'm often bothered by our inaccurate use of words for colour. A white man isn't white – he's pink (or purple if he drinks too much). A black man is brown. (It's even worse in Gaelic where a black man is *fear gorm* – a blue man.) I lived in China and I never met a yellow man there. Nor a yellow woman. Nor did I ever meet a red man in Canada. Hunting pink is red. Black coffee is brown; white coffee is beige. Black grapes are purple; white grapes are green.

A black eye is mauve or a nice shade of magenta, or even yellow, depending on how it was acquired and the fist that created it. Guinness (the 'black stuff') is dark brown. Same as coffee. White wine is yellow or gold. And even red wine can be purple.

My friend Gordon Baker had suffered for years from growing cataracts. It was so gradual he hardly realised how the world around him was fading. But, when he awoke from his operation, and looked through the window, he couldn't believe his eyes – literally.

'Is that house out there really that orange?' he asked his wife Helen in amazement. 'Is it really as bright as it looks?'

He told me later that lying there in bed, looking out across the River Lee at Sunday's Well in Cork, he had the mindful experience of a lifetime. 'It was sheer magic lying there, looking out at that incredible blue sky, seeing those columns of clouds, those lovely terraces across the river, one above the other, looking at all of those beautiful colours – it was a new world for me. A world I had forgotten.

'As my grandchildren would say today, it was awesome.'

Suggestions

- Take a magnifying glass into the garden on a bright sunny day. Focus it on a piece of paper until the focal point is a tiny dot. Then watch the paper burn. Actually you are really focussing infra-red rays, which are just below the visible spectrum. (As 10-year-olds we used to do it to classmates' necks using sunbeams from the window, during a boring summer class. I am not, however, recommending this.)

- After waking in the morning, pull back the curtains and hold your hand horizontally between yourself and the window. The top surface of your fingers will be blue (and not from cold, I hope, nor from circulation).

- Watch the light on people's hair in the street. Especially when the sun is against you – then you get rim lighting, and everyone looks like Marilyn Monroe. Well, sort of.

- Put a magnifying glass on a yellow part of your TV screen, and see what colours are really there. We're all being fooled, you know.

- Google Michael McCarthy's nature study *Kingfisher Blue, nature's most enchanting colour.* It's almost lyrical. You can still get it on the *Independent* newspaper's website – *www.independent.co.uk*

9: Touching with the eye

We only see what we look at. To look is an act of choice.
As a result of this act, what we see is brought within our reach,
though not necessarily within arm's reach

~ John Berger

Within two hours of where I live, you have mountains and desert as location.
I like the natural elements that abstract into light, texture, shape and shadow

~ Herb Ritz

The true worth of a man is not to be found in man himself,
But in the colours and textures that come alive in others

~ Albert Schweitzer

I search for the realness, the real feeling of a subject, all the texture around it...
I always want to see the third dimension of something...
I want to come alive with the object

~ Andrew Wyeth

When I was about eight years old, someone gave my family an exquisite and rather valuable ceramic vase. All I can remember was its marvellous shape, *and the fact that it was unglazed.*

Now that fact was important, hence the italics. Very important indeed. Because my mother (a together woman in all other ways) could – not – abide – unglazed ceramic. It set her teeth on edge – nay, it set her soul on edge. She went to pieces just looking at it, and wished *it* in pieces.

101

That wretched vase languished for ages on a top shelf of our scullery, until finally some man called to take it away (presumably summoned by my mother).

I remember her cringing in the scullery (the only time I ever saw her cringe – she didn't do cringing), pointing to the offending vase, and lisping (the only time I ever heard her lisp – she didn't do lisping either): 'Pleathe get that thing out of my thight. Thell it – do what you like with it. Justh *take it away!*'

The fellow touched his forelock and went off to spend my inheritance.

Now the lesson in this parable (God's truth, by the way), is surely as follows: although my poor mother never ran her hands over that vase's surface from the moment it was inflicted on her, she nevertheless knew exactly how it would feel were she to do so. And she knew it just by looking once at the offending article. Which means that looking can, in certain circumstances, take the place of touching. In other words, seeing is touching from a distance.

Five senses

Wasn't it psychologist Carl Jung who said that (apart from intuition) absolutely all our information comes through the five senses – sight, hearing, touch, taste and smell? The poet Rupert Brooke, who in his short life loved life so much, calls on all of them in his masterly poem, *The Great Lover*:

> These I have loved:
> White plates and cups, clean-gleaming,
> Ringed with blue lines; and feathery, faery dust;
> Wet roofs, beneath the lamp-light; the strong crust
> Of friendly bread; and many-tasting food;
> Rainbows; and the blue bitter smoke of wood;
> And radiant raindrops couching in cool flowers...
> And washen stones, gay for an hour; the cold
> Graveness of iron; moist black earthen mould...

Even in this brief extract it's clear that Brooke loved the texture of things – wet roofs, feathery dust, firm sands, cold iron, moist black earthen mould. But many of these textures are not actually fingered, but simply seen. In other words, touch can be achieved with the eye.

Some of our greatest satisfactions can come from the sense of touch. But many of us are scared of it, because of touch's intimate link with sexuality, where it is indeed paramount. But there is a world of difference between sexuality and sensuality. The latter is simply the joy we get from the senses. And especially the sense of touch.

Touch, as any blind person can tell us, can be a source of wondrous stimulation and joy. Fingers caressing a soft leather jacket; bare feet treading cool, damp grass; a cheek pressing against a fresh, cotton pillow; the feel of a rose petal between finger and thumb; sand between the toes; the sea up the nostrils at that first freezing June plunge into the sea; water sliding past as one races down a swimming pool; the crunch of pastry between the teeth; the crackle of autumn leaves under foot; fingers moving down the back of a beloved terrier, or feeling its damp nose.

As deaf-blind Helen Keller put it: 'To me a lush carpet of pine needles or spongy grass is more welcome than the most luxurious Persian rug.'

All this is the sense of touch. However it is intimately linked with the sense of sight. It is one of the magical things about our senses – sight and touch are so interlocked that with our eyes alone we can feel the texture of things.

The implications are wonderful because, mostly, touching things with our eyes can be a source of joy.

For instance it means we can feel the surface of things we may never actually reach. Like those mud flats on the lower Thames, where few people would dare walk (except those self-styled 'mudlarks', using things like snowshoes). As one local put it, 'This place is lethal. One step in the wrong place and you're up to your waist (and more) in mud.'

Yet the eye can feel the texture of any mud without our ever stepping on it. And the eye can rejoice when that mud turns to molten gold in the first rays of the morning sun.

Textures as seen

I already mentioned the mountains of Kerry after rain, and how they can sometimes create the illusion of being extraordinarily close. When that happens, my eye is allowing me, in its own way, to touch and feel a mountainside.

And if we ever look at the full moon through binoculars, we get a real feel for its surface. No wonder they used to think it was made of cheese – it does rather look like a Stilton. But if it's the edge of a crescent moon you look at, the eye meets something a lot rougher and meaner, something that might cut your fingers if you could run them over it.

The sea too has texture. I have seen it burnished bronze at sundown. Even clouds have texture. However in their case the texture is only in the eye of the beholder (what, by the way, isn't?). That floor of cloud seen from 35,000 feet looks so firm and solid that I sometimes feel I could just jump from the plane and bounce delightfully into the softness.

No wonder our forebears had the faithful departed playing harps while sitting around on clouds. Indeed it wasn't really till aeroplanes got us up there that we were quite sure they weren't sitting around like that. Come to think of it, why was it always harps? How boring: why not bagpipes?

It's not just distant things that reveal their texture to the eye. There were few things in childhood more joyous than breaking open the spiky green shell from around a chestnut, and gazing on that mahogany egg nestled in its soft white cocoon, a mahogany polished as no human hand could ever do. And realising that no one had ever before set eyes on it.

Every autumn I still do this.

Lovely too are the surface of rocks and stones, with all their textures that can be felt by the eye. A block of rough-hewn granite, sparkling with mica. A stone cross encrusted with lichen. Sand textured by the ebb tide. The grike-shattered limestone of the Burren. Window light glinting on the chancel walls of Iona Abbey. The coolness of Carrara marble. A rain-drenched pavement under lamplight. Green mossy stones on a seashore. A veined, stained, chalk cliff at Dover that seems so soft and fragile. Yet has endured, and protected England since history began.

On the Ayrshire coast, looking across to Ailsa Craig, there is a spot where a cluster of massive rocks is almost totally textured with lichen. I once saw those rocks in the sunlight of high summer, the lichen blazing yellow against a backdrop of deep blue sea. It was then I really understood why Vermeer so loved yellow and blue.

There is a tiny bay on Donegal's Atlantic coast where the stones are smoothed and rounded by eons of crashing seas. I can pick one and run my fingers over its gorgeous surface. But mostly I don't need to. I just walk along that beach, gazing down at a piece of pink granite, smoothed to a dinosaur egg; or a rounded black stone with a white streak running through it; or a strange, honeycombed piece of yellow rock I have never seen before. The eyes have it: they are all I need.

Incidentally Barbara Hepworth, who made such lovely abstract rounded sculptures, seems to have made it her life's work to do just with her chisel what the sea does to stones, but to do in days what took the sea millennia to achieve.

In the Rodin Museum in Paris there is a sculpture, *Danaïde*, that takes texture to its ultimate. The soft, smooth skin of a young girl emerges from a chunk of marble as coarse as the day it came from the quarry. The contrast is stunning.

Here is what the German poet Rilke said of it: 'It is wonderful to walk slowly about this marble, to follow the long line that curves about the richly unfolded roundness of the back to the face that loses itself in the stone as though in a great weeping, and to the hand which like a broken flower speaks softly once more of life that lies deep under the eternal ice of the block.' [27]

Seeing fabric's feel

There are few things that delight the eye as much as the texture of fabric. Each kind of material has of course its own unique feel to the touch, but the eye not only calls up that sensation but adds its own perceptions of sheen, shadow, pattern, colour and folds.

Have you ever really looked at the folds in fabric, on a bedspread, on a jacket, on a sleeve, or on your thigh? Run your fingers across the fabric in a circular motion: a Y-shaped ridge gently disappears into a U-shape as the fingers move, then folds into two parallel ridges ending in a T-shape. Which then flattens out, to arise again in the shape of an X. It is almost like miniature mountain ranges being formed, and I wonder did the Alps or Himalayas behave like this when they were being folded. Not quite as quickly, of course.

Various fabrics respond to the eye in remarkably different ways. Silk, of course, is unchallenged monarch – well, queen, with its unique feminine sheen and texture, in all its variations. There is shot silk that changes colour depending on its angle, as iridescent as a peacock feather. There is watered silk, beloved of bishops and cardinals, with all those interweaving ovals and circles and figure eights that change with the light, and look as if it the silk had been steeped in water and hung out to dry. Hence presumably its name. Although I don't think that's how they do it.

Silk may be top of the league, but that doesn't mean I have to like it. In fact I don't. I was once given a birthday present of a silk shirt which I detested from the start. I couldn't bear to wear it, as the sensation of silk surfaces rubbing together under my fingers would set my teeth on edge. In the end the very look of the shirt bothered me (not however quite as badly as that vase did to my poor mother).

My favourite fabric is corduroy. It plays with the light as no other material does – whereas folds in most fabrics create shadows, the folds in dark corduroy gleam brighter than the fabric itself. It's almost like looking at a photographic negative.

106

Writer John D. Sheridan once described the gleam on grey corduroy as being like the track of a snail at dawn. Snails may be no beauties, but their trails are a lovely part of the morning.

Since I was a child I always loved to let my eye follow corduroy's parallel ridges as they curve through folds like a ploughed field curving around a hillside. It's very like a Bridget Riley canvas, where all those parallel lines can make you dizzy if you gaze at them for any length of time. *

Harris and Donegal tweeds have a different kind of visual magic. Apart from the lovely patterns created in herringbone or similar weave, one of the achievements of these tweeds is to create a new colour by weaving wildly different colours together. I have a tweed jacket of a grey so warm that it nearly vibrates. It wasn't until I looked closely at the fabric that I saw it wasn't grey at all – it was made from equal amounts of tightly interwoven blue and beige wool. Which is exactly how some of those Impressionist painters would have worked, putting tiny points of blue and yellow side by side on the canvas, which the eye then merged and interpreted as green.

Forty shades of blue

Denim of course must be the most satisfying fabric of all to look at. It still has the texture of the tent material from which it derives, and the eye itself can actually sense that texture. But the eye can also savour the extraordinary gamut of blues that stride towards us down every street, ranging from the darkest indigo to the palest sky. I wonder how many hundreds of shades of blue do jeans come in. I've often tried counting while walking down a street, but usually end up bumping into people. And getting The Look.

And the things they do to poor suffering denim – fraying it to let the beige or light-blue weft show through; roughing it;

---

* When I was about two years old I had a brown corduroy teddy bear that came with me everywhere, a bit like Linus's security blanket. I often wonder if my fascination with corduroy comes from that little old bear.

wrinkling it; shrinking it; ripping it; writing on it – I think the word 'distressed jeans' probably says it all.

Yet the amazing thing is, no matter how much distress is inflicted, a youngster in denim always manages to look good, and older people in denim somehow seem to look younger.

It's a truism to say denim is the uniform of the world, but it does make one feel at home in strange or remote countries simply to see all those young people walking the streets in that friendly blue. Somehow I feel no harm could come from people dressed exactly as we are. While that of course might be somewhat naive, it is a fact that denim relaxes both the wearer and the viewer. Perhaps that is why it never goes out of fashion.

Furrow shine

Some time in the 1960s was the last time I saw a field being ploughed by a horse-drawn plough. The ploughman was the father of a friend of mine, and he was good. It was close to dusk as I watched him go around the field and do so again and again with astonishing precision.

But what I remember most is the shine on the sod as it curled away from the ploughshare. That coarse earth acquired the same sheen as the glittering blade that cut into it and turned it over. It shone like steel. I wonder now, had my fingers run over it, would it have felt as smooth and cool as the steel that had turned it?

I shall never know, but this I do know, and knew then – my eyes had again seen beauty.

Suggestions

- Google the painter Bridget Riley, then click on *Images* and take a look at those canvases with their parallel lines. Gaze at one and see if it makes you dizzy.

- Or google Barbara Hepworth, to see those amazing sculptures that look like something from the sea.

- If you have a mountain nearby, try watching it at different times of the day, in different seasons, in different weathers, and notice how its texture changes – from velvet to coarse rock to soft misted grey. Often in the course of a single day.

- Try the same with a nearby field, especially one on a hillside.

- When did you last pick up a fallen chestnut and open it? Do it once more this autumn.

- Try playing with those folds in fabric, to create mountain ridges on your bedspread. Or on your sleeve or thigh. *Your* thigh.

10: Just add water

There are always waves in water... churned up by winds which come and go
and vary in direction and intensity, just as do the winds
of stress and change in our lives

~ Jon Kabat-Zinn

Though inland far we be,
Our souls have sight of that immortal sea
Which brought us hither

~ William Wordsworth

Ocean: A body of water occupying two-thirds
of a world made for man – who has no gills

~ Ambrose Bierce

The cure for anything is salt water - sweat, tears, or the sea

~ Isak Dinesen

WATER doesn't always have a good press. Perhaps with good reason – it sank the *Titanic* (well, ice did, which is water at its wickedest); it's dreary to drink; it creates tsunamis; it drowns people; worse still, it ruins a glass of wine; it bursts pipes in winter and rusts them in summer; it floods towns; it wrecks summer holidays by raining and winter holidays by avalanching; it's the main ingredient of both typhoons and snots.

And it didn't do a mighty lot for Noah. Besides, it goes AWOL when you most need it, like in the Sahara. Or when pipes freeze.

Yet water is still the most precious thing in the world. And it can be the loveliest thing in the world to look at. And, since this is a book about looking, that's all we'll deal with here.

Ocean, lake, river, and stream are water's main habitats (apart of course from clouds, snow-capped mountains, glaciers, the Antarctic, London fog, the mist that does be on the bog, and the human body, which they tell us is up to 70 per cent water). And water appears so different in each of the above. But it's at its most magnificent in the ocean.

Ocean power

Whenever I think of the power of the ocean, I think of Mendelssohn's *Fingal's Cave*. They made a short film of it once, called *Moods of the Sea*, with the music in time with a monstrous green sea that savages the Isle of Staffa and smashes and smashes again at the cave entrance, whitening to a foam that surges out to be sucked back into the storm.

How the film crew ever survived to finish it I cannot imagine.

Awe is the only true response to ocean, especially to its ferocity. I have seen the Atlantic white with fury, with plumes towering hundreds of feet into the air as they are forced up cliff sides, between rocks or through crevasses; while the swelling ocean, with murderous intent, reaches towards where I perch, as if it's determined to suck me into its maw.

As indeed it has done to many before me.

It's wonderful to watch such a storm on an Atlantic headland of Scotland or Ireland. Or from across Galway Bay, out at Barna or Spiddal. From there Black Head looks through the murk like a giant whale, edged where it meets the water with a white lacing of foam that looks so delicate. Until suddenly one of those plumes soars, mighty even from this distance, and you realise what that white lacing is, and can do.

That great nature lover John Muir had a similar memory from his boyhood in Scotland:

> With red-blooded playmates, wild as myself, I loved
> to wander in the fields to hear the birds sing, and
> along the seashore to gaze and wonder at the shells
> and seaweeds, eels and crabs in the pools among
> the rocks when the tide was low; and best of all to
> watch the waves in awful storms thundering on the
> black headlands and craggy ruins of the old
> Dunbar Castle when the sea and the sky, the waves
> and the clouds, were mingled together as one. [28]

However the ocean does not need a storm to make it awesome. It is that anyway. Stand on any Atlantic cliff and look out to sea in any weather. See how the horizon is no longer straight, but curves around us to meet the headlands on either side. Use binoculars to watch a ship near the horizon sink slowly until only the masts are visible. Imagine how far below the horizon is Spain, or Morocco, or even Brazil, depending on which direction you are looking. Then gaze down at the whispering water far below, and realise that it hungers for you and will take you if it can.

If we ever have the privilege to be with someone who is seeing the sea for the very first time, then we realise the wonder of it all. We need just look at such a person's eyes as they gaze enraptured. We all had that wonder once, and we can have it back if we learn again to gaze and grow mindful.

Crossing the bar

It's almost a cliché of the romantic novel – the village where an old sea dog lives in a cottage above the harbour, spending his declining years wistfully gazing out to sea with his telescope. I found exactly such a place on the Isle of Wight called Freshwater Bay, near where the poet Tennyson once lived.

Not sure if there were any old sea dogs but, if I remember, the hotel was called the Albion. Whatever is the magic of the place, I spent my few days there gazing wistfully out to sea like any old sea dog.

This time I was experiencing a gentle ocean in all its summer loveliness. Ships passed far out to sea. Then one evening I saw a tall ship in full sail moving gracefully beyond the little bay against a strawberry sunset, perhaps heading for Portsmouth, and it was that *Players Please* packet come to life. I couldn't but recall Tennyson's words:

> And the stately ships go on
> To their haven under the hill:
> But O for the touch of a vanish'd hand,
> And the sound of a voice that is still !

I thought he might have written them here, but that's not possible, for Tennyson wrote those lines in 1835 and didn't get here until 1853. But I wonder if he wrote *Crossing the Bar* at Freshwater, not long before he got that 'one clear call' to put out to sea and meet his Pilot face to face.

Sea change

As the sea's moods change, so do its colours. It was James Joyce who coined the memorable phrase, 'the snot-green Irish sea'. Perhaps it occurred to him as a child when he lived in that house right on the beach at Bray, County Wicklow – the house in *Portrait of the Artist* where took place the most celebrated Christmas squabble in all of literature. I can just see the little boy wandering out to the beach to get away from it all, and gazing forlornly at that green winter sea. And probably sniffing and snivelling in the cold damp air. How could he not have thought of snots?

However the sea can have a whole range of greens, and a lot more lovely than Joyce's dreary snots. There's a very special green you get when you walk the beach at Inchidoney or at

Keel on Achill Island in high-summer sunlight. The sea is cobalt blue under a clear sky and the breakers gleam white as they crash on the sand. But there is just that moment when the sunlight penetrates each wave as it rises to topple, and the water under the crest glows with a translucent green that is purest emerald. Then crash, and all is white again. Then follows what Rupert Brooke calls 'the little dulling edge of foam, that browns and dwindles as the wave goes home'.

When a wave breaks, I've noticed it doesn't happen all at once. Rather it starts curling at one end of the beach, and slowly the curling and the toppling come rolling horizontally along the beach towards you. And that glowing green comes right along with it. There is no sight quite like it.

Easter Island

When we watch waves breaking on a shore it's salutary to remember that the energy within each one comes to us across the ocean for perhaps thousands of miles. Missionary Mick Caheny, returning to Europe from South America, once stopped off at Easter Island. He was pondering many problems about his future:

'But,' he told me, 'looking at those waves rolling in for 3,000 miles, I felt the insignificance of so much. Here am I worried, thinking I'm the centre of the Universe, and I'm not. Here am I halfway between two continents. I felt I had a unique chance to size up everything. There were longings in me. I'd walk around and look at the stone statues. I went with the fishermen and they'd cook the fish on stones on the shore. It was very Paschal.... It was like a great retreat: I relaxed in nature and stopped fighting against it.'

I think Mick Caheny says it all. When we gaze upon the ocean and let it work its magic on us, for all its restlessness it helps us grow towards peace.

Suggestions

- Try to get to a coast when there is a storm. Preferably a cliff top or a high road overlooking the ocean. Somewhere like Blackhead at the extreme end of Galway Bay. There you will see nature in all her ferocity. But beware: go only where it is safe. The ocean has a nasty habit of reaching in and stealing people away. It does so every year. So heed the warnings from met office and local authorities.

- The film, *Moods of the Sea*, which I mentioned in this chapter, is by Slavko Vorkapich and John Hoffman. Produced in 1941, it has been hard to come by. It has lately been released as part of a seven-disc DVD collection entitled, *Unseen Cinema*. However I've just found it on YouTube – just type in the title and there it is. Strangely, I seem to remember it in colour – but this is in black and white. It's still magical, though.

11: Lake water lapping

What would the world be, once bereft
Of wet and wildness? Let them be left
O let them be left, wildness and wet;
Long live the weeds and the wilderness yet

~ Gerard Manley Hopkins

Stillness –
clouds peak
in the lake

~ Kobayashi Issa

Take a course in good water and air; and in the eternal youth of Nature
you may renew your own. Go quietly, alone; no harm will befall you

~ John Muir

A lake is the landscape's most beautiful and expressive feature.
It is earth's eye; looking into which the beholder
measures the depth of his own nature

~ Henry David Thoreau

Walking on water is certainly miraculous,
but walking peacefully on earth is an even greater miracle

~ John Gray

THE sea can never be still, but a lake can. A sea can take on the colour of the sky, but a lake can mirror the actual sky itself. I think perhaps there lies the difference. So, while the magic of the sea is its restless energy, the magic of a lake is its tranquillity.

A lake is at its loveliest when there is no wind at all. For then it can do all its wonderful conjuring tricks with reflections. I sat by a little East Clare lake the other day, and there was nary a ripple on the surface. The pines across the lake were inverted in the water, so that if you were to photograph them you could hardly tell which way was up.

Above the lake was one of those stupendous skies with towering cumulus clouds. Within the lake those same clouds were twinned, inverted, seeming to descend as far down through the deep blue water as they soared high above.

Then, quietly, there swam across those clouds three little ducks together, one leading, leaving three V-shaped wakes. There wasn't a quack out of them, and I felt they too were relishing the stillness. They moved through those clouds without benefit of wings, and their overlapping wakes created brief ripples in the clouds before all became still again.

Giverny

Like any other body of water, a lake can get agitated, indeed nasty, as we know from what happened to the disciples on the Sea of Galilee. But the real loveliness of a lake is when it grows calm. The Impressionist painter Monet spent the last 30 years of his life simply painting the reflections of skies in his lake at Giverny (oh, well, his *pond* then).

I sometimes feel Monet could have done a lot more with those years, but those curved wall-sized paintings at the Orangerie in Paris capture, as no other canvas does, the wonderful interplay of water and sky in the reflections in Monet's lake.

Mostly what we ourselves see are two layers – the sky with its white clouds, drawn down to the lake surface and locked together with the water lilies. Some lakes near where I live have three layers. As I stand by the shallow edge of the lake, I can see through the crystal-clear water to the stones that lie on the lake bed, and the tiny fish that dart past. That's the first layer. Above that, lilies float on the lake surface, or reeds project from the water, and ripples shiver in a gentle breeze. That's layer two.

And finally, a few metres out from the shore the reflection of the sky takes over and clouds move among the reeds and lilies. Layer three. And on certain days in spring there is even a fourth layer – those myriad dragonflies and damselflies and mayflies that hover in their thousands just above the water's surface.

When a trout comes up for a mayfly, for one magical instant he unites all four layers – the insect above, the fish below, the lilies bobbing in the widening circle, and the ripple-splintered sky.

Beat that, Claude Monet.

Lake edge

The edge of a lake can be fascinating, and quite different from an ocean foreshore. Willows let their branches droop into the water; tree trunks on the margin often come up out of the water itself; stones by the water's edge can be sheathed in lush green moss. There are often no real waves, but what Yeats calls 'lake water lapping with low sounds by the shore'. The sight and the sound of that lapping can give one the same peace which they promised to the poet at Innisfree.

'...As the swan in the evening moves over the lake' – it's almost a cliché. But it isn't really. Of all the loveliest things about a lake, there is nothing quite like coming down a winding boreen to the water's edge, and seeing a couple of swans move silently far out on the water. It never fails to enchant.

Indeed enchantment is the theme of one of the most moving of ancient Irish legends – the story of The Children of Lir: a beautiful princess and her three brothers. A wicked stepmother turned them into swans, condemning them to spend 300 years on Lake Derravaragh, another 300 on the Sea of Moyle, between Scotland and Ireland, and the final 300 on the waters around Inish Glora.

As the last of the 900 years comes to an end, one morning the swans hear the sound of a church bell echoing across the water. The swans come to the island shore, and the monk who has rung the bell (it is Saint Patrick) comes out to meet them. He blesses them and sprinkles them with holy water.

Suddenly there on the shore is an incredibly old woman, with three very old men. The old woman puts her arms around her brothers and, as St Patrick baptises each of them, each sinks to the ground and dissolves into dust. That night St Patrick sees four swans winging their way through the moonlit clouds to heaven.

For some reason that legend touches something deep in me, but I wish I knew what.

Four years ago I went to Lake Derravaragh, just to see where the legend began. As I stood on the lakeshore, a golden disc of sun was sinking towards the horizon, putting a golden path across the lake. As I watched, a swan slowly moved into that path of light and for one extraordinary moment was silhouetted against the gold. I actually caught it on camera: The picture is now up on the website that goes with this book. (See back cover.)

I would like to claim that I saw all four swans at Lake Derravaragh, but there were only two. And the second one nearly spoiled the scene, as it was over among the reeds hunting for goodies, with its backside up in the air and its neck down in the water. Most undignified for a swan. Yet swans are forever at it (why do you think they have those necks?), and they can spoil any lake scene when they lose their dignity and behave like that. But, as I once heard someone say, sure they're only human.

There is a wonderful bronze sculpture of the Children of Lir (four swans sweeping into the sky) at the Garden of Remembrance in Dublin. This is the spot where Queen Elisabeth laid a wreath and stood with head bowed, during her 2011 State Visit to Ireland. This gracious gesture is now recognized as one the most significant and poignant moments of reconciliation between the two nations.

Suggestions

- To see Queen Elisabeth laying the wreath at the Garden of Remembrance, just google it on You Tube. (One of the best versions is *http://www.youtube.com/watch?v=99K4_iuA4eA*)

- Take a look at *Monet at Giverny* on Google. You'll see all the clouds in the water you could hope for there.

- Or go to the Orangerie, just off the Place de la Concorde in Paris, to see for yourself those vast curved Monet canvases extending across whole walls.

- If you would like to learn more about the Children of Lir, google *http://www.culturalireland.org/lir_intro.asp*. Or just type in *Children of Lir* and see what you'll get.

12: River and stream

Rivers are roads which move, and which carry us
whither we desire to go

~ Blaise Pascal

All rivers, even the most dazzling,
those that catch the sun in their course,
all rivers go down to the ocean and drown.
And life awaits man as the sea awaits the river

~ Simone Schwarz-Bart

Denial ain't just a river in Egypt

~ Mark Twain

Oh, is the water sweet and cool,
Gentle and brown, above the pool?
And laughs the immortal river still
Under the mill, under the mill?

~ Rupert Brooke

AS I write this, I can look through my study window down on the River Shannon which flows below me. Right now it sparkles in the afternoon sunlight. I have seen it pewter under a winter sky; Mediterranean blue in high summer; glinting at twilight; salmon pink at sundown; hidden deep under mist at dawn; laced with white-tipped waves in the high winds funnelled between the hills which here close in the river on either side.

I have also seen it still as a lake, mirroring our 12th century cathedral tower and the 16th century bridge. It's the longest river in the British Isles, and the moodiest stretch of water I've ever known. And I love it.

There are stretches of the Shannon that widen into lakes bustling with tourist traffic; and there are quiet backwaters at places like O'Brien's Bridge where you can walk the banks seeing little but wildlife, mirroring water, fish jumping, and the occasional angler.

All great rivers have their distinct personalities, and I am fortunate to have lived beside four of them – here at Killaloe by the Shannon; at Niederdollendorf on the Rhine where I stayed while studying German; by the Tagus at Lisbon, where I lived for a time as a Dominican friar; and at Camas on the Columbia River, which divides Oregon from Washington State, where I worked as a newspaper editor. All four great rivers are a feast for the eye in any weather, and all four are wildly different.

To sum up in a few words, the Rhine for me is Wagner and Lohengrin and Siegfried, almost sinister, with the Drachenfels and those castle-capped crags glaring down to where the Rhine Maidens still hoard their Rheingold deep beneath the waves.

The Columbia River Gorge is startlingly similar, especially to that stretch of the Rhine between Koblenz and Bingen – barges from Portland ply the waters past mysterious islands; hills sweep magnificently up from the river, in places becoming cruel cliffs. There is a crag very like the Lorelei – only here it is called Crown Point. And there is even a little town called Bingen (after the Rhineland town), which actually looks like a Rhineland village, having deliberately copied that region's architecture.

But one great difference is that no castles crown the crags here. The other difference is that a few short miles up river the scenery changes abruptly from lush green to brown desert, after the river cuts through the Cascade Mountains which catch all the rainfall from the Pacific. A dramatic scenic experience is to drive along the river from the green meadows and rain forests of the western side and see how, within what seems only minutes, the scenery changes to parched hills where rattlesnakes lurk.

The River Tagus at Lisbon resonates of seafaring and the 15th century Voyages of Discovery. There is the grim Tower of Belem, from whence the ships set out; the Memorial to the Discoveries – a 100-foot-high blade of stone, with 20-foot figures of the Discoverers along its base.

But the *Adamastor* says it all – a statue in a little public park above the Tagus at Alcantara. Portugal's national poet Camões chronicles, in his epic *Lusiadas*, the futile attempts of early navigators to pass the storm-bound Cape of Good Hope. So many lives were lost that sailors began to imagine the Cape as some kind of evil living thing, half monster, half mountain, that would never let them pass. A vision of this Adamastor appears in the epic, as a giant emerging from the sea before the ship:

> I saw a terrifying ghost of gigantic size, like the
> Colossus of Rhodes... its brows heavy with storms,
> its great beard tattered, its eyes gleaming like stars,
> its hair thick and wild. The vision spoke: 'O most
> fearless of all men, you have dared to go beyond
> what is permitted to mortal creatures... Massive
> and unseen by you, I am that which you call the
> Cape of Storm: my name is Adamastor.' He writhed
> and twisted in the air and, with a great cry,
> suddenly vanished from our sight.[29]

That awesome vision appears once more, now carved in stone, glaring out across the Tagus estuary whence those ships set out. A tiny bronze figure of a shipwrecked sailor clings to its base and, on a plaque beneath, are the words: 'I am that Cape: my name is Adamastor.'

Those are some of the great rivers, and there are so many more I may never get to see. I long to see the gorges of the

Yangtze; the majestic Zambezi; the Mekong; above all, the Amazon. I wonder if I ever will.

Walking by a river

Anyhow, for a feast for the eye, I am more than content with the littler waterways of home. One of the great joys for the eye is when one walks a riverside. I have walked the River Cam as far as Grantchester, and it is as lovely as Rupert Brooke remembers (except that the church clock stands not at ten to three – wouldn't it be a nice idea if they kept it as the poem asks?). I even peeped through the gates of the Old Vicarage, where I think Jeffrey Archer was living at the time. It was just like any old vicarage.

Near where I now live, the local Chamber of Commerce and some truly civic-minded people have developed a pathway along the Nenagh River, all the way from the town of that name to Dromineer on the Shannon.

It is a joy in any season. Come with me and you will meet my friendly swans; you will come across quiet pools reflecting the trees above; in those pools you may encounter what Yeats called 'a long-legged fly upon a stream' – those amazing insects that actually walk on water. To watch them is so mesmerising that you have to be careful of falling in.

There are places where the waters are shallow and you can see the shivering green fingers of underwater reeds that bend with the current, all pointing downriver; there are tiny rapids where the river tries to show how cross it can get – and that's not very.

There are calm stretches where little ducks share the space with lilies. There is a spot where a kingfisher flashes by and is gone, leaving you wondering if you have imagined it.

There are overhanging trees, still with straw and debris marking how high the winter flood water can rise; there are the muddy, miniature bays where the cattle come down to drink. There is a heron who flaps resentfully out of the water, to settle a hundred metres ahead, and takes off even more grumpily when you reach where he has landed.

There are grassy parts on the track whence, in early summer as you walk along, there arise clusters of metallic blue-green dragon flies or damsel flies. There is even a little weir over which the water slides with grace and smoothness, with its headrace leading to where a millwheel once turned.

And then there are those elegant stone bridges – three of them where little local roads cross. Built a couple of hundred years ago, each has stones of every shape and size, skilfully interlocked to create its arch, capped by a proud keystone.

Bridges

An aside about bridges: we miss seeing most of them. Why? Because we mostly drive across them. We don't even realise they are there – perhaps all we are aware of is a slight hump in the roadway or a road sign naming the river beneath. The thing is to stop the car and walk down the track to the river bank – there nearly always is a style you can cross, and a track down to the water, often worn by fishermen. It's there that you can see the bridge and the river in all their beauty.

At Poulaphuca in the County Wicklow is one of the most graceful bridges in these islands – a castellated archway perched high above a waterfall and the forested gorge below. (The Gaelic *Poll an Phúca* means a hollow or pool of the Puca – which is a kind of fairy.)

Yet most people drive across that archway without even knowing it is there. To see it you should drive into nearby Poulaphuca House, a classic country-house hotel, and from there walk down along a pathway above the little gorge. Finally, high above among the towering trees, soars the archway, a thing of considerable grace.

Bridges across canals can be especially lovely. Last summer I stopped to look at one crossing the Grand Canal a mile or two from Shannon Harbour, and got chatting with a local man who was fishing there. He called my attention to the stone plaque built into the bridge, giving its date and the name of the landlord who contributed to its construction.

Then he showed me a strange smooth groove running the full length of the inside of the archway, above the tow path. It was, he explained, the groove worn by two centuries of tow cables, linking the barges with the horses that pulled them from along the tow path.

It was then I noticed the canal surface. It was the stillest imaginable. A tree was mirrored in the water and through its inverted branches the afternoon sun winked up at me from the depths. Then the fisherman's line touched the surface, and I watched the widening rings slowly approach the tree. The branches wavered as the rings touched, and I saw the immersed sun shiver through the water. It is one of those mindful moments I shall remember.

Tow paths are the great joy of canals. A river may or may not have a pathway along its bank, but a canal invariably has. This means we can pretty well traverse England, Ireland, France, the Netherlands or Germany, and perhaps many other countries, walking the towpaths of their canals. And what magic lies in wait for our eyes. Whereas a river pathway may meander off into a field or, worse still, end at a fence put up by some landowning cretin.

On the water

While walking by a river is one of the greatest visual joys I know, going out upon the water is a surprisingly different kind of joy.

My first memory of being on a river was at Maidenhead on the Thames. I must have been quite young but I do remember that my Aunt Betty took us out in a rented boat. It must have been a brilliantly sunny day, for my abiding childhood memory is of an expanse of dazzling water all around me; the oars of a passing eight cutting through the sparkles and creating more of them; someone leaning out to balance a tilting sailboat; cruisers churning gently up and down past us.

And I have a vague memory too of some idiot racing by and creating a huge wake so that everyone started yelling and swearing and shaking fists.

There's always one like that.

Renting a cruiser on the Shannon can be a uniquely mindful experience. It's as if you leave the everyday world behind – there are no cars, no roads, often no people, except perhaps a couple in a rare passing cruiser who silently, smilingly salute as they go by.

All around are reeds, and water hens with their little bobbing heads; a couple of disturbed ducks bursting into the air; the inevitable heron reluctantly lifting off the water; some little swimming creature that might be an otter; a couple of cows curiously watching you go by; hedges ending at the water's edge; and the sky, a gigantic blue-and-white dome above that flat expanse. And the cloud reflections from that dome, writhing and twisting in the boat's wake.

Something quite extraordinary happens after a while – time seems to stand still and you grow totally relaxed. After the first day you feel you have been a week on the water. I don't quite know why this is – could it be because things pass so slowly by? Or does one's heartbeat slow down? I'd like to think it does. Or could it be simply the effect of Mindfulness?

And then, if by any chance you espy a road in the far distance, especially with a car moving along it, you almost resent it. What's it doing in this wilderness? Those things don't belong here. Leave us alone, will you.

It's all an illusion of course: we can never be that far from roads or cars, or, uh, people. But it's one of the loveliest illusions I know.

According to sociologist Robert Levine, when time seems to stand still, what we are experiencing is 'natural time' (as opposed to 'clock time'), which is what we experience when enveloped by the forces of nature.[30]

He gives the example of the late writer Alex Haley: 'One of the reasons he loved to cruise the sea on small freighters was what it did to his sense of time.' Haley did his best writing while at sea, and observed, 'Once you're at sea for a couple of days, time becomes meaningless.'

Salmon of wisdom

Remember dendritic? A great river, fed by tributaries, in turn fed by streams which get their waters from babbling brooks? Salmon of course could tell us all about that, knowing how to find their way back from the great ocean through that dendritic puzzle to the very stream from which they came. No wonder the salmon is the symbol of wisdom and knowledge for the Celts.

Only once in my life did I ever see one spawning – in the shallowest of streams, in a remote Michigan forest four hours drive north of Chicago, and twenty uninhabited forest miles from a hamlet called – Dublin.

I still remember the wonder of that sight.

In the British Isles our salmon don't have to travel so far. Our streams are not so remote, but that indeed is part of their charm. They're easy to get to, for us as well as the salmon. I love to follow a little stream back into the mountain where it began. My favourite one near here grows steeper and narrower as you climb along it, finally squeezing its way between great sprayed boulders of limestone.

Glens are where many great rivers have their beginning – those forested clefts in the hills, with water gurgling down between their moss-covered rocks and trees, tumbling white from one clear pool to the next, where the shy deer come to drink. The very word is magic – Glen Shiel, Glen Orchy, Glencoe, Glendalough (*Gleann dá Loch* – Glen of the Two Lakes), Glen Trool, Glen of the Downs, Glen Affric, The Devil's Glen, the Seven Glens of Antrim. The word 'glen' itself seems to promise trees meeting over tumbling waters, and stunning visual beauty.

It nearly always delivers.

Suggestions

- Read *The Lady of Shallot* by Tennyson. The poem gives one of the most evocative descriptions of a river in all of literature: 'Willows whiten, aspens quiver, little breezes dusk and shiver, through the wave that runs forever, by the island in the river...' Just Google it and you can get the whole magnificent poem.

- Consider a river-cruising holiday, just to experience time standing still. There is very little skill needed to operate a family-sized cruiser, and little danger, provided you wear life jackets.

- To rent a family cruiser in Britain there is excellent help on *http://www.holidayuk.co.uk/afloat/book.htm*. This website helps you choose a route, shows where to start from, and finds you a boat.

- For excellent value in Ireland, on both the Erne and the Shannon, and the various canals, google *Emerald Star*. There are several other boat-hire companies, and you can find them by googling *Shannon cruising*.

- Or if you prefer to be catered for, there are floating hotels with every comfort. Google *English Holiday Cruises* for luxury cruises on several of Britain's rivers. For the Shannon, google *Shannon* Princess. This floating hotel even offers golfing cruises. Why not, given that there are thirty golf courses along the 200 miles of the Shannon?

13: Lore of the living

I think I could turn and live with animals,
they are so placid and self-contained,
I stand and look at them long and long

~ Walt Whitman

The bird of paradise alights only on the hand that does not grasp

~ John Berry

God sleeps in a stone; dreams in a flower; moves in an animal

~ Anonymous

I ask people why they have deer heads on their walls. They always say
because it's such a beautiful animal. There you go. I think my mother is
attractive, but I have photographs of her

~ Ellen DeGeneres

'HAVE you looked closely at a mussel shell recently? They're beautiful things: not a standard slate grey, as you might think, but glistening with colour and pattern, from blond streaks and blue highlights to graded tortoiseshell stripes of brown, caramel and café crème. It seems almost a shame to cook them.'

Lucas Hollweg wrote that in a recipe for *The Sunday Times* and, if his cooking is a good as his power of observation – and his writing – then no wonder he is a celebrity chef.

Think of it: there must be few things quite as hectic as a restaurant kitchen, yet this chef could find time to notice an insignificant little mussel, to gaze at it and to admire it. And then to recall its living colours. There's a man with the gift of Mindfulness.

A mussel is a living thing. Well, maybe its shell isn't, same as my fingernail isn't alive. But let's not make too fine a point of that. The point I do want to make is that of all the things in nature, those things that live and move and have their being are the greatest source of the Joy of Looking.

Especially the wild things. Padraic Pearse longed to see 'little rabbits playing in a field, lit by a slanting sun.... things young and happy.' As I write this there's a baby rabbit lolliping around the grass outside my window. I'm stopping now to watch the little nose twitching as it explores its new world. I find that when I watch a wild thing for any length of time it has a strangely calming effect on me, almost euphoric, and friends have told me the same thing. I know I've said it before, and will say it again, but I cannot help repeating it. I think it's all part of Mindfulness.

Foxes

Some months ago I had a close encounter with an urban fox. It was the night of a full moon, well after midnight, and I had just parked my car in a quiet suburban side street in Somerset. Not a soul was around, but then I noticed the silhouette of what looked like a silent dog sitting in the middle of the moonlit street just ten feet away. I looked again, and discerned a strange bushy tail, stretched along the ground, nearly as big as the creature itself. Even though it sat sideways on to me, the head was slightly turned and I knew it was watching me.

We both stayed gazing at each other, silent and unmoving, for at least ten minutes. I don't know what the fox felt, but once again I felt that strange peace.

I am sure we would have stayed an hour, just like that, but my wretched mobile phone chose that instant to ring. In the moment it took me to grab it and switch it off, the fox had disappeared, silent as ever.

It can be even more wonderful when trust develops between a human and a wild creature, provided that trust is not abused. Since that encounter with the fox, I have been introduced to a pair of foxes who have become friends with my friends Harvey Wasserman and Sarah Daniel. They live in the wilds of the Burren – the foxes and the folks – and every day the foxes come to the kitchen door and jump up at the door handle, demanding to be fed. I had the experience of holding out a piece of bacon and having the fox take it from my hand. I'm not sure which of us was the more nervous. (By the way, I won't do that again, as I have learnt it can give foxes wrong ideas.)

I am aware of the controversy in Britain about urban foxes. I know that they are accused of hunting in packs, and of killing pet cats, and of lots of other enormities. I have no intention of taking sides: just let me refer the reader to *www.thefoxwebsite.org.* You may be surprised by what you find there.

A few years ago a pair of collar doves began visiting my deck. I would spread some peanuts, and gradually began placing them nearer to where I sat. At some point I just put the peanuts on the table in front of me, and the doves started feeding happily from right beside me. Finally I got to holding out my hand with the nuts in the palm, and – I could hardly believe it – one would perch on the tips of my fingers and happily devour the nuts, while the other waited its turn (probably the male, letting the lady go first). It was extraordinary to feel the little talons tighten around my fingertips, as the wings fluttered to maintain balance and the bobbing head pecked away at my palm. (I actually have a picture of this, which, by the way, you can see on the website.)

It got to the point where I could go out to the deck, imitate the *whoo-whoo-WHOO* call of a collar dove and, from across the Shannon, two tiny dots would appear, fluttering bigger and bigger until they landed on the rail of my deck. And thence to my hand.

Those two collar doves came daily over a period of two years. Often they would peep in at my study window asking me to come out and play; other times they would spend the whole day sitting in the creeper above my deck.

To my lasting shame I ended the friendship. There came a bit of a scare about bird flu, and people told me I might pick up something from the doves. So I simply stopped feeding them. They continued coming for a while, looking forlorn and hungry and sad, and then they just didn't come any more.

If only I could have them back now.

Grace & beauty

The most marvellous thing about living creatures must surely be their grace. When I was about ten I used to cycle down to the nearby docks to watch the seagulls. Just to look at them riding the wind was a source of wonder: they could be almost motionless in the air just ten feet above me, with their wings in that elegant shallow curve, moving a fraction every now and then to adjust to the breeze with a mastery that was incomparable. I still love to watch them, especially out at sea when they follow a ship.

There is beauty in all living things. There is the beauty of shape – the incomparable grace of a racehorse; the sheer mass of a bull; the ease of contented cows; the elegance of a stag.

There is the beauty of texture – the pulsing dampness of a frog's skin; the rippling muscles in the shoulders of a foal; the mop of hair tumbling down the forehead of a lovely mare. It was Marianne Moore who asked, 'Which of us has not been stunned by the beauty of an animal's skin or its flexibility in motion?'

In the way creatures move there is indeed great beauty – the forked swoop of a swallow low across a field; the serpentine curving of an eel in the shallows; the sinuous undulating way a squirrel runs; the abrupt little movements of a robin as he comes close to spy on you; the canter of a pony over a hill against the sky; the scamper of a spaniel along a seashore, its ears pinned back by the wind.

Starlings

To me the most wonderful movement of all is when a vast number of creatures – fish or birds – move in unison. I recently watched a gigantic dark cloud of starlings wheeling above the twilit Shannon right across from me here: one moment they stretched out in a line a hundred metres long; suddenly they clustered into a globe; then they became a giant funnel swirling through the sky like a tornado and it seemed almost frightening. It made me think of one of those Old Testament plagues descending upon the Egyptians.

Then they became almost invisible as they wheeled away to show only the edges of their wings; and then, as if obeying some incredible design, they formed an absolutely perfect teardrop shape – a zeppelin in the sky – curved at the front, and tapering gracefully back to a sharp point at the rear. The front of the teardrop was denser, like a kind of warhead, where the starlings were more concentrated.

It was as if the whole flock had suddenly acquired one single mind, become one single body of which the individual starlings were only cells. Luckily I had my camera to hand and managed to get a photograph of it. (It's that picture on the book's cover.)

This is known as a *murmuation* of starlings and can contain more than 100,000 individuals (some authorities say half a millon). There are some incredible videos of these murmurations on YouTube. There is an astonishing one taken at Gretna in Scotland -- just google *Starlings at Gretna* to watch it on You Tube. It is almost terrifying to watch a shape in the sky like a giant winged dragon coming towards you, suddenly becoming a gigantic blanket in the sky that looks about to descend and smother you. Once again it makes me think of the biblical Plagues of Egypt coming to destroy the land.

I have been reading some of the comments on this particular video. A man called Scott Masson writes from Oklahoma that he had seen something similar there: 'It had the most profound spiritual effect on me. I can't even explain it or put it into words. After an incredibly difficult week in my personal life, this one moment completely shifted everything. I now all of a sudden have renewed hope about life and the world in general. Witnessing natural phenomena such as this is a gift.'

Surely it's the gift of Mindfulness.

Just up from my home, at Lough Derg on the river Shannon, are regularly some of the most wonderful murmurations I have ever seen. Recently two young English women, Sophie Windsor Clive and Liberty Smith, out canoeing on the lake, captured a two-minute film of one such murmuration, which has become an international wonder on the Vimeo website with three million hits at the time of writing this. To see it, check Suggestions at the end of this chapter.

How do the starlings do it? No one really knows. Some suggest it's an instance of chaos theory. Scientist Wayne Potts believes it works like a chorus line at the Folies Bergères – one individual initiates a movement, and the others follow within milliseconds. Certainly recent studies indicate that starlings have a reaction time of between 20 and 100 milliseconds.

But how could that explain a sudden perfect teardrop shape? Could any bird brain dictate such a shape in an instant, never mind conceive it? Biologist Rupert Sheldrake suggests a phenomenon which he calls morphic resonance. The theory suggests that the flock operates in some kind of field of influence – a 'morphic field' which, Sheldrake says, provides a 'structured context within which the animals' communications and responses occur'.[31]

In more recent studies Sheldrake concludes that telepathy is more pervasive than we ever guessed, and that a mind stretches far beyond the skull which we thought confined it. Perhaps like radio waves? Could this help to explain murmurations?

Italian scientists Dr Michele Ballerini and Dr Andrea Cavagna have been studying the starlings of Rome, using synchronised movie cameras to capture the movements in three dimensions, and physicist Irene Giardina suggests that starling flocks are 'a critical system', somewhat similar to crystals uniting at a critical temperature or avalanches forming at a critical point of tension.

But no one yet knows how this criticality is actually created or maintained. Apparently it is similar to what operates in proteins and neurons, according to some universal principle yet to be understood.

It seems that every individual starling may at a critical point be connected to some single invisible network, or even together become temporarily cells of a single entity.

To me that sounds very much like a single mind taking over. But I'd better leave that to the scientists, who tell us the jury is still out. And anyhow, as a BBC commentator put it, we don't always need to ask why – 'sometimes we should just sit back and enjoy the show.'

Comical critters

Living creatures can be graceful; powerful; awe inspiring; beautiful; frightening – they can also be very funny.

Take farmyard dogs, for example. Essentially they are bullies. As I hike past a farmhouse one of these critters invariably comes sneaking out, crouching close to the ground, with malign intent. If I run, or shrink into the hedgerow, he's delighted and advances, showing his teeth. (There is even one that won't let me walk the street of a certain village.}

However, bullies are invariably cowards, and dogs are no exception. So I stop and stand my ground. The dog stops, unsure what to do next. Then I advance menacingly, raising one fist with an imaginary stick. The dog lets a howl, and runs yelping back to safety with his tail between his legs.

Occasionally, if I wait, he will slink back out after a while, once more close to the ground, but this time cringing, with an ingratiating smile on his face. Or peer over a wall, begging for forgiveness and understanding.

Exactly like the office bully.

And I accept him graciously, magnanimously, as I would the office bully.

Dogs can be such fun. There's a red setter in a cottage some miles from here and, whenever I happen by, I stop the car, hoot the horn and climb out. Out prances the dog and drops a stick at my feet which I must then throw for him to fetch. The game could go on forever. I've even got to know the family, introduced by their doggie.

Dogs are funniest when left inside a car. They become totally territorial. Sometimes, if I am in an irresponsible mood, and if the owner is nowhere near, I like to put my face to the car window and watch the paroxisms of fury inside. The smaller the dog, the meaner it gets.

Except police dogs – they're both mean *and* large. And the one time I got what I deserved was when I peeped in at a police dog in a squad car in Seattle. Unfortunately the car door hadn't been properly shut...

My late friend Rebecca Millane maintained that God must have a sense of humour. Just look at the waddle of a duck, she used to say. Or the mournful face of a bulldog. (How could you not be mournful with a face like that, she'd ask.) Or watch a dog facing down a cow. Or a cow family seemingly posing for the camera. Or two cats mating in the middle of the street. Or is there anything quite as ridiculous as a poodle? (Rebecca wasn't exactly gone on poodles.)

Last summer I saw a hawk hovering high over my garden. I knew it as a hawk from the wings far up close to the head, but whether it was a sparrow hawk or a merlin or a falcon I would not know. It was almost still in the air, with just a slight flutter at the serrated wing tips.

But that was the only thing up there that was still. The hawk was being bombarded by what seemed dozens of swallows. They dived it and veered away at the last moment, turning to come back again to the attack. And back again and again. It was like watching Spitfires attacking a Heinkel 111 in the Battle of Britain. Finally the poor old hawk bowed to the inevitable, side-slipped and veered away. I almost felt sorry for it.

I was out for a walk a few days ago when I saw a herd of cows charging furiously down a long, hilly field. About ten metres in front of the herd lolliped a hare, obviously thoroughly enjoying the chase. Every now and then he would squat for a moment and look back at the charging cows. Then he'd take off again. At the bottom of the field he simply disappeared into a neighbouring farmer's garden, leaving a lot of very cross cows.

The caws of dissent

There is a colony of crows in a stand of trees at the Lakeside Hotel just down from where I live. They are like one ghastly family of humans that you might see on TV – the Royles or people like that. The screeching and the fights that go on, the sulking and the huffing and the puffing, the settling of scores, the squawking, the reconciliations and the settlings down, and the bullying and the chasing of some poor nerd-bird, provide me with endless merriment.

My friend Fiona Clark-Echlin thinks they even seem to hold parliament each day. One crow croaks away as authoritatively as any prime minister, and everyone listens attentively. Then there is a chorus of squawks that sounds exactly like 'hear-hear', and then the PM starts again. Another chorus. Then, as if a division bell rings, they all suddenly take off in every direction. To vote, or to their constituencies? Who knows?

Incidentally, anyone know the collective noun for crows? It's 'a murder of crows'. Apt enough, betimes.

At night these crows all fly home together right past my deck. There is an air of joyous homecoming; the conversations are animated; they are hurrying to get back. And then there are always the few solitary latecomers, flapping along forlornly as though they have missed whatever fun was planned for the evening.

They've obviously been out working all day – bird work, presumably. Very intelligent work, by the way: I have seen them carry walnuts high in the air, and drop them onto concrete so that they break open. I have caught them taking my hanging basket of peanuts off its hook to spill it open on the ground. They then swagger along my deck rail to defy me. And when I chase them, for the sake of the littler birds, before they flap away they give me such mocking, contemptuous looks that I am convinced they are laughing at me as much as I laugh at them. Forget what I said about bird brains.

Suggestions

- To see that amazing flock of starlings filmed by the two girls on Lough Derg, just google *Murmuration from Sophie Windsor Clive* on Vimeo. You can also see it on *http://www.rte.ie/news/2011/1107/starlings.html.*

- Almost everyone has the opportunity to feed birds, and it is one not to be missed. It is the one thing that can bring wild nature right into our lives. We don't need a garden, or even a back yard. A balcony will do. And even without one, we can always hang a feeder outside a window.

- If you do feed the birds, get one of the *Observer Series* on British & Irish Birds, or some similar book. There are lots of them. Some are listed in the Bibliography at the end of this book. In no time at all you will be able to identify every little creature that comes to your feeder. If you want to see the extensive list of *Observer* wildlife titles, google *http://en.wikipedia.org/wiki/Observer's_Books*

- Besides the two starling videos mentioned in this chapter, there are lots of other starling pictures and sequences on both Google Images and YouTube. Just type in *starlings.*

- But don't just google. Get out there and find the starlings for yourself. Where to find them? The Royal Society for the Protection of Birds can tell you where. Just google *RSPB*. Their Johann Holt says that many nature reserves have starlings, and many roost near well-known tourist destinations like Brighton Pier, Gretna Green in Dumfries and Galloway. Holt: 'Several of our reserves make great viewing spots too. These include Leighton Moss, Lancashire; Saltholme, Middlesbrough; Ham Wall, Somerset; Newport Wetlands, Newport; and Snape, Suffolk.' They are commonest in southern Britain, but are found all over Ireland. You can be fairly sure of when to look for them as their timing is precise from day to day. Holt again: 'In many cases they are like clockwork – you know that at a certain time in the evening the sky will start to turn black, and it's mesmerizing watching the flock grow and grow.'

- If you do go starling watching, why not film them? Your smart phone is quite sufficient, or even a simpler mobile phone – it's all Sophie and Liberty had, but of course a camcorder would be even better.

- You could also join a bird-watching club. Clubs know exactly where to find, not just starlings, but rare seabirds and waterfowl and birds of the forest. And they frequently organize outings to go find them. Especially if you live in a city it is a wonderful way to stay in touch with nature and also to learn about it.

- You can listen to Rupert Sheldrake on *www.sheldraketv.com*. He is well worth your time.

- By the way, the photo of those collar doves coming to my hand should be up on the website now (address on back cover).

14: The littlest things

If you think you are too small to be effective,
you have never been in bed with a mosquito

~ Betty Reese

Hey! Don't swat:
the fly wrings his hands
on bended knees

~ Kobayashi Issa

There is nothing, sir, too little for so little a creature as man.
It is by studying little things that we attain the great art
of having as little misery and as much happiness as possible

~ Samuel Johnson

Some of nature's most exquisite handiwork is on a miniature scale, as anyone
knows who has applied a magnifying glass to a snowflake

~ Rachel Carson

Without a seed there would be no plant

~ Geshe Rabten
(Treasury of Dharma)

THERE is a poignant scene towards the end of the film, *A Man for All Seasons*. Thomas More has been condemned to death for refusing to endorse Henry VIII's divorce. Suddenly the screen fills with the cheerful close-up of a bumble bee buzzing busily in the heart of a rose.

Then the screen widens to take in what lies beyond the rose bush. It is the scaffold, the block, the axe, and the black-clad, masked executioner.

Whoever filmed that scene was mindful of of tiny things. There is a whole world of such things out there – things living and non-living – that most of us never even notice, simply because they are too tiny to attract our attention.*

Take the snowflake, for instance. Of course we are familiar with those big plastic six-pointed stars that hang in our supermarkets at Christmas, but how often have we actually seen a real snow crystal close up?

If I catch a snowflake on my sleeve, and get down close to it before it melts, I see that it is made up of lots of minute six-pointed stars, every single one different from any other that ever was or ever will be.

There are other shapes too, stellar plates and dendrites, columns and needles, but the stars are best. They mesmerised Henry David Thoreau, as he wrote, in 1856: 'How full of the creative genius is the air in which these are generated! I should hardly admire more if real stars fell and lodged on my coat.' [32]

These snow crystals are tiny – you could fit several on the nail of your little finger. So a very good way of seeing them is to carry a small pocket magnifying glass.

Pocket lens

A pocket magnifier is not just for looking at snowflakes, however. I have actually started carrying one pretty well all the time in the glove compartment of my car. There are so many tiny things to look at, if I make time to look at them. Which I try to do. Sociologist Robert Morrison MacIver always carried a pocket lens which, he said, 'greatly extended the scenery'. He

---

*I believe it was Patrick Carey, an Irish film maker famous for his documentaries, which include *Yeats Country; Errigal; Oisín;* and *The Port of Hull.*

was forever looking for design, detail, and colour in tiny things like leaves, twigs, mushrooms, seashells, feathers.

Environmentalist Rachel Carson, author of that glorious book, *The Sense of Wonder,* maintained that a pocket lens actually brings a new world into being: 'A sprinkling of sand grains may appear as gleaming jewels of rose or crystal hue, or as glittering jet beads, or as a melange of Lilliputan rocks, spines of sea urchins and bits of snail shells. A lens-aided view into a patch of moss reveals a dense tropical jungle, in which insects large as tigers prowl amid strangely formed, luxuriant trees.' [33]

She maintained that any tiny creature, once viewed under a lens, reveals extraordinary complexity and beauty, for the lens helps us escape the limitations of the human-size scale.

Insects

So now for insects. This is a dicey one, for not all of us are enamoured of the critters. As Astrid Alauda said, 'Cockroaches really put my all-creatures-great-and-small creed to the test.' Ogden Nash put it even better:

> God in His wisdom made the fly
> And then forgot to tell us why

And yet insects are the most fascinating of all tiny things. If only for their complexity – it's hard to believe that a gnat has muscles to drive its wings, cavities to hold its blood, air tubes to take in oxygen, eyes vastly more complex than mine, and a brain to drive the lot. All miraculously packed inside that airborne speck.

It is the sheer beauty of insects that fascinates more than anything. I have had some strange visitors indeed to my front door in all shapes and colour. Even the hated wasp is lovely to look at. Wait until July, then put out a jam jar with a little jam or honey left on its rim, get out your pocket lens and wait for that first wasp. You will see a stunning study in yellow and black – not just that striped Kilkenny or AEK Athens football jersey on the abdomen, but a head of dazzling yellow set off by a pair of great black sunglasses such as Bono or Elton John might wear.

On a warm afternoon last summer I strolled past a buddleia tree outside a rural bungalow in Devon. At first I thought the tree was just in blossom but, when I looked again, the blossom seemed in motion, and I realised it was quivering with butterflies. They were mostly tortoise-shell but I counted five different species altogether. One tortoise-shell was so drunk with nectar that I got within a couple of inches of him and could watch his proboscis, like a tiny elephant's trunk, probing the riches of each blossom.

The young woman of the house came out and I asked her had she noticed the butterflies. She hadn't. When she saw them she called her three children, and my last sight as I walked away was of a family entranced.

The fly is up

Butterflies are tops in the insect beauty league. They're often called flying flowers or aerial blossoms. But they're hard pressed in the pageant by dragonflies and damsel flies (I find it hard to tell the difference between these two, except that the latter folds its wings when at rest). I understand that both are considered a primitive form of insect since their wings are not locked together but operate separately. For that very reason they remind me of those early biplanes, and all I can say is that, primitive or not, they are creatures of extraordinary beauty.

I can never forget a hot summer's day in the gardens of Quarr Abbey on the Isle of Wight, where I encountered what were literally swarms of these magnificent insects hovering and darting above the ponds. Their blue metallic bodies danced as if in time with the shimmering sun-kissed water.

I remember another time when I saw them in their thousands. I was walking along the bank of the River Suir near

Clonmel: the grass was high and, at every footfall, swarms of damselflies rose into the air in clouds of blue sparks. It was like having a firework display at my very feet.

A close third in beauty must be the mayfly, that tiny creature that comes up from the depths of a lake to live for just three days, indeed sometimes only for a few minutes, which time the male spends making love, or trying to, without even bothering to eat. The mayfly is elegant with its three long tails, and the big front legs for grasping the loved one.

Few things are more delightful than to be down by a lakeside during those short weeks when the mayfly is 'up'. The lake is dotted with small boats containing people who should be at the office but are out sick, dapping for the trout that go berserk after the mayfly. I remember once being down by a lakeside and encountering a cloud of mayfly all engaged in their brief but frantic courtship. Suddenly hundreds settled on my car, covering it all over, and some even landed on my fingers, which could hardly have been mistaken for mates. I don't know what the poor things were thinking.

The courtship dance of such little creatures is as elegant as any ballet. Especially lovely to watch is a cloud of midges, particularly when a shaft of evening light catches them, as they bob and whirl and move up and down with all the grace of a Viennese ball. Of course this is best viewed from a vantage point of some feet away, and a dab of insect repellent can also be helpful. (I didn't say midges were friendly – I only said they were nice to watch.)

Hover & dance

My favourite of all is the hoverfly. A childhood memory is of being often in our garden on a summer day and watching this tiny creature, striped like a wasp but only a fraction of its size, simply perched in mid air just in front of my five-year-old face, seemingly gazing right into my eyes. I was never scared, as they had told me it didn't sting, and that the stripes were just to scare off enemies.

149

Then suddenly it would vanish, to reappear three feet away as if by magic. Always it stayed absolutely still, with just a slight blur where its wings ought to be – I now know that those wings were beating at 250 times a second, which is why they were scarcely visible.

And even that record is broken by the dancing midges, whose wings beat at the quite unbelievable rate of 1,000 times per second. Per *second*, not per minute. Think of it – it's surely one of nature's most astounding feats.

The poor benighted housefly is almost as good when it comes to high-speed wings, and its aerobatic agility is incomparable. It can take off vertically in an instant; do cartwheels in the air; fly on its back; do spectacular split-second turns; land upside down on the ceiling. It never, ever stalls. And it sees you coming – that it certainly does.

When it does, it can react in one three-hundredth of a second.

Next time why not first admire it before you swat it? There is a lot to admire. Last word to Stephen Dalton: 'Apart from the development of the brain, the fly is almost as complicated and miraculous as man, possessing everything necessary for its way of life... with sophisticated tissues and mechanisms for operating the wings. Yet, without a second thought, we can destroy it at a single stroke!' [34]

Eight?

Joseph W. Krutch presumably loved his fellow men, and probably his dog. But there he drew the line: 'Two-legged creatures we are supposed to love as we love ourselves. The four-legged also can come to seem pretty important. But six legs are too many from the human standpoint.'

So how about eight?

There's a lot to be said for spiders, actually. Obviously I don't mean tarantulas – I'm thinking of the domesticated little creatures that cause those cobwebs which I've just noticed on my study ceiling as I write this.

Spiders can be friends. I have one that travels everywhere with me. He, or she, has spun a web between my car's wing mirror and the window. So far she has managed to survive the wind and the rain and several hundred-mile drives. It helps that I haven't washed my car for some considerable time.*

There is also a spider outside my back door, that comes down on its thread every morning and stays looking at me for a while – at leasts I think it's looking – before scurrying back up again. Obviously I don't know what it's thinking, but *I* am thinking that for the first time I am actually getting acquainted with an individual spider. Not just any old spider, but the same one every day. I am actually getting to know a spider. Could we become friends? Watch this space.

Whatever about friends, spiders can certainly be mentors, as one was for Scottish freedom fighter Robert the Bruce. At one point he had taken refuge on Rathlin Island, off the coast of Antrim. He lay on a straw bed close to despair, after six attempts to win in battle against Edward I of England.

Then he saw a spider trying to spin a web between two beams. A thread hung from one beam, and the spider on the end of it was trying to swing it to the neighbouring beam as the start of its web. Bruce watched it try and fail six times. On the seventh, it succeeded. Bruce said to himself, I failed six times against the English: if this wee spider can do it on the seventh try, then so can I.

And so he did, eventually becoming King of Scotland after driving out the English at the Battle of Bannockburn in 1314.

A spider's web is certainly one of nature's loveliest gifts to us. Webs have been around for 140 million years, as evidenced by one preserved in Early Cretaceous amber in Sussex. It is their intricacy, their ingenuity of construction, with the

---

*Only just this morning I found a second web attached to my wing mirror. I'm not sure whether I'm now hosting two spiders – spouses, perhaps – or whether it's just one particularly hard-working spider. I think I'll put the picture of my spiders' web sites up on my own website.

151

spreading rays and the cross lines always denser towards the centre, that make them look like tiny nebulae.

There are two occasions when webs are particularly lovely. Both are in early morning. One is after a white frost, when every tiny thread turns white from its coating of ice. The other is when dew collects on the filaments, and condenses into rows and rows of the littlest pearls imaginable.

Once I was in an early morning train from London to Edinburgh. It was at the end of winter, before the gorse blossom, and at first I couldn't understand why all those acres of gorse bushes beside the tracks seemed to be in blossom, but a blossom that was eerily white. Then I suddenly realised that I was looking at millions if not billions of spiders' webs, completely enwrapping the gorse, and every one of them gleaming white with morning frost.

Ever smaller

Then of course there is the world of the smaller yet, but for that we need a microscope. Whenever I've had the opportunity to peep through one, to discover what I'm really made of, partly scared me but partly reminded me there's a further world in there which I must really get around to looking at.

Maybe the almost unbelieveable things which an electron microscope reveals has eroded the status of the old-fashioned microscope (what they now dismissively call a 'light microscope', as opposed to an electron one). Yet the experts tell us that any venerable microscope with its lenses and eyepieces can give us an extraordinary insight into the wonder of life.

Professor Brian J Ford, president of the Cambridge Society for the Application of Research, and visiting professor at Leicester University, actually laments one result of electron microscopes. In a lecture delivered at Trinity College, Dublin, he suggests that we are looking at smaller and smaller components of reality, and losing the bigger picture (within that tiny world). 'We are developing all these techniques which allow us to see more and more about different bits inside cells.

It's as though we are hell-bent on this reductionist thing – it really is like you are analyzing the ink on the page that makes a note, but I want to hear the entire symphony.

'The talk… is who has got the highest magnification and the best and the biggest, but you can't just keep analyzing scrambled eggs and hoping it will tell you about bird life.'

Ford wants us to use microscopes to look more at whole cells, and to make people more aware of what they are. 'It should be illegal,' he says, 'to get to the age of 12 and not have looked through a light microscope and seen the cells we are made of.'

Suggestions

- If you do decide to carry a magnifying glass, go for at least a 5x – that is, one that magnifies five times. Better still, get a 10x. Get a light plastic one, which is easy to carry, and costs very little at one of those pound or euro stores.

- Take a look at some of the snowflake sites on Google – a particularly good one is *www.snowflakes.com*. Then await winter and get out and look at the real thing.

- Since I wrote the above I have managed to get a little digital microscope, and it's amazing. It's like a small flashlamp, with a USB cable to connect to the computer. You just put the lens close up to something tiny like a wasp's face, press a button, and hey presto, there's old wasp grinning from the laptop, 400 times bigger than he ought to be. You can get one for about €80.

- Get hold of Stephen Dalton's *Miracle of Flight,* [35] published by Merrell in London (*www.merrellpublishers.com*). The section there on how insects fly is an enthralling read, and the ultra-high-speed photos will certainly make you look more respectfully at the next fly you meet.

15: Line, shape, pattern

The ear is as much offended with one even continued note,
as the eye is with being fix'd to a point, or to the view of a dead wall

~ William Hogarth

Before the Roman came to Rye or out to Severn strode,
The rolling English drunkard made the rolling English road.
A reeling road, a rolling road, that rambles round the shire,
And after him the parson ran, the sexton and the squire;
A merry road, a mazy road, and such as we did tread
The night we went to Birmingham by way of Beachy Head

~ GK Chesterton

And while I stood there I saw more than I can tell and I understood more than I
saw; for I was seeing in a sacred manner the shapes of all things in the spirit,
and the shape of all shapes as they must live together like one being

~ Black Elk

For life is but a dream whose shapes return, some frequently, some seldom,
some by night and some by day

~ James Thomson

'THE most beautiful aircraft ever to have graced the skies' – words used to describe the Lockheed *Super-G Constellation*. They appear on the website of the Airline History Museum of Kansas, and most aviation enthusiasts would agree with them. I certainly do.

The original Constellation design appeared shortly before World War II, and spent its first years in the drab olive green of the military. However it came into its own after the war, when a lengthened version, the *Super-G,* appeared in the red-and-white livery of Trans World Airlines. That was the iconic one.

It was the line of the fuselage that made it beautiful. It was shaped like a very shallow, horizontal S, with the front end seeming to droop slightly, while the rear curved upwards to carry the elegant triple oval tail fins. The S shape was emphasised by the curving red-on-white stripe that ran the full length of the plane. Other airlines followed suit, with their own versions of the S stripe. Lufthansa had a particularly elegant stripe in blue and yellow.

What was it about the shallow S-curve that was so satisfying? And why does that same curve always seem to please our eye wherever it occurs, whether it be in the side-view profile of a female figure, or the line between *yin* and *yang,* the sensual curve of a Christmas cactus, or the 'rolling English road' beloved of Chesterton, as it curves around hill and dale?

The 18th century English painter, William Hogarth, in his *Analysis of Beauty,*[36] put forward the theory that the serpentine curvature of an S-shaped line is far more lively and exciting to the eye, indeed more like a living thing, than a boring old straight line where nothing much seems to happen. Be that as it may, it certainly seems that Hogarth's Line of Beauty continues to please the eye today.

I find it everywhere – in country laneways; in cumulus clouds; in hills and dales; in the leg of a Queen Anne chair; in the path of an eel in the shallows; in the curved back of a shark; in plants and trees; in hedgerows; in Joyce's 'swerve of shore and bend of bay'; in the neck of a swan; in a cobra poised to strike; in the trunk of an elephant; in the silhouette of a beautiful woman; in the profile of forehead and nose; in the undulating way a squirrel runs – and it's always fascinating to encounter.

But there are many other different lines that give us pleasure, especially when they combine in a design, as they do so elegantly in Chinese characters, or when they come together to create a shape. I have often thought that the letters of our own alphabet, while lacking the astonishing variety of Chinese characters, sum up some of the lines and shapes that most please our eyes.

The letter **A**, for instance. It suggests inherent stability – an athlete with feet apart; the Pyramids of Egypt; Mount Fuji; hands joined in prayer, like the ones Dürer drew. It is also railway lines leading into the distance.

B is the belt on a big bulging belly. **C** is Joyce's swerve of shore and bend of bay. It is also the waning moon, while **D** is the crescent moon.*

H is the goalposts dear to rugby and hurling fans; it's also a bookshelf, a barred gaol window; a house with chimneys; the horizon; a soldier surrendering. **I** is Salisbury Cathedral spire pointing to heaven or indeed any ancient church tower above its tombstones; the old mill chimneys of the Black Country; every phallus that ever was; the appliance symbol for *ON*; Big Ben and the vertical element in architecture. It is the forefinger raised to instruct, the middle finger raised to insult, and the downward thumb in a Roman amphitheatre. It is also a line of coke. And it once again is the World Trade Centre.

J is a hook, which in nature is nearly as prolific as is dendritic – it is the talons of eagle and the cruel beak of a hawk; it is our fingers curled to lift; it is the curve of a left hook in boxing; it is an elephant's trunk when feeding; it is those horrid wire coat hangers that get so entangled; it is the curled tail of a scolded doggie and the claws of every cat; it is those

---

* If the moon would just decide grow the other way round, it would be a lot easier on all of us, for then C would be the crescent moon, which would now be shaped like a C instead of a D, and D would be the waning moon, which is a D shape. But there's not much chance of that. Contrary old thing that moon. The French have the same problem by the way – their words are *crocher* and *decrocher* for the moon growing and waning.

berries that cling to our clothes when we pass through a field (which, by the way, inspired *Velcro*, which depends on hundreds such tiny hooks).

One of the most pleasing sights in the sky are those little hooks at the end of mares' tails – *cirrus uncinus*, I think they are called. It's as if the high winds up there had decided to give one last graceful little flick to their handiwork, just to finish off, like. As a painter might do before laying down the brush.

L is Beachy Head or the Cliffs of Moher rising straight from the sea; it is the right angle that has been integral to human constructs since before Euclid. **M** is an avenue of cypress trees vanishing into the distance. **N** is old slanting tombstones in a cemetery, or the diagonal bar on a farmyard gate.

O is the harvest moon; the earth and every planet; it is the human face; the wheel that revolutionised human life; a hula hoop; the widening ripples from a splash; the clock that governs our life and the fruit that nourishes it; it is the @ in an eMail; a snake with its tail in its mouth (the Celtic symbol of eternity); that astonishing Eden Project in Cornwall; the appliance symbol for *off*. It is the zero which the Arabs gave to mathematics and made the modern world possible. But above all it is the beginning of all life, from dinosaur eggs to the human ovum. And the source of that life – the light-giving Sun. And the ultimate source of all – the curved Universe.

Come to think of it, that *on-off* symbol that we find on so many of our appliances could be the sperm penetrating the ovum – ⏻.

S of course is Hogarth's Line of Beauty. It is the Serpentine in Hyde Park; the path of a snake; a curving hedgerow; it is many a boreen in County Clare and many a curving road through the Mendips, especially that wonderful one through Cheddar Gorge. **T** is a tower crane; a one-way road sign; the Scales of Justice. It is also, sadly, a gallows and a crucifix.

U is the turn we're not supposed to make on a motorway. It's also a valley gouged out by a glacier; and the curved pipe that traps the water to make possible our indoor loo. **V** is a valley worn down by a river. It is also a volcano erupting; the first shoots of a crocus; it is all of perspective – lines meeting at their vanishing point; and Churchill's enduring symbol for victory.

W is a line of mountain peaks; the swell of the ocean; the furrows in a ploughed field. **X** is every crossroads; it is the mark used to vote but also to delete; it is all crossed swords and the symbol for battles fought. And, when warped and twisted, it can become the swastika – its German name, *Hakenkreuz* means 'hooked cross'.

Y is every tree, every rib cage, every wishbone, every wine glass, and that fork in the road where Robert Frost took the road less travelled by. **Z** is the warning sign for electricity; the slashing cut that Zorro made with his rapier on the forehead of corrupt politicians (what a capital idea). Its slanting bar gives rigidity to every gate, every crane, every girder bridge, every biplane wing. And hideously, when doubled it is the symbol for the Nazi SS – although in that case it is actually a distortion of the letter S – ⚡ (see page 167).

Patterns

A pattern is one of the most satisfying of all the things an eye can discern. Its essence is repetition – mostly a recurring sequence of certain elements, like lines or dots or squares. There are the deliberate ones created by ourselves, such as parquet flooring, lattice work, herringbone tweed, polka dots, chessboards, flowered curtains, the drawings of MC Escher, or those splendid patterns in the sky drawn for us by the Red Arrows.

I remember how once, at an airshow in Britain, the youngsters directing cars in the parking lot sent our red car to a particular spot. It was only when we climbed out that we saw all the other cars were red. Behind us was a line of silver cars. Behind that was a row of black ones. Then a row of blue ones. And so on. The kids were having an absolute ball creating a pattern all of their own – and a very large pattern it was.

If I remember rightly, the rarer green or yellow cars were relegated to the far end of the parking lot, since they didn't fit in with the pattern. But no one seemed to mind – indeed we all enjoyed the creative prank.

It is the patterns in nature that are the most satisfying of all, since we do not create them, but rather have to discern them. One could spend a lifetime seeking out such patterns – indeed some scientists and mathematicians do precisely that. Some patterns are of course easy to find, like the columns in the Giant's Causeway, or a honeycomb – but even there the wonder is, how did the bees find out that hexagons were the one of the few shapes that could fit nicely together? Who ever told them about tessellation?

One of the most stunning use of the hexagon must surely be those domes of the Eden Project in Cornwall. Those extraordinary structures of Jay Baldwin, made of interlocking hexagons, enclose the world's largest greenhouse. They look just like giant bubbles coming up out of the ground.

Recognising patterns can be fun. Divide 81 into 1 – you will get 0.012345679...012345679.... Keep going and those figures will keep recurring forever. That's indeed some pattern. But it is rather visual patterns that delight the eye – the ripples on a lake that keep repeating; the widening circles when a stone drops in a pond; ancient ridges on a hillside from long vanished cultivation; Atlantic waves rolling in towards a beach; the way grazing cattle or sheep seem to position themselves in a field, almost equidistant from one another; the V-formation of migrating geese; the shape of a fern.

A fern indeed has an especially interesting kind of pattern, since its smaller leaflets are scaled-down approximate copies of the fern itself. And that is repeated on the yet smaller growths that make up the leaflets. The same is roughly true of a tree – branches often approximate the shape of the tree itself. This *fractal pattern*, as I think it is called, can be found throughout nature, in clouds, snowflakes, coastlines, frost ferns on a window pane (no wonder they're called ferns). It's even true of broccoli.

Moving patterns

There is a phenomenon worth looking for called the interference or *moiré* pattern. One instance is when you walk past a row of park railings, with other railings behind it, perhaps at right angles. As you walk, the railings play all sorts of tricks on the eye, appearing thick, then thin, and even sometimes seeming to undulate or dance if they are in any way curved. You get especially satisfying effects from the criss-cross mesh on those gantries across the M5 motorway: as the car moves towards them the meshes on either side interact, creating what seems like bigger and bigger meshes. You might even get the effect with chicken wire in your own garden.*

That same moiré effect is actually the bane of digital camera manufacturers, as the pixels within a camera can interfere with patterns in pictures being taken, giving unwanted results. They have to add a special filter to counter it, at considerable cost.

A few days ago I was swimming in the pool at my local leisure centre. After some lengths I stopped to rest at the shallow end and I noticed something that intrigued me. The sun was shining in through the big windows and the whole white-tiled wall opposite me had turned into a giant fireplace with dancing white flames. However the flames were sunlight reflected off the water surface.

---

* Something akin to this, but in the realm of sound: I vaguely remember, from when I was a very tiny child, listening to German bombers overhead, heading for their target. The sound was up and down, a sort of slow *woo-WOO-wah, woo-WOO-wah*, a second or two between the loud *WOO* and the next. It was both sinister and terrifying. In later years my engineer brother-in-law Chris Bruce explained it to me: every couple of seconds the beat of those hundreds of engines, thousands of cylinders, all synchronised and gave that terrifying *WOO*.

The rhythm of the reflections seemed exactly like the rhythm of the flames of a coal or turf fire, where flames leap and dance as if to some music we cannot hear. It is a dance that can mesmerize if we gaze mindfully into a fire for any length of time – a thing I love to do.

Sometimes I wonder if this rhythm runs through more things than we can imagine. I have seen almost exactly the same rhythm in the courtship dance of a shower of mayflies just above a lake and in the dance of midges in my garden at evening. I wonder if lake water lapping has a similar happy rhythm. As Rupert Brooke put it so beautifully – 'There are waters blown by changing winds to laughter, and lit by the rich skies all day...'

Maybe indeed the crashing of Atlantic breakers on our coasts is the same, if somewhat slower and more solemn. Eva Gore-Booth summed it all up so beautifully, in her poem *The Little Waves of Breffny*:

> The great waves of the Atlantic sweep storming on their way,
> Shining green and silver with the hidden herring shoal,
> But the Little Waves of Breffny have drenched my heart in spray,
> And the Little Waves of Breffny go stumbling through my soul

So is this the rhythm of the Universe? The dance of the galaxies; the beat of our pulses; the rhythm of our breathing (which I have heard said matches the rhythm of surf on the shore); the rhythm of the seasons; the leap of life and the dance of death? Is it all part of the great cosmic dance that the Hindus call The Dance of Shiva?

Spirals

I mentioned the lines and shapes suggested by the alphabet. However there are many more and we could spend a lifetime exploring them. Some shapes are flat; others are solid. And lines and shapes do matter to us: do we not all have our favourite cup, our favourite drinking glass? Don't we spend ages selecting spectacle frames?

Manufacturers know that all too well. Cars sell on their sleek lines; supermarkets are cluttered with packaging in all sorts of intriguing shapes – everything from deodorants to chocolate boxes. I even bought detergent lately because it was in an elegant oval package. I won't make that mistake again: the package was nearly impossible to open and the liquid splattered all over the place when it did open.

My favourite shape of all is the spiral. Like dendritic, it is everywhere in nature – from the barred galaxies in our night skies to the DNA within us; to the curve of a wave around a surfer; to shells on the seashore and the homes that snails carry on their backs; that tiny curled-up spring of a butterfly's feeding tube; tornadoes; a hurricane seen from a satellite; the whirlpool of water leaving a basin.

There is an astonishing spiral in the centre of a sunflower. The tiny seeds arrange themselves in a spiral pattern that curls clockwise. But, if you look again you see another spiral going the opposite way. The two spirals seem to cut into one another, so that curved lines appear to run everywhere. It's almost mesmerising. You get the same effect in marigolds and even the tiniest daisies.

Apparently it is nature's way of fitting as many seeds as possible into the space. I read somewhere that this is a consequence of the mathematical *Fibonacci Sequence*, which can give rise to a number that occurs throughout nature – 1.618 – called *Phi* (ф) or *The Golden Mean*. The flower uses that number in a particular way to determine the angle of each seed in relation to the previous one, and that angle is always 137.5 degrees called – what else? – *The Golden Angle*. This angle results in those lovely curved rows of seeds, which squeeze in as many seeds as possible.*

---

* The Fibonacci Sequence is as follows -- 0, 1, 1, 2, 3, 5, 8, 13, 21, 34, 55, 89... and so on. It's got by adding, say, 1 to 2 (= 3), then 2 to 3 (= 5), then 3 to 5 (= 8) then 5 to 8 (= 13), and so on. If you divide any of the pairs into one

It is this same Golden Mean that governs much of nature, even how leaves position themselves on a tree so each gets the maximum exposure to light. It even governs the proportions of our bodies (see page 212).

We can see it in any supermarket in the surface of pineapple. Those spiny bumps ('eyes') on its surface follow the same pattern as the seeds in a sunflower, for the very same reason - to fit in as many as possible. The seeds on a pine cone do the same. Indeed, once you become aware of it, the pattern seems to be everywhere. (See Suggestions at the end of this chapter.)

Whirlpools

Regarding the whirlpool leaving a basin, It is regularly claimed such a whirlpool always flows in an anti-clockwise direction in the northern hemisphere, due to the earth's rotation (the *Coriolis* effect) and that, no matter how hard we try, we cannot alter this. It is also claimed that in the southern hemisphere it flows in the opposite direction, and that, at the Equator, it doesn't swirl at all. This view has had considerable airings on TV – for instance in The Simpsons episode 'Bart vs Australia' and The X-Files episode *'Die Hand die Verletzt'*.

It is certainly true of the great anti-cyclones of our weather systems, but scientists say that there could be no such effect in such small things as hand basins or baths or loos. Nevertheless take a look at Suggestions at the end of this chapter, to find some very interesting demonstrations.

There are also the spirals we humans create. We were at it three thousand years ago when we carved those lines at

---

another – eg, 21 into 34 – you approximate this Golden Mean (1.618...) If instead you divide the larger into the smaller, you get just 0.618. Multiply that by 360° and you get approximately 222.5°. Subtract that from the full 360° and hey presto you get 137.5° -- the sunflower's favourite angle for positioning its seeds. An interesting sideline to this is that petals on flowers often follow this Fibonacci Sequence – an iris has three petals; buttercup and columbine have five; primroses and delphiniums each have eight, a marigold has 13; an aster has 21; and michaelmas daisies have either 55 or 89 petals.

Newgrange. Our present-day spirals are everywhere in modern life. There are the flat ones, such as the grooves on a DVD, the three-dimensional ones like springs, screws, nuts and bolts, screw caps, irrigation pumps, spiral staircases and the path traced by helicopter blades.

And of course that crucial, precious, most utterly indispensable item in all of human civilization, without which life as we know it could simply not survive – *the Corkscrew*.

Watching a revolving spiral can be fun. It is almost impossible to keep the eye from moving up along the spiral until it comes to the top. Try doing it with a corkscrew, preferably before that second glass of wine.

Then there are rectangles. We take them for granted, I suppose because most man-made things are that shape, be they houses, doors, books, fields, and those smart phones we spend so much of our time gaping into. But nature has her rectangles too, and some can be lovely. Is there anything more graceful than a thoroughbred horse viewed sideways on? My favourite living rectangle is our Rosie, the wee Scottie right now asleep at my feet, leaning her chin on my right shoe. Rosie is actually two rectangles – the briefcase-shaped little black body, plus the square head out in front, the whole set off by three spikes – two ears and a tail. But even when viewed head on, Rosie is still a rectangle.

Three dimensions

Three-dimensional shapes are perhaps the most fascinating of all. In particular, the sphere, which presents the smallest possible outer surface of any shape. I think earth and the planets are spheres because their own gravity forces them into the most compact possible shape. The same shape is particularly familiar to us from the balls used in various sports (with of course the honourable exception of rugby).

For me the most delightful sphere of all is the soap bubble, which I've enjoyed from childhood to this day. It too is spherical because that is the least surface area required to enclose a volume of air, and thus the most efficient (same as a balloon). When two bubbles join they flatten their common surface, again to get the least surface area. Foam is simply millions of bubbles doing just that.

One of the most astonishing sights I have ever seen is of flurries of sea foam rising from the Atlantic and being wafted skywards in an up-current, like giant pizza-sized snowflakes that have lost their way. I have seen it twice in my life – once from that cliff road at Slea Head on the Dingle Peninsula, and once at Fanad Head in Donegal.

A bubble's iridescent rainbow colours come from the thinness of its skin – as thin as the light waves which interact with it causing interference. I think.

One of the loveliest ever depictions of bubbles was by artist Sir John Everett Millais, who painted his little five-year-old grandson gazing up at a bubble he has just blown. It became famous for generations when it was used as an advert for Pears Soap. But Millais had a darker intent when he painted that picture: he wanted to show the fragility and brevity of childhood. For also in the picture is a pot with a growing plant, but beside it another pot – this one broken. (By the way you can see the picture by googling *Millais Bubbles*.)

Incidentally that little boy grew up to be an admiral in the British Navy. Inevitably the poor fellow was known all his life as – well, what do you expect? Bubbles, of course.

The teardrop is another elegant shape in nature. Rounded in front, and tapering elegantly to the rear, it is the perfect shape for passing easily through air or water. The bodies of birds are teardrops. So are many fish. And surely the beauty of a shark is its shape that grows more slender all the way to the tail fin. Every drop of rain is moulded by the air into that same shape.

And as usual, we humans have copied it: the teardrop is basic to aircraft bodies and aerofoils. Sadly it is also the shape of bombs and mortar shells. We degrade so many lovely things.

For me the most significant of all teardrops are the two that curve into one another in a 69 shape to represent *Yin* and *Yang*

166

– one black, one white, each with a dot of the opposite colour, giving us the promise that darkness contains the beginning of light, yet warning us that light contains the seed of darkness.

Shapes of good & evil

There are certain shapes that connote things far beyond them, things holy, and we find it hard to view them as simply shapes. The Cross will always mean Christianity, as the Eight-Spoked Wheel symbolises Buddhism; as the Crescent means Islam, and the six-pointed Star of David stands for Judaism.

But certain other shapes connote sheer evil – the swastika; but also the two zig-zag lines on an SS-uniform collar – *ᛋᛋ* – the S-shape at its most malign. It was created in 1933 by graphic designer Walter Heck, who was paid 2.50 Reichmarks for it. That zig-zag shape was taken from the old Viking writing, the *runes*, and originally signified the sun or life-force (*sowilo*). The Nazis made it a symbol of victory: for the rest of the world it remains the symbol of one of the most monstrous organisations in history.

A former German soldier who had fought in Russia once told me that when they put a wooden cross on an SS-man's grave, they bent both the arms downward. That, he explained, was the Viking rune for death.

Today we see that same arrowhead symbol used by the Campaign for Nuclear Disarmament – aptly, for it still signifies death. Ironically it has gradually become the worldwide symbol of peace.

However the runic death symbolism is just a coincidence, as its designer, Gerald Holtom, did not have that in mind at all. There is a letter from him that explains his intention:

'I was in despair. Deep despair. I drew *myself:* the representative of an individual in despair, with hands outstretched outwards and downwards in the manner of Goya's peasant before the firing squad. I formalised the drawing into a line and put a circle round it.' [37]

That may be how it began, but the symbol has long since come to mean more. Eric Austin, who actually created the first placards with the symbol, has added his own interpretation of the design: the downward-sloping lines have long been associated with the Death of Man, and the circle means the Unborn Child. Others point out that the symbol incorporates the two semaphore signs for *N* and *D*, standing for Nuclear Disarmament (*N* being represented by downward sloping arms with flags, and *D* being the two arms placed approximately vertically).

Suggestions

- Hogarth's Line of Beauty can be found, not just in paintings, but in lots of things in nature – trees, rocks, animals, clouds. Try looking for it.

- To see a video of sea foam coming up from the sea, go to You Tube and type in *Cliffs of Moher sea foam rising*.

- There are some wonderful illustrations and explanations of the Fibonacci Sequence on Google, particularly from Dr Ron Knott of the University of Surrey (type in *Fibonacci numbers and golden section in nature*).

- While in your supermarket, go to the fruit department and pick up a pineapple. You will be astonished at how those spiny seed bumps on its surface arrange themselves – in a curving line clockwise, and another curve anti-clockwise. Just as in the sunflower. (There's even a third line, running nearly from top to bottom. See if you can see it. And if you feel like counting the bumps in each line, they seem to fit the Fibonacci Sequence – 8, 13, 21).

- It can be fun to think up shapes that correspond to the letters of the alphabet. There are many more than the ones I listed in this chapter. Listing them can make us aware of all the beautiful lines and shapes around us. It can be a great party game, too. Why not send suggestions to our website and blog? Address on the back cover.

- And how about blowing some bubbles? It's still as much fun as when you were a child. Any toyshop will sell you bubble mix, or you can make it yourself. Here's a great recipe from the National Wildlife Federation: ¼ cup of liquid dishwasher detergent; ¾ cup of cold water; 5 drops of glycerine (which you can get from your local pharmacy).

- Do seek out those moiré or interference patterns. They are everywhere, and are truly a feast for the eye. If you want to get a first taste of them, try the Internet, with YouTube *Moire patterns*. What you see there will amaze you. But then get outside and find them for yourself. They are a lot of fun.

- Take a close look at a fern as you walk along by a hedgerow, just to see how its smaller leaflets imitate the shape of the main frond. If you can't find any ferns, try You Tube. Best is *2D IFS Fractal: Fern Zoom revisited.*

- If you want to see more of those incredible fractals, google You Tube *Fractals*. What you will see will dazzle you.

- To get demonstrations of water swirling north and south of the Equator, as well as on the Equator itself, type into You Tube *How does water flow?* Seeing is believing. Or is it?

16: Mindful of the night

*I often think that the night is more alive
and more richly coloured than the day*

~ Vincent Van Gogh

Whoever thinks of going to bed before twelve o'clock is a scoundrel

~ Samuel Johnson

*Ah, Moon of my Delight who know'st no wane,
The Moon of Heav'n is rising once again:
How oft hereafter rising shall she look
Through this same Garden after me -- in vain!*

~ Rubaiyat of Omar Khayyam

Nothing like a nighttime stroll to give you ideas

~ JK Rowling

*I will love the light for it shows me the way, yet I will endure the darkness
because it shows me the stars*

~ Og Mandino

RACHEL Carson tells of one moonless summer night on the coast of Maine. She had gone with a friend to a headland almost surrounded by the waters of the bay. They lay down and looked up at the millions of stars that blazed in the darkness.

Apart from a few lights in cottages far across the bay, she and her friend were alone with the stars. 'I have never seen them more beautiful,' she writes in her wonderful book, *The Sense of Wonder*. She describes the constellations hanging in the black sky, the great river of the Milky Way, a meteor burning its way across the sky, a blazing planet low on the horizon:

'It occurred to me that if this were a sight that could be seen only once in a century or even once in a human generation, this little headland would be thronged with spectators. But it can be seen many scores of nights in any year, and so the lights burned in the cottages and the inhabitants probably gave not a thought to the beauty overhead; and because they could see it almost any night perhaps they will never see it.' [38]

Go out into the dark

It's the old story of familiarity. And it's also the Tower-of-London syndrome – if it's something we can see any time, we mostly never bother to visit. Yet the sky at night is literally the greatest show on earth – no, the greatest show beyond the earth. It is our one and only glimpse of the Universe.

For once in this book I am going to ask the reader to actually take some action. If tonight promises to be a clear night without a moon, will you take a pair of binoculars, go outside and train them on the night sky? If tonight is not clear or moonless, will you do it at the first opportunity? You won't regret it. It could even change you. It could be your first experience of Mindfulness.

It is hard to believe what even small cheap binoculars can show. What appeared to the eye as just a few bright stars in a black sky turns out to be more like the sands of a seashore – but a seashore where every grain glows, a sort of plasma of billions of tiny pinpoints of light.

It is at this moment that the sense of wonder clicks in, when we realise that each of those pinpoints could be a sun like ours, perhaps with a complete solar system, or even be a galaxy containing hundreds of millions of such solar systems, or a supernova, or a giant red star. There's even one galaxy we can see with the naked eye – the one in the Andromeda Constellation. (It goes by the romantic name of 'M31'.)

And then we realise that we are looking at some things as they were fifty million years ago, or even much more, since the light has taken that long to get from them to us. So they may now be changed utterly, or not even be there at all.

I have even wondered whether, if the Universe is circular, we might even be looking at ourselves out there. But I don't think anyone yet knows.

We can feel wonder just by reading about the Universe; even more wonder when we look at those pictures from the Hubble telescope – but it is only when we actually gaze at the living night sky itself that we realise we are truly looking out into the Universe. What we can feel then is awe. It can be close to a spiritual experience.

I make a habit of sitting out on my unlit deck on dark, clear nights, sometimes with my binoculars, sometimes without. But always just gazing – and contemplating. There are times that I have had the strangest sensation of just hanging off the edge of the Earth as it hurtles through the Universe, with only gravity to hold me in place. There are other times when I realise I am not just looking out at the Universe – I am in the middle of it. Or rather, I *am* the Universe, albeit a minute part of it. I literally am star dust.

There are other times when I find myself contemplating that most frightening question which physicists are now calling the ultimate quantum puzzle – does the Universe exist when no one is looking at it? Does it exist independently of measurements? Is there any reality out there at all?

Not that I reach any conclusions. I am no quantum physicist, nor am I an astronomer. I just love looking at light. And night.

Anyone can

A sense of inadequacy puts many of us off star gazing – a chart of the night sky can look so daunting, and all those sketches of hunters or great and little bears require an awful lot of imagination to see those same things in the night sky. I do not believe any of this really matters when we gaze in wonder.

However it does help to recognise the most prominent of the star arrangements, and night after night they become old friends. Like Orion the Hunter – once we are shown the line of three stars that are the studs on his belt, we really can imagine the rest of him quite easily. And if we join those belt stars and project the line downwards, it will bring us to the brightest star in the sky – Sirius, or the Dog Star.

Just about everyone can recognise The Plough – four stars for the corners of the blade, and three more to make the handle. Frankly I think it looks more like a saucepan, and I can never understand why they keep calling it The Great Bear. That's certainly pushing it. Or indeed The Big Dipper doesn't mean a whole lot either.

There is one thing about The Plough that I do find satisfying: If I join the two stars on the other side from the handle, and project the line upwards, I reach a fairly nondescript star that never moves. It's Polaris - the Pole Star - around which all the sky revolves.

Then there are the Pleiades – a blur in the night sky which turns out to be six bright stars when you put binoculars on it. They call them the Seven Sisters, but one of the sisters seems to have gone AWOL. Apparently these sisters are near neighbours of ours, relatively speaking. Only 440 light years away. And actually there are far more stars in the cluster than even binoculars can reveal.

I have real trouble with the Milky Way. The way people talk about it it sounds like a brilliant highway of light right across the sky (our galaxy seen edge on), but I can never see anything as spectacular as that. I can just about see something, it but it certainly isn't that brilliant. Maybe it's where I live, or maybe it's my eyesight.

I used to have trouble with the planets too, apart from Venus, of course, which is mostly around when the sun is

174

setting or has set. I tried various charts, and I had a couple of books on the night sky, but I found them difficult. Quite often a brilliant planet would be sitting up there for days, and I wouldn't know whether it was Jupiter or Mars or what. And when I asked, people would just shrug their shoulders – sure who cares what it is?

Well *I* cared. I used to be reduced sometimes to calling our nearby observatory and asking someone there. They were always patient. Nowadays however I just get *The Night Sky* on the Internet and I learn exactly what planets are up there. (See Suggestions at end of this chapter.)

A friend recently showed me his new smart phone, and he was delighted with one of the apps that showed the night sky. It was nighttime so we went out to the garden and he held the phone upside down against the sky. It was all there on the screen, an exact replica of the sky above. There in the corner of the screen was Jupiter. Then I looked at the sky itself and there gleamed old Jupiter himself, just where the phone said it would be.

That's what I want for Christmas. The phone, not Jupiter.

Telescopes

On the other hand, maybe I'd prefer a telescope. The one I have is useless. As far as I can see, many of them are. Of course I went for *el cheapo*, forgetting the motto, 'Buy cheap, buy twice'. To begin with, the instructions are useless, yakking about Barlow lenses and reflectors and eyepieces, but explaining nothing about their function or how to use them. The wretched thing is also wobbly, and there seems to be no relation between the small finder scope and the telescope itself. I can find nothing I look for in the sky. Besides, all this crouching or bending down to peep through the telescope is hard on my back. So for the moment I am sticking with binoculars.

What I am trying to say is, if it's a telescope you're looking for, don't buy cheap. Remember the above-mentioned motto. But, more importantly, I am saying we don't need all that fancy equipment just to enjoy the night sky. In fact we don't need anything. Just our eyes and a sense of wonder.

Light pollution is the great enemy of the night sky. And it is getting worse. I am lucky to have a deck and garden in the countryside, with very little ambient light. Nevertheless I take great joy in driving out into the hills around here, where there are simply no lights at all. Out here the sky becomes, as Shakespeare put it so beautifully, 'the floor of heaven... thick inlayed with patines of bright gold.'

Unfortunately if you live in a city the night sky is almost lost to you. But only almost lost. It may mean a considerable drive, and a rare occasion, but if it is as magnificent a sight as Rachel Carson says, it surely is worth it. Wouldn't any journey be worth making, *to look upon the Universe*?

Suggestions

Going for a walk at night has become something of a lost art. Increasing road traffic is partly responsible for this. But it is still well worth doing regularly, especially if there are country lanes in the vicinity. The only absolute essentials are a reflector jacket and a flash lamp.

- Whatever about telescopes, at least buy a reasonably good pair of binoculars. Get them as light as possible, as your arms can tire with prolonged star gazing. Also, very large binoculars can be difficult to hold steady.

- One of those folding fisherman's chairs is a useful accessory.

- There are lots of astronomical societies worth joining. Best are often ones linked to a nearby observatory. To get an exhaustive list, google *List of astronomical societies* on Wikpedia.

- I find that winter months, especially November, yield the brightest and clearest skies. Besides, the stars come out earlier, so we don't have to stay up late. But wrap up well, as star gazing generates little movement, so can be cold.

- To know what stars are out tonight, google *earthsky.org/tonight* – or– *amazing space: tonight's sky.*

- To find where best to see the night sky, google *Britain's best star-gazing sites.* It's a *Daily Telegraph* website, and excellent. Also try the National Trust's website – *Star-gazing sites.* In Ireland almost anywhere away from towns is suitable, and the *Astronomy Ireland* website is brilliant for listing events both earthly and celestial.

17: Work of human hands

These I have loved... the keen
unpassioned beauty of a great machine

~ Rupert Brooke

The artist... remains within or behind or beyond or above his handiwork,
invisible, refined out of existence, indifferent, paring his fingernails

~ James Joyce

All labour that uplifts humanity has dignity and importance and should be
undertaken with painstaking excellence

~ Martin Luther King, Jr

Every noble work is at first impossible

~ Thomas Carlyle

In designing hardware to be used every day, it was important to keep
both the human aspects and the machine in mind.
What looks good also often feels good

~ Michael Graves

THE Spitfire is generally reckoned as the most beautiful military aircraft ever built. Yet RJ Mitchell had no thought of beauty when he designed it. He wanted simply the most efficient possible carrier of aerial guns that could be powered by a Rolls-Royce Merlin engine. He certainly got that, even though he never lived to see his creation go on to save Britain and become 'The First of the Few', along with its Hurricane sister fighter.

Why is the Spitfire such a beautiful thing? Surely because it so perfectly fulfils its function. Just that. There is nothing added simply to make it beautiful.

An aeroplane, any aeroplane, is the epitome of beauty deriving from function. Everything is designed to make it fly efficiently, safely, and fast. With nothing added.

And the results can be breathtaking. To stand at the end of a runway and watch an Airbus 380 rotate and claw its way into the sky must be one of the most magical experiences of modern times. It is the modern equivalent of standing on the railway footbridge at Kenton, as I often did as a youngster while visiting my Aunt Betty, to watch those magnificent steam trains thunder down to London, and to be engulfed in the steam and smoke that swirled up around the footbridge.

Helicopter

I think a helicopter taking off is still one of the most extraordinary sights in the world. The way it gives the lie to gravity is something I never cease to gaze at with wonder whenever I see it happen. Especially one of those massive military choppers with rotor blades so long that they droop when still.

I still remember my amazement the first time I ever saw a helicopter take off – It was one of the last times Hendon opened to the public, and the chopper was a now-vintage Westland-Sikorsky Dragonfly. My main emotion that time was a feeling of terror that one of those whirling blades might come off and decapitate me.

I used to ride a helicopter from time to time when I was a news reporter more than 30 years ago in the Pacific Northwest (Washington State). I wrote a piece about it for an American newspaper at the time, and I'm including part of it here, as it still sums up for me the sheer visual and sensual wonder of that astonishing piece of technology. Here a couple of extracts from it – I called it *Chopper lifts off*:

'Riding a helicopter must surely be one of the most exhilarating experiences in life. For me there are few highs to equal the moment of lift-off, when that incredible machine spurns gravity with such splendid assurance.

'It's wonderful to watch how, at gentle touch of the Master's hand, this jumble of bits comes together as a pulsating, living thing. First there is a call of 'Clear!' and a whine begins somewhere behind our heads, quickly rising in pitch. The rotor blades start moving slowly overhead. Faster and faster then they turn until they are lashing above our heads like a couple of fearsome whips. The note of the engine grows shrill, and the whole machine is one great shudder.

'The pilot's left hand slightly twists a motorcycle-type throttle on the end of a control lever, the vibrations become smoother, and the rotor fades to a ghostly parasol above our heads.

'There is a few seconds' pause.

'The pilot's fingers tighten around the left-hand lever and ease it up a little, gently. Something strange and subtle happens to the machine. It remains on the ground – just. But now it weighs almost nothing, and it tells us so through our bodies. The pilot is feeling the skids just teetering on the asphalt. Another second or two, poised.

'Suddenly, but with gentle precision, the left-hand lever comes smoothly back and up, simultaneously the right-hand lever moves forward and a foot pedal moves with it. The world outside simply falls away and opens out below us; the tops of the evergreens are suddenly tiny points far below; the Olympic Mountains rise up beyond the trees, and we are soaring, and my heart and mind are soaring too.

'Now I know how an eagle feels.'

Perhaps the difference between contemporary and Victorian manufactured products is that the Victorians thought that beauty was some kind of extra to be clapped on afterwards. Back then they would put cast-iron curlicues or wreaths of metal roses onto factory machines to make them look prettier – I seem to remember some such iron delicacies on the great 19th-century factory engines at London's Science Museum. I have even seen little iron dolphins carved on a cannon to make it nicer for the gunners. Even Singer sewing machines, up to the 1950s at least, had pretty little flowers painted on them, presumably to gladden the eye of the seamstress. As if beauty were an ingredient you just add, like sugar to a cup of coffee.*

But you can't do that to an aeroplane. Or can you? – I'm hesitating even as I write this. For the sheer colour and designs on the various airlines at Heathrow can be very lovely indeed. And I will always relish the era when British Airways gave over the tail fins of their 747s as giant canvases for artists from around the world. What a pity they don't do it any more.

Perhaps the answer is that no aeroplane really needs anything further to make it beautiful – its sheer gleaming functionality is all it ever needs. So it's a very real challenge indeed to add colour and line to such beauty without actually spoiling it. And I think only really gifted artists or craftspeople can do it, and happily most airlines have the wit to seek them out.

I once had a neighbour whose job is painting aeroplanes. His name is Robin 'Chippy' Carpenter, and he is an artist to the finger tips. One of his finest achievements is a stunning Hawker Hunter that regularly does the airshows – it is painted

---

* In 1913 Austrian architect Adolf Loos published a stinging essay on the practice of slapping ornaments onto machines. In 'Ornament and Crime' he asserted that 'the evolution of culture marches with the elimination of ornament from useful objects'. He said it was a crime to waste the effort needed to add ornamentation, and called it 'degenerate'. Strong words.

with a blazing white nose fading to yellow, then orange, then red. It's as if the tip of the nose is white hot.

Sometimes alas aeroplane painting doesn't quite work out, leaving certain airliners looking like giant bananas or flying billboards. But mostly the view of the ramps through the windows at any airport is a joy to the eye – a festival of colour and shape – and a welcome relief from the ugliness that awaits you as you turn away from the terminal window – that misery of serpentine queues and incomprehensible screens and snippy check-in clerks and turdish sausage rolls and the hairy legs of scurrying holiday makers and the flashing lights of rampaging baggage trolleys.

It's why I sit beside a window whenever possible.

Gratitude

I feel a sense of gratitude whenever I climb into an airliner. I find myself thinking of all those people who have made possible this incredible piece of technology that has so changed our world. I think back to the two young fellows at Kill Devil Hill, struggling to get their Wright Flyer into the air. I remember two engineers on opposite sides in the war, Hans von Ohain and Sir Frank Whittle, who independently developed the jet engine which, with just one moving part, takes us across a continent or an ocean in a short few hours.

Then I remember the thousands of workers – engineers, metal workers, riveters, welders – at Boeing or Airbus, who put this incredible thing together. And the workers who produced the hundreds of miles of copper wire that go into a modern aeroplane, and the miners in Chile who dug out the ore to make that wire. And the scientists who created the carbon fibre to hold it all together. And the pilot into whose hands I entrust my life, who has to undergo such rigorous and regular checks, both of competence and health. And the dozens of air-traffic controllers who shepherd us safely through those teeming skies. I could go on and on. In a sense all these people are present in that plane, for it would not exist without them. How could I not feel gratitude?

This morning as I pulled on my jeans, I noticed the astonishing detail of those front pockets and their stitching, and I thought of some poorly-paid woman in Bangladesh who would have done that stitching for me. That set me thinking of cotton pickers in Uzbekistan who, in spite of machines, are still doing back-breaking work so that those women would have something to stitch, so I could have a pair of jeans. And then I recalled Thomas Hood's poem, *The Song of the Shirt*, about the cruelty of early Victorian England:

> With fingers weary and worn,
> With eyelids heavy and red,
> A woman sat, in unwomanly rags,
> Plying her needle and thread —
> Stitch! stitch! stitch!
> In poverty, hunger, and dirt,
> And still with a voice of dolorous pitch
> She sang the 'Song of the Shirt'
> ...
> Work — work — work!
> My labour never flags;
> And what are its wages? A bed of straw,
> A crust of bread — and rags.
> That shattered roof — this naked floor —
> A table — a broken chair —
> And a wall so blank, my shadow I thank
> For sometimes falling there!
> ...
> Oh, Men, with Sisters dear!
> Oh, men, with Mothers and Wives!
> It is not linen you're wearing out,
> But human creatures' lives!
> Stitch — stitch — stitch,
> In poverty, hunger and dirt,
> Sewing at once, with a double thread,
> A Shroud as well as a Shirt.

Plus ça change; plus c'est la même chose. This poem makes me realise that little has changed in two centuries except the geography of exploitation. So to my gratitude for the jeans, should I also add guilt? Yes, if I am indifferent to what goes on.

Yet what can I do? What can one person do? It is here that Mindfulness comes in: if it is taken up around the world, then more and more people will be concerned for the sources of our goods. If this concern were to become widespread it could have a significant effect on exploitation. This is already happening in certain commodities like coffee beans.

Looking good

Jaguar Cars had a motto years ago – or maybe the motoring journalists invented it – 'If it looks good, it *is* good.' I think it was uttered in reference to the Jaguar XK 150, or maybe the E-Type. The motto meant that if Jaguar got a design truly functional, then the appearance would take care of itself (more or less same as the Spitfire). And it certainly was so – car after car that the company produced looked unerringly right.

They were so different from the then prevailing tradition of 'styling', where, especially in the USA, a car's shape was dictated by the need to look exotic in a showroom, rather than meeting any particular function. Hence the fatuous fins on the 1959 Cadillac Eldorado, the tailfins on the Chryslers, the massive chromed grilles nicknamed 'the dollar grin', the go-faster stripes, the spoilers, the lashings of bright metal, the mock air intakes, the faired-in rear wheels, the V-windscreens (which must surely have been copied from the Douglas DC-3).

There was actually a right old war of words between two of the big US companies, about which of them had been 'first with fins.' Some tailfins even turned out to be actually dangerous, even on parked cars. There was a famous civil case, *Kahn v. Chrysler*, where a seven-year-old on a bicycle was alleged to have collided with one of those fins and to have suffered a head injury.

185

Nowadays those companies at least claim to make things functional. But one wonders how far they have succeeded. The SUVs of today, whether from Germany, Japan or Korea or the US, are surely the least functional of any automotive product – four-wheel drives and massive proportions might perhaps have had some function on a prairie ranch, but are utterly unfunctional for carting children to school or for negotiating the crowded streets of cities. And something unfunctional – dare we say dysfunctional – is ugly. There is nothing quite as ridiculous as a horde of those massive machines, complete with their redundant and rarely-used four-wheel drives, tractor-sized tyres, bull-bars and spot lamps galore, vomiting out fumes and blocking up the street outside a suburban school, each waiting to pick up some diminutive child.

To me the ordinary motorcycle is one of the loveliest of all machines, simply because of its honesty. It hides nothing: it lets it all hang out. Everything is functional; nothing is covered up. The fins are there to cool the engine, or the radiator is right up front to do the same; disc brakes gleam around the wheel hub, for all the world to see; wires wind wherever needed; spark plugs perch pertly atop the cylinders; exhausts curl gracefully around from the engine; mirrors are huge and functional.

Wouldn't it be lovely if they made cars as honest as this?

Intrinsic beauty

The beauty of a motorcycle is intrinsic: it hasn't been slapped on afterwards. Happily we have mostly moved on from the Victorian idea of beauty as an optional extra. Modern industrial designers now realise that beauty can be intrinsic to a product – so that the slenderness of an Apple-Mac laptop is lovely to look at before it is ever switched on; and indeed the gracefulness of something simple like an electric kettle can enhance a kitchen counter top.

However here lies a danger – the danger mentioned above – that companies put things like deodorants or perfumes or even washing powder into especially elegant, or rather, fancy containers, and have us buy things for the packaging rather than for the content. (I have just replaced the word 'elegant' with 'fancy', because elegant means, as I already quoted from the OED, 'pleasantly ingenious and simple'. That, these containers certainly are not.)

Which means we need to be on our guard against the seduction of prettiness for its own sake. Once again we are back to the question of beauty as a result of function. The only function of such packaging is seduction of the shopper, and thus it can hardly be called beautiful.

Windmills are among the most loved and lovely features of a Dutch landscape. Yet they were not designed to be lovely but simply to work – they were just pumps to clear water from the lowlands, or machines to grind grain. And they could hardly have been called elegant – just four big sails whirling around like a toy in a giant child's fist. Yet elegant they certainly were – are – if we again take that word in its strictest meaning – pleasantly ingenious and simple.

For centuries windmills were hardly noticed, as they had been around for so long. But as people grew to love landscapes, helped undoubtedly by painters like Hobbema, they grew to love and cherish their windmills. And that eventually made them beautiful. How could something *become* beautiful? Well, if we take Aquinas's definition of beauty as 'that which pleases when seen' *(id quod visum placet)*, than something that begins to please the eye surely begins to become beautiful.

It's all in the eye, as they say.

All of which should give us comfort when people rail against the new wind generators appearing on hills and ridges throughout these islands. Undoubtedly there will come a time when their sheer elegance (remember that definition?) will make them beloved silhouettes on many a horizon. And people will wonder how anyone could ever have rejected them (as Parisians once rejected the Eiffel Tower but grew over the years to cherish it as the graceful symbol of Paris).

A tall ship

Tall ships in their day were simply the most efficient form of pre-steam travel, built expressly to harness the wind just as windmills had been. But now they are regarded as among the most beautiful artifacts ever created, although they were not built for beauty but purely for function.

When I was 15 years old I became fascinated by a maritime painting I found in an art book. It was entitled *Off Valparaiso*, and was by one Thomas J. Somerscales. A full-rigged clipper plunges towards the viewer through a jade-green Pacific, with the Chilean coast a faint line to starboard. The great ship leans in the wind as it shakes out its royals and top gallants and hoists its flying jib. The painting has such exuberance that you can nearly taste the salt on the wind. I remember thinking at the time that that ship must be the most beautiful thing I had ever seen in my life. Some day, since I could never now see the ship itself, I must at least get to see that painting.

The canvas was in the Tate Gallery, according to the book. Ten years later, when visiting the Tate, I remembered *Off Valparaiso*, and went looking for it. It was nowhere to be seen. I asked at the desk and, after some checking, they told me it had long since been moved down to the Royal Naval College at Greenwich.

Many years went by and I found myself at the Greenwich Royal Observatory. I remembered the painting again, and decided to walk down the hill to the Naval College and see it. Alas, the college had just closed its doors for the last time.

Perhaps the painting is back on a wall of the Tate, or maybe it's just in storage somewhere. I haven't got around to checking. Anyhow I don't need to now, as I have lately found that very same painting in a pub at Clonakilty, Co Cork. At the very back of the pub, filling the whole end wall, hangs my *Off Valparaiso*. Hardly the original, obviously, but an exquisite replica: that ship and its Pacific swell fills the whole wall and those top gallants still snap in the salt-drenched breeze.

Finding that painting did not quell my longing to see a tall ship for myself, however. And so, a couple of years ago, I contrived to sign on as trainee crew on the three-master barque *Jeanie Johnston*, as it sailed down the Atlantic out of Galway. It was a brilliant experience of living in the Now, and it brought home to me the sheer wonder and beauty of what human hands can make. Here is what I wrote at the time, in *Cara*, the Aer Lingus magazine:

'A tall ship under full sail ploughs the Atlantic at dead of night. Sea hisses and sucks at the hull; canvas rumbles and snaps; all around me, timber talks to itself in creaks and groans. Above me, two faint stars move sideways past the mizzen masthead, and slide slowly back again to starboard. To port, a lighthouse flashes thrice before the swell comes up to hide it, then emerges to flash again, this time four.

'There's the smell of timber too, but mingled with rope and tar and salt on the wind – a wind that sighs past my ears. And the feel beneath my hands is of wood and brass, and my muscles ache with the pulling of it. *For I am at the helm.*

' "Keep her on two thirty," a young, quiet but firm voice says, out of the darkness behind me. "Turn two degrees to starboard, then hold her there and she'll come around herself."'

The trouble is of course that, when you're part of something, you don't actually see it. Certainly not the whole thing. So I never really saw the *Jeanie Johnston* under sail, except to look up at the masts from the deck and to watch the marvellously professional crew in action. Or to see her docked, with her sails furled.

So there was one more thing to do.

And I did it. When the Tall Ships leaving Waterford assembled four miles south of Hook Head for the start of their international race, I contrived again – one has sometimes to do a lot of contriving to get to see great sights – I contrived to be aboard a fast tender full of photo journalists recording the event. We darted in and out among those magnificent ships, earning and deserving summary abuse from certain of their crew.

I will never forget suddenly seeing the great Russian four-master *Mir* (one of the world's biggest) bearing right down on us, so that its sails towered high above us. At that moment I forgot the danger, and found myself thinking that a tall ship under full sail, built not for beauty but simply to harness the wind, is nevertheless one of the most sublimely beautiful of human creations.

Just before we slid out of the way I managed to get a rather good picture of *Mir* (which I'm told means 'peace', by the way). So now I have my own *Off Valparaiso*. It will shortly be on the website. Watch this space.

Suggestions

- Google *Song of the Shirt* for the text of that poem.

- Airports can be such miserable places these days that anything which makes them bearable is to be cherished. So try getting by a window, as I do, to watch the comings and goings on the apron and runways. A plane taking off is still as magical a sight as ever.

- Instead of envying the high-end cars of the very wealthy, why not simply admire their beauty? – beauty which *you* can see and enjoy, whereas the occupants cannot, since they're locked inside. And certain cars can be very beautiful objects indeed.

- If the annual Tall Ships Race is due into any port near you, I beg you not to miss it. Google *Tall Ships* to find out where. But don't just go to the quayside: find a place where you can see the ships at sea – a cliff top, perhaps, or the narrow part of an estuary. Ask where the best viewing point is: locals can always tell you. But get there early.

- It's better when the ships are leaving port, at the end of the festival, as they all leave at short intervals, whereas you often have to wait hours between ships that are arriving. Besides, you have a better chance of seeing them under sail when they are leaving.

- If you can manage to rent a boat, or get a place on one, you will be able to get right down among the ships as they get under sail far off shore. A call to the local tourist office of the festival port can help here. Or better still a call to the organizers of the festival.

18: Mindful of people

The most precious gift we can offer anyone is our attention.
When Mindfulness embraces those we love,
they will blossom like flowers

~ Thich Nhat Hanh

The face to meet the faces that we meet

~ WB Yeats

In all men there is to praise and to blame:
The blame ignore, the praise then only proclaim

~ Nasser Khossrow

Under 18 there are no ugly girls

~ Chinese proverb

For thou hast made him a little lower than the angels,
and hast crowned him with glory and honour

~ Psalm 8

What a piece of work is man

~ William Shakespeare

RECENTLY I had to go to Seattle on business, and the day finished with a couple of hours to kill before my bus to the airport. So I just sat at a sidewalk café table near Pioneer Square and drank beer. Just doing that brought me the kind of fun I had almost forgotten existed.

In France they call it 'watching the promenade'. You sit outside the Deux Magots across from St Germain-des-Prés, and simply gawk at the folks as they pass by. When your beer or your crème runs out, you tinkle a coin on the outside of the café window, and out comes the waiter with another one.

What's so wonderful about looking at people? I had never really understood until I started writing this book. Perhaps it is that it puts one is in a relaxed and mindful mood, with leisure to wonder what kind of business is that alpha male into, or what sort of a fellow got that girl pregnant, and does he treat her right.

Well for a splendid two hours I find myself sitting outside that Seattle pub, in a marvellously mindful-of-people mood. Long slender girls are serving long slender glasses of beer, and the sunlight drives through both the blond hair and the blond beer, so the glasses seem filled with liquid gold. Another beer? I really shouldn't. But then, I'm not driving, and the airport bus is only a few blocks away. At least I think it is. Well, in that case...

A couple of tables away, a moustachioed professor type is holding forth to a 19-year-old student. She hangs on every word, eyes and ears and mouth open wide, and downs her beer almost without noticing it. Beside the prof is a glass of pale white wine, almost untouched. A Japanese chap who could be businessman or tourist, or a cross between both, stops to gaze at the café tables, digital SLR camera dangling. He comes in, sits down and orders a beer. I suddenly realize the camera is up to his eye, and that I am part of the picture. Automatically I pull in my paunch, then say, what the hell, no one will ever see the picture anyway, and let the paunch back out again.

A man passes along the sidewalk, chuckling happily to himself. Either someone around the corner has just told him a good joke, or he is merrily off his head. An important-looking fellow, complete with bowler hat, pin-stripe suit and tightly-rolled umbrella, bustles along, trying hard to look like a London stockbroker. One of those unbelievably pretty girls passes by, dressed simply in tee shirt and jeans, and conversation everywhere falters until she disappears around the corner.

Three earnest businessmen are discussing something important: I overhear the word 'collateral'. Ties come off, and soon jackets follow. A bus rolls by with a superbly painted giant fish on the side of it. Is the fish really so marvellous, or am I just marvellously mindful? Or is it just the beer?

Now the sun is slanting down the street towards us, putting a halo-like rim of light around every head, and the sidewalk tables become a photographer's dream. The fellow with the camera has also noticed it, and is clicking merrily away.

A few yards down the street some senior citizens sit on park benches under a complicated wrought-iron structure that looks surprisingly like the entrance to a Paris Metro. For some reason I get the feeling that the senior citizens have been sitting there even longer than the wrought-iron structure.

The worshipful student's glass is empty again, and the professor's wine remains untouched. My glass is empty too, but it's time to go. I head for the bus station thinking how good it is for once not to have to drive a car. And to know that a comfortable 747 is waiting at Seatac Airport to whisk me across the Pole to London and its rain.

Well, at least it is a change from the normal routine. And was it not Aristotle who said, centuries ago, 'Change is of all things the most sweet'?

Peoplewatching

Watching people has been one of the greatest of all visual joys down the centuries, as testified by writers from Hilaire Belloc (*The Path to Rome*) to James Michener (*Drifters*) to Peter Mayle (*A Year in Provence*) to Heinrich Böll (*Irish Diary*) to Desmond Morris (*Peoplewatching*) all the way back to 12th century Gerald of Wales (*Topographica Hibernica*). It still is a joy, as testified by singer Jack Johnson, who celebrates 'just watching the other people watching me'.

The Spanish have long brought this to a fine art with their *paseo* – a nightly performance deliberately designed for people watching, where everyone parades up and down the promenade after dinner – to see and to be seen. The tragedy is that we in these islands never really got much of a chance to watch people – one, the weather is extremely unhelpful; two, the *paseo* never caught on, probably because of that same weather; three, we didn't have pavement cafés like they have in Paris. So all we really had was church, where we did most of our people watching during those sermons.

For some reason we thought that only places like Paris could have pavement cafés, and one of the great joys of going to the continent was to sit outside one like the Deux Magots and watch the world go by. No wonder Joyce and Beckett and Ezra Pound buggered off to Paris.

Thank heavens we have finally realised that of course we can have those cafés – in spite of our miserable weather. For once that dreary defeatist phrase 'It-would-never-catch-on-here' has given way to those two splendidly mindful words of Bernard Shaw, immortalised by John F. Kennedy – *'Why not?'*

Even pubs have eschewed the alcoholic gloom for which they were famed at least in Ireland, and have popped a couple of tables and chairs outside the door. Simple solutions like barriers to keep off the wind, canopies to keep out the rain – all while waiting for the one wonderful day when the sun might deign to shine. And when it does – or rather, *if* it does – don't our cafés, and even our pubs, surpass themselves?

Of course much is due to the smoking ban – if you want to smoke, you go outside whatever the weather. So a table and chair can be helpful. Most solutions are pragmatic, anyhow.

But we also have one new place for people watching – the shopping mall. And if we can for a brief while take our mind away from retail therapy, that other wonderful therapy of people watching is right there for all to enjoy, without even the fear of rain.

The beautiful people?

Many years ago I was in a queue at a football stadium and, as the line was long and looped past me on either side, I had plenty of time to look at other people. I remember making a startling discovery – that most people are not particularly good looking. Fine folk to be sure, decent people no doubt, but simply nothing to write home about.

Which brought me to two interesting conclusions. The first is that we plain people are the norm. And isn't it rather nice to be normal? Well, if we're normal, we can only conclude that those rare beautiful people are *abnormal* – freaks, in other words. Which is my second conclusion.

It's a comforting insight, though, is it not? That we're the norm, I mean. (An insight of course that I would immediately jettison if a fairy godmother suddenly made me beautiful. For the moment, however, I can take comfort in that insight.)

However, if beauty is 'that which pleases when seen', as Aquinas says, then far more people are beautiful than the ones glaring haughtily from the glossy magazines. In other words, we're all pretty lovely, particularly if we're loved. (So forget what I just said about people being plain. It's all in the eye.)* As Rogers and Hammerstein put it in *Cinderella*, 'Do I love you because you're beautiful, or are you beautiful because I love you?'

Beauty of sport

Outside of ballet, sport is probably where we see the human body at its most sublime. To watch a backhand stroke at Wimbledon is to see beauty in motion.

Rugby might hardly make a claim to be graceful, but watch a well-executed tackle in slow motion, as the body slants

---

* In rural China a thin woman is considered ugly and far from eligible, because she would not be able for the hard work of farming. Whereas the ideal of beauty in Edwardian England was a delightful plumpness. Take a look at those old postcards. The same in 17th-century Holland – just look at the fine hefty lassies in Reubens's paintings.

forward and the arms come out to enwrap the foe and slide slowly down. It can be beautiful, albeit uncomfortable for the tackled one.

Indeed, slow motion more than anything else captures the beauty of sport. A striker dribbling the ball around an opponent to score that goal; a rugby wing weaving through the opposing backline for a try. Indeed one of the most beautiful movements in rugby is a line of backs moving like migrating birds, where one takes the lead with the ball, then cedes place to another.

What could be more graceful than a hurler balancing a ball on the tip of his caman as he runs; or a basketball player reaching up to touch the ball into the net; a high diver leaving the board with arms as wide as wings; the winning moment of a 100-metre dash, when the loping stride slows and the arms rise in triumph? All such are the human body at its most sublime.

But for me the most graceful thing I ever saw in my life was little Nadia Comăneci at the 1976 Olympics, when she flicked that wrist at the very end of her performance on the uneven bars. Can any who saw it forget that moment?

It can be an interesting experience to watch a football match without bothering about the score. Not always easy to do but, if it's between teams that mean nothing to us, it can be enjoyable. For then we can concentrate simply on the extraordinary skills and grace of these magnificent performers.

It reminds me of the tale about the Englishman watching a match between Celtic and Rangers in Glasgow. He was obviously unaware of the sectarian tensions, and enthusiastically applauded achievements by either side. An onlooker listened for some time, before muttering, 'Must be one of them atheists!'

Spoilers of looking

But whether lovely or unlovely, people are fascinating. However the joy of our looking can be blighted by what I call the spoilers of people-watching.

I can best explain this by citing a memory from childhood. I was about 11 years old and was walking home from town with my mother. Just up ahead of us a 13-year-old called Norma climbed across a fence from the nearby field, hopped down onto the road ahead of us, before scampering past us with a cheery hello. I had long been mesmerised by Norma's long legs and that blond hair to her waist, and that little upturned nose, and the cluster of freckles, but was still paralysed by pre-teen shyness.

'Isn't that an absolutely beautiful sight?' my mother said.

I just grunted.

And then she said something I have never forgotten: 'You know, it's so easy to be envious of the young.'

As I grow older now myself I often recall that piece of wisdom from my mother, who must have been gently chiding herself. She obviously was aware of how envy could spoil her Joy of Looking. As it can spoil ours. One can envy a young couple obviously head-over-heels in love; or that rich lawyer in wig and gown outside the courthouse; or that young fellow climbing out of a Ferrari that he certainly shouldn't be able to afford. (I mean, what's the world coming to, anyway?)

I once myself had a convertible that looked far more expensive than it really was, and I regularly got hostile and envious looks, particularly when the top was down ('going topless', as I called it). I remember once we drove into a car park in Edinburgh that was full of leather-clad motorcyclists, and one of them yelled across – 'Aye. Wouldja just look how the effin rich live!'

As I immediately turned the car around to leave, I called across to him: 'Your effin Harley cost five times as much as my car.' I then gunned the engine and ran for my life.

So now when I see a really magnificent car I often say to the driver, or signal with finger and thumb together, 'Wow, what a lovely car!' The pleasant surprise, indeed the joy in the driver's face, can itself be a joy to see.

Enough about cars – this is about looking at people. Envy is not the only spoiler of people watching. Contempt is another. It can be so easy to dismiss and ignore someone as unattractive, or obese, or from a class lower than one's own, or from an age-group higher than one's own, or of a colour other than one's own.

There is a 19th century story about two freshman medical students on a train to Lille, who sneered across at a little old fellow in the corner who was telling his beads and obviously praying. It was only the next day that the world-renowned professor giving the inaugural lecture turned out to be the little old fellow. His name was Louis Pasteur.

There are other spoilers too, and even sexuality can be one of them. By which I mean that if one notices only the sexually attractive, then the roving eye misses all the other interesting and truly beautiful people so well worth watching. I think that is what women mean when they say that at a certain age they become invisible.

But undoubtedly the greatest spoiler of people-watching is prejudice. For prejudice (from the word *pre-judge*) projects onto people a picture already formed. So we see what we would like to be there, rather than what is. And what we would like to be there is mostly ugly.

Geraldus Cambrensis

THE nastiest piece of prejudice I have ever read was written by that 12th century cleric, Gerald of Wales. He toured Ireland and wrote his report expressly to justify the Norman invasion of 'the barbarous Irish'. Here is a small taste of Master Gerald:

> Nor have I seen in other nations so many persons
> blind from birth, so many crippled or defective in

various ways. While the physique of well-formed
individuals is very fine indeed, as good as
anywhere, and those so gifted grow up very
handsome indeed, nevertheless those to whom
nature refuses such gifts grow up hideously ugly.
But this is a nation truly outside the law of God,
given over to adultery, incest, illegitimate births
and wrongful marriages, so it is no wonder that all
this foul perversity should corrupt nature itself. It
seems to me that God in his justice has allowed
nature to reverse its own laws and to generate such
horrors, so that those who ignore both their
consciences and their God, should often have to
suffer the misery of ugliness and blindness.[39]

Empathy

Whatever about the spoilers of people-watching, there is one
thing that enhances it beyond measure. It is that wonderful
aspect of Mindfulness which we call *empathy*. The Oxford
Dictionary defines empathy as 'the ability to understand and
share the feelings of another'. Some say it is the most
important quality in all aspects of our life, as it is the seedbed
for kindness, generosity, compassion and care. Others go so far
as to say that the survival of the human species may ultimately
depend on empathy.

Certainly it utterly transforms the way we look at people.
When we see that young couple hand in hand we can rejoice in
their joy. We can share in their hopes for the future. Our
hearts can go out to them for the problems they are bound to
face. When we see a father hugging his little daughter we can
be close to tears for the love we are seeing. We can look at
children learning to draw, and feel the joy of their creativity.
When we see a group of teenagers we can imagine their hopes,
fears and uncertainties.

201

An obese person sits across from me in the Piccadilly Line – I try to imagine what grief and suffering must have brought that degree of comfort eating. And that further grief of having other people glancing and looking quickly away. Or perhaps there is no grief – perhaps this is a happy mother of many children, just with some incurable weight problem that she is coping with.

That elderly gent across there who looks so cheerful – surely he must have a happy life? Does someone love him to bits, to make him that cheerful? And that fiftyish man over there who holds his left hand to stop it shaking. Is it drink? Or some nervous disease?

Just trying to understand how all these people must feel – the happy, the cheerful, the morose, the grief-stricken – can tune us into what Wordsworth called 'the still, sad music of humanity.' As Thich Nhat Hanh puts it: 'The sufferings of others is our own suffering, and the happiness of others is our own happiness.'

The world-renowned photographer Ernst Haas had a way of looking that was honed by empathy. Journalist John Kord Lagermann recalls being taken around New York by Haas, who pointed out an elderly couple climbing the steps of a brownstone house, 'who paused for a moment to look at a young couple swinging by. An ordinary enough scene but, viewed in an imaginary frame with all else excluded, it made a picture of unusual force and poignancy – one that, until then, I would have missed.' [40]

Faces are the most interesting. Anxiety can etch a face. Humour can put little smile-lines at the corner of eyes and mouth. Anger or disappointment can make a tight line of the mouth. Arrogance can curl the upper lip and make the nostrils flare. Love can put a sparkle in the eye. Goodness can shine from a face.

Actually nothing, but nothing, can outshine goodness. It cannot be hidden, and we cannot not notice it. Encountering goodness – and we instinctively know it when we do, rare though it may be – is the supreme experience of the Joy of Looking.

'I don't like that man,' Abraham Lincoln once said. 'I don't like his face.' When an aide remonstrated, Lincoln replied, 'After forty, a man is responsible for his face.'

But even if there is little to recommend the appearance of someone, I find myself coming back to a legend from 11th century Persian poet Nasser Khossrow who, surprisingly, wrote about Christ. The story goes like this: 'Jesus one day walked with his disciples and they passed by the carcase of a dog. The Apostles said: "How foul is the smell of this dog." But Jesus said: "No pearls are whiter than its teeth!"' [41]

The way we look at other people is actually one of the best indications of how well or badly we ourselves fit into our world. Respect for others usually indicates we fit well. If we are short on empathy, we fit rather badly indeed. I think Albert Einstein put it best, in a letter he wrote to a distraught father who had lost his young son, and had asked Einstein from some comforting words:

> A human being is a part of the whole, called by us Universe, a part limited in time and space. He experiences himself, his thoughts and feelings as something separated from the rest, a kind of optical delusion of his consciousness. This delusion is a kind of prison for us, restricting us to our personal desires and to affection for a few persons nearest to us.
>
> Our task must be to free ourselves from this prison by widening our circle of compassion to embrace all living creatures and the whole of nature in its beauty. Nobody is able to achieve this completely, but the striving for such achievement is in itself a part of the liberation and a foundation for inner security. [42]

Surely what Einstein is referring to is Mindfulness, even if he does not actually use the word.

Suggestions

- Thich Nhat Hanh's book, *Peace is Every Step*, is a marvellous guide to empathy with others and with our world. Here is a brief sample: '...See yourself in the... child starving, in the political prisoner... in everyone in the supermarket, on the street corner, in a concentration camp, on a leaf, in a dewdrop... the rain of Dharma will water the deepest seeds in your store consciousness, and tomorrow, while you are washing the dishes or looking at the blue sky, that seed will spring forth, and love and understanding will appear as a beautiful flower.' Get that book. Details are in the Bibliography.

- Read Desmond Morris's *Peoplewatching*. It tells about far more than just reading body language, and you will never quite see people the same way again. Indeed his final chapter is about living in the Now rather than in the future or the past, although he doesn't actually use the word 'Mindfulness'. Details in the Bibliography at the end of this book.

- Try occasionally watching a football match on TV where the score doesn't matter to you, where you don't feel so emotionally involved. Just watch it for its grace and beauty, especially the rerun of some action in slow motion.

- Tennis is among the most graceful of all sports. Try watching it just for its beauty of movement. (I've been doing that since Little Mo.) Again, the slow motion reruns show it best.

- The best people-watching can be had on public transport. The trick is to position yourself where you can see as much as possible. And don't forget to eavesdrop – the late Maeve Binchy made a career out of it.

- Google *Nadia Comăneci* on You Tube. You won't regret it.

19: Mindful of oneself

Nothing could be more absurd than to despise the body
and yet yearn for its resurrection

~ Wendell Berry

Our body is precious. It is our vehicle for awakening. Treat it with care

~ The Buddha

Often the hands will solve a mystery
that the intellect has struggled with in vain

~ Carl G. Jung

You got a body to die for

~ Dizzee Rascal

O wad some Pow'r the giftie gie us.
To see oursels as ithers see us!

~ Robbie Burns

WHEN did you last look at your hands? I don't mean just see them – we see them every day as they minister to our needs. But *look* at them? I mean trace those extraordinary lines etched into the palm before we were born, or follow the veins on the back of the hand (dendritic, again, by the way), or examine those half-moons on the nails?

When did you last examine those minute ridges that make you unique – what we call fingerprints or, strictly speaking, epidermal ridges? Can you remember yours without looking? Are they arches, loops, whorls or are they tiny gothic arches with flying buttresses? And how do they differ from one finger to another?

I know people who couldn't answer that, because they haven't really truly looked at their fingers since childhood. I'm not sure I can answer it myself. [Note to self: must take a peep shortly.]

We hardly notice our hands, yet their evolution is what allowed us to use tools and create our world. They are the most precious gift to us from our ancestors. Thich Nhat Hanh puts it so beautifully: 'If you look deeply into the palm of your hand, you will see your parents and all generations of your ancestors. All of them are alive in this moment. Each is present in your body. You are the continuation of each of these people.'

And if we have forgotten just how precious our hands are, there is a neat little reminder in Julius Caesar's memoir, *The Conquest of Gaul*, written two thousand years ago:

> Caesar realised that the conquest of Gaul could never be successfully concluded if revolts like this were permitted continually to break out all over the country; and that his kindness and mercy were so well known to everyone that people would not think him cruel if for once he came down hard on the rebels. So he decided to make an example of the defenders of Uxellodunum and thus deter all others. Therefore everyone who had carried weapons had their hands cut off. They were then turned loose, so that everyone should see the fate that awaited evildoers.

It is a sad fact that we are hardly aware of our body until it creaks or groans or yelps. Yet the only thing we truly possess is that body, which also happens to be the most stupendous creation in the Universe. Literally. The sun bubbles away up there, but it doesn't have a heart to beat or lungs to breath. And it can't see us, whereas we can see it. It doesn't even know it's there. It can't even enjoy being the sun. Whereas *we* can enjoy *it*. And enjoy being us.

It's extraordinary to think that, until we humans came on the scene, the Universe had no one even to know it was there. No one even to look at it, to see it, appreciate it. No one to be mindful of it. What kind of existence was that, simply not being known? No audience whatsoever? Almost a non-existence, surely. So, in a sense, the Universe needed us. Needed someone to know it, anyhow. (Unless it already had Someone...? But that's outside the compass of this book.)

Yet, even though we humans are the most extraordinary thing in the Universe (as far as we know), how many of us ever look with awe and wonder on the quite incredible organism that is oneself – a self-organising structure that functions without a single wheel; that stands erect and moves on two feet without tottering; that navigates by vibrations of light and communicates by vibrations of air; that can reproduce itself; and, above all, that is able to become aware of itself and ponder its existence.

The first step in that awareness is surely to look at oneself. First with wonder. Then with awe. Then with love. And then with gratitude. Then with joy. And finally with Mindfulness. But do I ever do it? Do I ever look at myself?

'Know thyself,' Augustine said. Surely the best place to start is the body, although I doubt if that was exactly what the good man had in mind.

Don't look now

Unfortunately the Puritanism of past centuries still lurks within us to make us diffident about looking at our body. It was a lot worse in my childhood, when there was an imaginary dotted line below the navel, and anything beyond that was out of bounds. Nobody actually said so, but we absorbed the attitude by a sort of osmosis.

There were Things down there that were not particularly nice: one had to cope with them of course, but looking upon them, gazing upon them was, well, simply not done. It was not quite *terra incognita*, but gettin' there. Here be dragons, as the ancient maps used to say. Dragons that might raise their heads.

It was even worse in earlier generations: years ago a very old priest told me that, when he was in a Roman seminary, anyone taking a bath was given something like an Oxo cube to dissolve in the water, so one would not get to look upon whatever lay below the waterline. He also remembered a plaque on the bathroom wall: *Dio ti vede* ('God sees you').

I think much of this went back to the daft dualistic notion that the soul (good) was imprisoned within the body (bad). Even Shakespeare expressed this notion in *The Merchant of Venice*:

> Such harmony is in immortal souls;
> But, whilst this muddy vesture of decay
> Doth grossly close it in, we cannot hear it

But even in the last couple of centuries Puritanism ruled OK in pretty well all religious denominations, where threats of insanity or blindness were regularly invoked to control adolescent behaviour. It reminds me of the tale of the mum saying to her son, 'Tommy, if you keep doing that you'll go blind!'

'C-could I do it till I n-need glasses?' was Tommy's reply.

In the matter of looking upon our own bodies, are we all that enlightened today? There are a couple of things that still deter us from looking at ourselves too much. One is a fear of vanity, particularly if we're good-looking. Another is fear of being upset if we think we're not so good-looking. That is by far the greater danger.

The first is often inculcated by parents ('Don't keep looking into that mirror, dear'). There is a fear of vanity, and an even greater fear of narcissism.

The second fear, of being plain looking, is mostly groundless. In spite of what I said earlier, most people, while not perhaps models, are actually better looking than their own self image. I actually know some really fine-looking people, men and women, who actually think they look awful. And it very often goes back to something said in childhood: a cruel playground reference to the size or shape of a girl's bottom; a boy being told by a jealous classmate, 'Sure what girl would look at *you* !'

Jon Kabat-Zinn has some comforting words on this:

> Maybe the fear is that
> we are less than
> we think we are,
> when the
> actuality of it
> is that we are much much more [43]

One of my greatest joys is photographing the children of my friends, especially teenagers. So often, particularly young women, have such angst about their appearance, even though they may be very beautiful indeed. However, sometimes I have managed to photograph such a young person, where the camera zeroes in on some striking loveliness. Result: the young person is transformed and grows into confidence, simply by seeing, in a photograph, how lovely she really looks.

Women's magazines have a lot to answer for, by focusing on almost impossible female figures, even though some of magazines now claim to have renounced airbrushing. If you have ever had to deal with someone with anorexia – as I more than once have had to – you will know the devastation caused in young people's lives by the incessant false images in the media. Perhaps the answer is in looking more at the ordinary people around us to realise that we too are normal and – as I said in a poem they won't let me publish here – that 'the beauties are freaks'. (I might just put that little poem in my blog up on the website. They can't stop me.)

There is a really helpful blog on all this by bestselling Irish author, Sinéad Moriarty. See Suggestions at the end of this chapter.

Perhaps in might be a good idea to introduce a course in schools along Robbie Burn's lines of 'see oursels as ithers see us'. Youngsters could be shown how media-imposed norms of physical beauty are false. They could be taught to look around them to realise that the average person looks nothing like that, and that the youngsters themselves are average – that is, *normal.* As said above, it's the so-called 'beauties' that are freaks. It could work wonders for teenage angst and bring a rare sense of security. And it might head off both anorexia and bulimia which, in my experience, cause so much wretchedness. And far too often, death.

'Know thyself'

Nevertheless, whatever our self-image, I believe we should, must, become familiar with our own bodies. And one of the best ways is first to look at each part of ourselves separately, and grow in wonder at what an incredible thing that part is. But then also to see it also as part of the whole wonderful human body.

The eye, for instance – perhaps the most incredible thing in all of life. We're told it's nature's camera – but being told is not the same as actually realising it, seeing it for real – by looking at how the iris narrows to cut down bright light, just as a camera lens does. Close your eyes in front of a brightly-lit mirror, then suddenly open them and you will see the pupil go from wide to narrow before your very eyes.*

Or look at the eyebrow, how it's designed to catch sweat before it enters the eye. Blink, and see how you have just used

---

* Darwin once said his blood ran cold every time he contemplated the complexity of the eye. According to British biologist Brian Goodwin, 'the eye developed independently in more than 40 lineages during evolution'. So now some scientists are wondering if there are some sort of blueprints out there quite apart from natural selection.

the fastest muscle in your body – it can blink five times in a second.

I have just suggested that we look at the eye as a single entity. But while doing so with any part of one's body, we need to keep in mind how it relates to the whole. Maybe indeed a reason why people have a bad self image is that they look at thighs, paunch, chin, ears, only as if they were individual items instead of parts that fit the whole body, and fit rather well indeed.

So after we have viewed each part, we should then look at ourselves as an integral whole. That way we don't get obsessed by a thigh or a chin or a hairline, once we see how it all fits so splendidly together.

Anything viewed out of context can be visually vulnerable. Imagine a plateful of ears – with all those hollows and ridges and lobes – they would a look lot less pretty than a plateful of fried eggs. (Brendan Behan once described someone or something as looking like 'a plateful of mortal sins'. Wish I could remember who.)

Come to think of it, an ear *is* a bit like a fried egg – a rather badly fried one, at that. Yet it can be neat on either side of one's head. Try a head without one.

Even an eye is no beauty away from a face: 'Out, vile jelly,' says that Shakespearean nasty in *King Lear,* as he is gouging out the eye of the Duke of Gloucester. Which brings that hideous comment from Regan: 'Let him smell his way to Dover.'

Nevertheless we must admit that the gouger had a pretty good grasp of an eye. *Ouch.*

A nose on its own is a rather plain looking thing, too, with its pear shape and those two silly little holes. It actually can look ridiculous, and nobody showed that better than Woody Allen when he put some assassinated dictator's nose all by itself on the operating table. They were going to try cloning the original owner from his surviving nose, if I remember rightly.

Picasso, as we know, played around a lot with the furniture of the face. He had a particularly interesting take on noses:

211

> People take notice, however, when a nose is
> sideways, but I deliberately painted the nose
> sideways. You see? I did what I had to, so as to
> force people to see a nose.

There you go: even Picasso noticed we don't notice noses. Yet what a nose can add to a face. Again, try one without it.

Golden Mean

Remember the Golden Mean (1.618) and all that extraordinary carry-on inside a sunflower? Well it seems that we use it too in our bodies. Your height is 1.618 times the distance from your head to your finger tips. And that latter distance is 1.618 times the distance from your navel back up to your head. Or indeed from you elbows to your head. And that last distance is 1.618 times the width of your shoulders, or the length of your forearm or of your shin bone. There's lots more – proportions of parts to each other and to the nails, toes to feet, forearm to hand – enough to make one dizzy. Leonardo's *Vitrurian Man* (familiar from the *Da Vinci Code*) shows those proportions brilliantly.

Now don't go measuring yourself just yet. All this presumes that one has the ideal human body, which really only exists in classical Greek sculptures by Phidias and the like. None of us quite makes it. So don't start measuring and then getting upset. It's when we measure lots of people that the average is as above.

Even those Fibonacci numbers (0, 1, 1, 2, 3, 5, 8.... See page 164) turn up in our bodies. There is one torso, one head, one nose, one belly. Two of the following – arms; legs; eyes; nostrils; lungs; breasts; kidneys; testicles or ovaries; feet; hands; ears; buttocks. Three parts to each finger, and three knuckles. (Even the thumb has three, which you will know if you get arthritis.) Throw the thumb in with the fingers and we get five digits, another number in the sequence. Five toes, too.

I can't think if there's eight of anything. Internal organs, perhaps? How about teeth? Aren't there about 13 each, top and bottom? (I'd count mine if I had any.)

Hairs on the head? Could the number of hairs be way up the Fibonacci Sequence, around 2584 or so? Dunno. However I am pleased to declare that the hairs on *my* head fit exactly into the sequence – down at the lower end.

Zero, to be precise.

Our bodies really are incredible. And they're all we've really got. And surely they're there to be enjoyed. And that joy leads us to Mindfulness. As does wonder. The wonder grows the more one gazes – for, no matter what its shape, we possess the most incomparable thing in all the Universe (unless something from outer space turns up to trump us – which is why I wish they'd stop sending those messages out there).

As usual, good old Will Shakespeare says it best, in *Hamlet*:

> What a piece of work is a man, how noble in
> reason, how infinite in faculties, in form and
> moving how express and admirable, in action how
> like an angel, in apprehension how like a god! The
> beauty of the world, the paragon of animals

So maybe we should forgive him his 'muddy vesture of decay'.

Suggestions

- One of the most brilliant books about looking at the body is actually written for children – *Looking at the Body*,[44] by David Suzuki with Barbara Hehner. Read it and you will never see yourself the same way again. It can be got from Amazon, but I've just discovered you can download the whole thing free from *www.arvindguptatoys.com/arvindgupta/suzukibody.pdf*.

- To see how the Golden Mean works in the human body, google *The Math behind the Beauty*, or type in *http://www.intmath.com/numbers/math-of-beauty.php*

- *Body Image* is a blog by best-selling Irish author Sinéad Moriarty, which brilliantly discusses how to guide young women through the fear of obesity. (*www.sineadmoriarty.com*)

- If we practise looking with Mindfulness at the so-called plain people we encounter in street or public transport, especially looking for their good points, we will find them a lot more beautiful than at first sight. We will also realise that being loved makes one lovely.

- If you are a teacher, would you consider what we discussed about trying in school a 'Robbie Burns workshop', – on seeing ourselves as others see us? I would love to know if it would work. If ever you do, please let me know. You could put a comment on my website and blog – address on back cover.

20: Mindful in the city

We don't have to travel far away to enjoy the blue sky. We don't have to leave our city or even our neighborhood to enjoy the eyes of a beautiful child. Even the air we breathe can be a source of joy

~ Thich Nhat Hanh

Two men looked out from prison bars,
One saw the mud, the other saw the stars

~ Frederick Langbridge

In Rome you long for the country;
in the country – oh inconstant! –
you praise the distant city to the stars

~ Horace

Towered cities please us then,
And the busy hum of men

~ John Milton

What is the city but the people?

~ William Shakespeare

WHEN I talk of Mindfulness, people sometimes say, approximately, 'It's all very well for you, living in the countryside among all those lovely fields and forests. But we have to live in the dreary streets of this city of ours [whichever]. What's to to be mindful of here?'

Whenever I hear things like that I think of Ernst Haas (whom I cited in the last chapter). He was an Austrian photographer who moved to New York in the early 1950s. He was already famous by then, as a key member of the Magnum Photo Agency. After he arrived, *Life* magazine asked him to do a 24-page colour-picture essay – 'Magic Images of a City'. The result was sensational.

It could be said that Ernst Haas helped New Yorkers see their city for the very first time. Those wonderful photos showed to people facets of the city and its life they had simply never before seen. Or rather, had never before noticed, for those scenes and angles and details had always been there. It simply took the mindful eye of an Ernst Haas to discover them.

For he knew how to look. And where to look.

So, while people tramped past an oily puddle on a pavement, he would stop and look, and find there a rainbow of oil on water. A lake in Central Park might reflect an inverted skyscraper. Double-lens tourist telescopes at Battery Park could look like heads on spikes. A close-up of the barb on barbed wire became a shape of elegant but cruel curves. Lovers kissing brought sunshine to a street. A cluster of graffiti became the cave pictures of Lascaux.

And it wasn't that Haas made the commonplace beautiful: he simply perceived the beauty in the commonplace. 'No matter where you go,' he once said, 'you are surrounded by pictures. The trick is to recognise them.'

One might answer that New York is special, and that few other cities are half as glamorous. But it wasn't glamour that Haas saw – it was detail – the things we hurry by. And such things are in every city and town.

Sources of joy

While starting to write this chapter I found myself listing the things that can give joy to the eye in any city, be it Glasgow, Boston, London, Dublin, Manchester, wherever. Every city has 'that little tent of blue that prisoners call the sky,' as Oscar

Wilde put it. And the clouds up there are as lovely as clouds anywhere, even if we sometimes have to crane our necks to see them.

Cities have inhabitants – imagine one without them – and those inhabitants are the most fascinating part of any city, grist to the mill for that people-watching we discussed earlier.

Many streets have trees, which can look as gorgeous in spring or autumn as any tree down the country. Some cities have the most splendid murals – sometimes whole gable ends are scenes in themselves. There are invariably statues, commemorating people or events, some commemorating mighty heroes, others just quirky or humorous.

Dublin is famous for its whimsical statues, mostly down on street level. There's Molly Malone, close by Trinity College, 'who wheeled her wheelbarrow, through streets broad and narrow, crying cockles and mussels, alive, alive O'.

Then there's James Joyce, dapper with cane and straw hat. And those two housewives, sitting chatting on a park bench. It's a mild shock to sit by them and find they're made of bronze.

Galway too has a bench, this one with Oscar Wilde sitting, large as life, chatting with Estonian writer Eduard Wilde. The sculpture is a gift from the Estonian people.

Bridges can be works of art in themselves and often incorporate hidden history. Blackfriars Bridge in London, for instance – those pulpits above the bridge's piers honour the Dominican Order, known as the Black Friars, near whose 13th-century priory site the bridge was built. The Dominicans are the Order of Preachers, hence the pulpits.

And always there are the churches – with their steeples and clock towers and restful interiors, fascinating old inscriptions, and sometimes what Milton called 'storied Windows richly dight, casting a dimm religious light'.

There can be mist or fog to soften silhouettes and skylines and the harsh edges of streets. Even pollution can make for marvellous sunsets – and not only sunsets: in Beijing the sun at midday is often a golden disc like a sunset high above one's head, all due to the pollution.

There are reflections after rain, especially lovely under lamplight; and damp pavements and plain street fronts can turn gold when an evening sun pours down a street. There are flowerbeds, and flowers tumbling from window boxes.

There is that magic moment in every city – beloved of the painter Whistler – when the lights are just coming on, yet that clock tower or bridge is still silhouetted against the dying light of the sky. And of course a city after dark can be transformed, especially with the floodlights that can make even dreary buildings look magical. And even those neon signs can often add their own garish charm.

Pigeons rule OK in city squares everywhere from Trafalgar Square to St Mark's in Venice; there are the flocks of doves that wheel above the rooftops everywhere. I can never forget the ones in Beijing – hundreds all fitted with tiny bamboo whistles attached to their legs, that made a hauntingly lovely sound as they dived and wheeled high over Changan Boulevard.

Parks

I often think that parks are the escape valves of a city. Even if we are confined to the everyday of pavements grey, we can mostly find grass within walking distance. Also trees and water and bird life and many of the things of the countryside. Granted those keep-off-the-grass and dogs-on-short-leads notices, a park is still a mini countryside, be it Hyde Park or New York's Central Park or Dublin's Stephen's Green.

The finest parks are those where you can almost forget the city, except for the traffic murmur from beyond the trees. My favourite of all is the one at Chiswick House in West London. I have a friend who lives nearby and sometimes takes me there to meet her heron. *Her* heron? Well, as soon as my friend appears at the edge of the lake there's this heron that flaps up into the air to cross the lake and land at her feet. It looks quite miffed if not immediately presented with its customary daily ration of sprats.

This is the park that gave birth to the English Landscape Movement, so it's no wonder it is such a truly lovely place to visit. Its 18th century owner, the Earl of Burlington, drew his inspiration from a grand tour of Italy, and you can almost imagine the gardens as a part of Italy with their Palladian villa, ancient Roman sculptures, the narrow lake that winds through the trees like a river and the ornamental stone bridge that could have been taken from the Arno in Florence.

This park, left to ruin for years but now restored, is for me the epitome of what green can do for any urban area. As the then British Tourism and Heritage Minister John Penrose said, 'Chiswick House Gardens is an oasis of tranquillity right in the heart of bustling London... This beautiful landscape will bring hours of pleasure to tourists and local residents alike.'

Looking up

One of the things we often forget in any street is to look up. Shop windows are designed to rivet our attention but, if we can forget them for a few moments and look up to the levels above them, we can often find fascinating details in the most mundane of streets.

Intricate victorian brickwork, gothic casements, curved balconies, carved stone plaques and curious faces carved in granite, glaring gargoyles, everything from quirkiness and humour to downright beauty – there is a whole wealth of detail high above the hurrying hordes, all of it waiting forlornly for someone just to stop and look upwards.

Mind you, if you do stop to stare upwards you are likely to get The Look. What's wrong with *him*? Some sort of vision he's having? Or is it just a crick in his neck? Worse still, other people may start staring upwards too – not to admire some nice brickwork but in the hope of seeing someone about to jump.

Actually one of our entertainments as nasty youngsters was for a few of us to stand in a street gaping upwards, just to see how many passers-by we could trick into gaping up along with us. Of course in those days we didn't really notice the nice brickwork.

London of course is an up-gaper's dream. Oxford Street alone, with those massive ionic columns above Selfridges, more than you would ever see on any Greek temple – I think I once counted 22 along one façade. Or that Underground entrance with its red-brick carbuncles and circular windows; or nearby Duke Street with its granite and red-brick bays leaning out over the street, its pointy-roofed dormer windows, and those massive Victorian chimney stacks which are surely danced around by sweeps from *Mary Poppins*.

I am always delighted by the quite ridiculous follies and turrets and domes that top so many of our downtown buildings. So up there maybe is a white limestone thing with columns through which the wind whistles, that might contain the tomb of some unknown soldier if only it weren't away up so high; over there a copper-green dome that could well grace a church but is perched atop a department store; right above me, a round cone-capped turret that might have been pinched from Neuschwanstein except that it's made of red brick and clings to the top corner of a bank.

I sometimes wonder what these things are like inside. Do bankers hold their banquets beneath that green dome? (Should that read 'do banquers hold their banquets...'?) Does some starving servant eke out a life within that turret? Or is some wretch chained up there? Or could you swing a cat in it? Or has anyone ever been in it since the day it was built?

How dreary would our cities be without such follies. They make our skylines lovely even if they can't quite match Prague or Barcelona or Bruges. And if we never get to find out what goes on inside them, they are still fun to look up at – that is, if we are mindful enough to look up.

Bleak?

So much for downtown, but what about our bleak highrise estates? Nothing much to look up at there, except washing hanging out. It is a fair point, and one that is not easy to answer.

Is it naïve to think that one can find beauty beside the graffiti of some of our housing estates? That we can find it without the help of drugs? All I can venture right now is that if Victor Frankl could find a glimpse of beauty in Auschwitz, then perhaps it is possible for others. And if it is possible, it will be by dint of learning to look with Mindfulness. And perhaps if enough people learned to look for what is beautiful, and to care about it, then it might lead to things being made more beautiful.

I recently had the privilege of working on writing skills with a group of inner-city youngsters in a certain city. Having quit school early, these had been invited back to try and finish their education. These really had been deprived in many ways – one eighteen-year-old had lost both her brother and her boyfriend to suicide.

One of the group's projects was a small volume containing stories, essays and full-colour art work. The result was an utterly stunning achievement, making it perfectly clear that these youngsters had creativity, imagination, talent, longings, and now at last the beginnings of Mindfulness and of hope. Several may become artists, at least one will surely be a novelist, and all are developing confidence.

If the word education is from the Latin *e-ducere* (to draw out), then this project, these youngsters, and the wonderful team running the project, are drawing out the wonders that lie within every human being, and are reaching Mindfulness.

- Joining clubs for outdoor activities is one of the best things a city dweller can do. It can be hiking, birdwatching, hill climbing, photography, canal walking, boating, sailing – the list is endless. The great thing about clubs is that you meet similar-minded folks, which means you don't feel so lonely while doing all that mindful gazing, or when getting The Look.

- You can find all the clubs you want on the Internet. But beware: if you just google *Clubs in London*, for instance, you'll mostly get nightclubs and DJ bars, which is not exactly what we have in mind here. Always add an adjective – rambling clubs, hiking clubs, adventure clubs, bird-watching clubs, Sunday-walkers' clubs. That sort of thing.

- There may even be a Mindfulness club or society in your city. Or at your local university. See page 300 for contacts both in the UK and Ireland.

- Try being a tourist in your own city. I once lived for some years in a city which I shall call Dundreary, as it would be regarded as a very dreary city indeed. It was only when I knew I would soon be leaving it that I decided to spend my final three months as if I were a tourist. It was only then I discovered all the wonderful things I should have seen long before.

- Most cities offer organised day trips out of town that only tourists seem to avail of. They're not expensive and it is amazing how much loveliness lies within half a day of any city in Britain or Ireland. Remember even the dreariest cities often have fascinating hinterlands. Don't leave it all to the tourists.

- Actually no city is really dreary. Every single one has its history, its art, architecture, museums, galleries, parks. It is we who are dreary, unmindful of such riches right under our noses.

- Maybe towns and villages don't have all those things. But they have something else – green fields and woodlands are never far away, with their leafy lanes and forest walks. And at least you get a chance to see clouds and stars without going too far.

- Remember the Tower-of-London syndrome? – natives of London don't bother going to the Tower, never go up the London Eye, never go to Madame Tussauds, or the Planetarium, or the Houses of Parliament. So if you're a Londoner, google *Things to see in London* and simply take it from there. How about things to see in Birmingham, or Glasgow, or Belfast or Limerick? Just about anywhere. Try googling, and you will be astonished.

- When walking down High Street, don't forget to look up. Remember? But be mindful of that manhole.

21: Looking at landscapes

*The world is wide – no two days are alike, nor even two hours; neither were
there ever two leaves of a tree alike since the creation of all the world*

~ John Constable

*Each day I live in a glass room unless I break it
with the thrusting of my senses and pass through
the splintered walls to the great landscape*

~ Mervyn Peake

The lake and the mountains have become my landscape, my real world

~ Georges Simenon

*The artist is a receptacle for emotions that come from all over the place: from
the sky, from the earth, from the scrap of paper, from a passing shape, from a
spider's web*

~ Pablo Picasso

*I make it an infallible rule when travellg. abroad to see as little of the scenery
as possible; thus the mind is not unsettled and disturbed by wild excesses of
Nature and barren deserts such as the Scottish Highlands. My invariable
custom is to attempt to drink a bott. of port for each league travelled*

~ Squire Haggard's Journal of 1778

THE word *landscape*, like so many other words, needs to
be rescued from the computer, which has demeaned it to
mean a horizontal page as opposed to a vertical one
(*portrait* – another demeaned word).

225

Yet the word *landscape* still resonates. It conjures up for me a hiker coming over a hill to gaze upon the valley stretched out below, as Wordsworth did above the Wye, upriver from Tintern Abbey. Or a Donegal farmer leaning on a gate, surveying with pride his fields wrested from those reluctant rocks. Or that rolling English road beloved of Chesterton, winding through hills and dales.

We got the word from the 16th-century Dutch, who were the first to shift the term (*landschap*) from a mere tract of land to something beautiful in its own right, particularly as reproduced by a painter. Now the word has come back to just a tract of land, preferably beautiful but not necessarily so – how about 'an urban landscape', 'a barren landscape' or 'an industrial landscape'? Beautiful? Debatable. However, for our purposes here, let us take landscape as beautiful.

A landscape can mean so many different things to different people. Saint Benedict saw Monte Cassino as a remote hilltop above the Liri Valley on which to site his monastery away from worldly things; a German artillery officer saw that same mountainside as an ideal location for his guns, covering that same Liri Valley.

Pilgrims for centuries have seen the valley as the path to Rome. Geologists see that whole terrain as a valley swamped with lacustrine mud, overlooked by a volcanic peak veneered with rock prone to landslides.

And military historians see that same geology as the reason both for the effectiveness of the German Gustav Line, and why the American troops got bogged down for four months in what was one of the daftest undertakings of the war.

'I am prepared for defeat,' wrote General Fred L. Walker in his diary even before the battle.

When I visited there last year I saw Monte Cassino differently again. What I saw was a scene almost like Tibet's Potala – a peak crowned with a massive rectangular cluster of buildings, gleaming in the sunlight. And the hills around them like islands rising out of the encroaching mist.

That's because that evening I was looking with the eye of a tourist. Or maybe of a photographer. But the following morning, with the help of our gifted guide, I saw it differently, as a piece of history. Not just as the site of that horrific Italian Campaign, but as the site of all the battles that preceded it down the centuries, which destroyed the monastery four different times, and was sacked by nasties from the Lombards to the Saracens to Napoleon's troops and, uh, the Allies. But also I learned that it was once, before all this, a shrine to Apollo.

The past

One of the most exciting ways to look at a landscape is to wonder what happened there. We can do it anywhere. I live on a bluff in Killaloe that slopes down to the River Shannon. Now Killaloe was once the capital of Ireland, from 1002 to 1014, in the time of High King Brian Boru. On the skyline across the river from me is Kincora, the site of Brian Boru's palace (there's a church built on it now). A half-mile further upriver is Boru's fort to guard the river, and that circular fort still stands, twenty feet high all around. So I look out at my garden and realise that Boru's troops may have camped right here, where I plant roses today. Or maybe enemy troops, massing to attack across the river.

I look down at the Shannon below my window and imagine Viking ships sailing upriver (which they did) and pulling into the bank, to disembark those horned savages who swarm up the hill to massacre man, woman and child on the very spot where we will sleep in peace tonight.

It may have happened. It probably did. But the fun is to imagine. A bit more fun that being massacred.

There are of course the classic places for such imaginings, such as battlefields. I once took a solo trip on a motorcycle through the World War One battlefields of Northern France, where my Uncle Paul Rice had perished as a very young soldier.

I remember coming into Albert, where the great golden statue of the Virgin had hung horizontally from the church tower all during the campaign. (Soldiers used to say that when it fell the war would end.) I went into a bar across the square from the church, where the statue is long since back in its place atop the church tower. I asked the young barman about the story.

He shrugged: 'Don't know much about it. That's years ago,' he said (approximately). 'There's a few photos around the walls here, if you care to look at them.'

I don't blame him for his indifference. Who would want to remember such horrors? He and his people must have spent the last several generations trying to forget.

But for seekers like us, it's grist to the mill. Except that a couple of days later, after seeing trenches and shell holes and mine hollows and memorials and cemeteries galore, I ended up at a nearly empty campsite where I could not stop weeping. I will never forget how the woman who ran the campsite hugged me until I came to my senses.

So be wary of battlefields. Or maybe not. Do you ever wonder, when you read of battles like Marston Moor, or the Yellow Ford, or Bosworth Heath where poor old Richard III got his come-uppance, what these places are like now? I'd love to visit a few more of them. I believe at Bosworth Heath there is some sort of plaque identifying exactly where Richard offered his kingdom for a horse, and got a halberd into the back of his skull instead. One could do a lot of imagining there. (Soon there will probably be a plaque in that Leicester car park where his bones have been lying for 530 years.)

A warning, though. I once heard of a fellow who was cycling through an area where some 16th century battle had been fought, and found himself suddenly among galloping horses and flashing sabres and screaming, dying men. A time warp?

Rolling roads

What I love best in landscapes are what Chesterton called 'the rolling English roads', or what in Ireland are called boreens. The little roads, in other words. They are like ribbons that bind the land together.

For me the loveliest of all are the roads that crisscross the Cotswolds. We lately spent another wonderful holiday exploring them, and every twist and turn there brings a joy to the eye. A road curves through tunnels of trees; there's a brief view down to the church tower of Chipping Campden; a honey-coloured farmhouse by the roadside seems to glow in the evening sunlight; further on, the church tower of Stow-on-the-Wold is glimpsed atop its hill; and then comes that Venice of the region, where the streets almost dip into a little river with its ducks and drakes – Bourton-on-the-Water. There's nowhere quite like it.

And the friendliness of the people: at one point we were down in a valley village called Naunton, nestling under a yellow hillside of rapeseed. The village has a lovely church set in a rolling green churchyard. But the church was locked, as it was late evening. In no time a woman came up the hill towards us with a key to the church. 'Take all the time you want,' she said, and sat on a bench by the church to wait.

Another road I enjoy is the tortuous A595 that follows the Cumbria coast, hemmed between sea and mountain. It is a road to be enjoyed, rather than to be hurried along. If you are heading north there are glimpses of the Irish Sea, perhaps with the last of the evening sun glancing off it. There are hills and dales and hairpin bends galore – it's the outside rim of the Lake District of course. And hamlets where the road narrows between houses straight out of a calendar picture. And on a good day a chance of seeing the Isle of Man.

But that lovely rolling road leads alas to – Drigg, where they dump nuclear waste. And worse still, to Sellafield, where they create that waste. And beautiful, Drigg and Sellafield certainly are not.

Some of the loveliest roads are on the Scottish isles. Even though the Isle of Arran is only 19 miles long and 10 miles wide, it has the most breathtaking little roads around the perimeter and across the mountains, with stunning views and the quirkiest, loveliest town names – Lochranza, Sliddery, Lamlash, Shiskine, Corrie, Samox. It's nearly worth going for the names alone.

Among my favourites are the little roads in Ireland – what they call 'boreens' (which is simply the gaelic for 'little road' (*bóithrín*). It seems that Ireland has more roads per square km than any other European country – which probably goes back to the huge pre-famine population. But, in spite of the brilliant new motorways, the little roads are still there, and they are a dream to explore.

The ones I like best are those with a line of grass up the middle of the road. They are quite literally the roads to God knows where. These little boreens weave in and out through every county and can often lead to scenes of stunning beauty that few tourists ever get to see. The real adventure of touring in Ireland is to get off the beaten track and explore these pretty-well unbeaten ones.*

Mindful ways to look

The most satisfying way to look at a landscape is just to drink in its beauty. To see how that curving fence leads you eye right into the middle of the scene. Or how those overhanging branches act like a frame to the landscape (remember Belloc seeing the Alps?). Or how that steeple in the distance is like a finger pointing heavenwards out of those gently curving fields. Or how those hills grow fainter, one behind the other, like in an oriental painting.

There are two ways to look at a landscape. I can take in the whole impression at once, just letting the beauty wash over

---

* Kathleen's uncle, Colum Quigley, once told me that he remembered how there always used to be *two* lines of green up the middle of these boreens. He asked me to guess why. I did. *Can you?*

me. Or I can scan the view, letting my eye rove over it, taking in one component, then another – line, balance, shape, pattern, texture, lighting, movement, trees, hills, sky, structures, human figures. Either way has its particular satisfaction. Most of us do both anyhow for, when we do scan, we nevertheless end up noticing how the various items knit together to create the complete scene in all its loveliness. So we are once more viewing it as a whole.

People sometimes say to me that one would really need the eye of an artist to see the beauty of a landscape. Nothing could be further from the truth. We need not an artist's eye, but a mindful one. Nature's loveliness is for everyone, and we can all develop the skill of looking, as well as any artist. It's simply that the artist calls on some further skills with paint and brush, or with camera and lens, as well as the skill of visualising the scene within the limits of a rectangular frame.

However, landscape painters do a signal service to the ordinary viewer: they call our attention to the beauty that is out there, which we might otherwise miss. John Constable does this incomparably. As he once wrote: 'Water escaping from mill dams, willows, old rotten planks, slimy posts, and brickwork, I love such things.' His *Sketch at Hampstead*, in the Victoria & Albert Museum, shows us how the last flare of the setting sun can render a field as blazingly golden almost as the sun itself. His *Stonehenge* calls our attention to how low slanting light can texture earth and stone so we feel it without ever touching. And it also shows us how splendid a rainbow can be.

Constable also presents us with wonderful viewpoints that we can still return to. I have always admired his canvases of Salisbury Cathedral viewed from the Water Meadows: well, only recently I went there with my camera and the view was exactly the same as it had been two hundred years earlier. I got almost the same picture – except, well, I'm no Constable, and a camera is not quite the same as a paintbrush.

They must have a wonderful city council in Salisbury which, down all the years, has allowed no buildings to spoil that classic landscape. In fact I have heard that it permits no edifice of more than two storeys within the city, which means that the spire, tallest in Britain, can be seen from almost anywhere.

Paul Henry's canvases remind us that mountains can be purple even when bereft of heather. Or mauve, or magenta or pale blue – whatever the wilful western weather dictated at the time of painting. Or they can give us a green mountainside with a tiny white cottage perched at its foot. His canvases remind us too to look upwards, to see how those mountains can be utterly dwarfed by the colossal cumulus clouds of the Atlantic seaboard. I have gone into Connemara with my camera, to see if I could find what Paul Henry showed us. I was amazed at what I found. (I'll be putting some of the pictures up on the website.)

Claude Monet shows us how dramatic can be a silhouette against a brightly-coloured evening sky, as in his *Houses of Parliament* (in the Musée d'Orsay). He teaches us how the very sky can drop down to live among the lilies in tranquil water; his series on Rouen Cathedral shows us how the grey west front of a church can become blue in morning light, change to dazzling white under the noonday sun, and then turn gold at evening. He even helps us see the beauty of man-made things, especially steam trains and railway stations. But above all he reminds us that we do not really see things at all – what we see is merely the light that comes from them, light which can magically change itself and the things we think we see.

David Hockney presents landscapes in a particularly lovely way. His fields spread out like a quilt; his rolling roads wind in and around hillsides that would have delighted Belloc and Chesterton. Just google *David Hockney* to see what I mean.

Galleries

People used to be scared of art galleries, and I find that some still are. The hushed atmosphere; the silent, watchful functionaries who make us feel like potential thieves; on the first walls those varnished brown rectangles from a bygone age that means little to us; those arrogant aristocrats sneering down from their massive gold frames; or worse still, those funny faces with eyes or noses in the wrong place – it all can be rather daunting.

Yet there can be no better place for learning mindful looking. The funny faces can wait: what I often suggest to a diffident gallery visitor is to go straight to the landscapes – anything from Corot, Cezanne, Monet, Turner or Van Gogh to Whistler, Roderic O'Connor, Jack B. Yeats, Thomas Ryan, David Hockney, Graham Sutherland.

Of the last named, Kenneth Clark wrote: 'Graham Sutherland has described how, on his country walks, objects which he has passed a hundred times – a root, a thorn bush, a dead tree – will suddenly detach themselves and demand a separate existence; but why or when this should happen he cannot tell us, any more than a rider can tell us why his pony shies on a familiar road.' [45]

That surely is what mindful looking is all about – not just passing by, but really *seeing* something for the first time. Even something tiny or seemingly of little consequence. There is no joy quite like it. And artists and art galleries can call our attention to such things.

If we then learn to appreciate them, eventually we get to appreciate the funny faces too. But, as they say in Gaelic, *sin sceal éile* – 'that's another story', perhaps for another another time or another book.

Of course if one had the gift of being a landscape painter – would that I had it – one would enjoy a heightened adventure of looking and seeing. But few of us have such a gift, although far more have it than realise it. However, if we are not able to handle easel and brush, there is another instrument which, if used with skill, can help to transform us. I mean, of course, the camera, which the following chapter is about.

- Looking at the works of great artists is an excellent way to learn to appreciate landscapes. Click on *Google Images*, for any of the following, and you can have a mini landscape gallery right at home – David Hockney; Constable; Corot; Turner; Thomas Ryan; Cuyp; Roderic O'Connor; Alfred Sisley; Jack B Yeats; Monet; Claude Lorrain; Paul Henry (artist); Hobbema; John Piper; Francis Danby; Cezanne; Van Gogh; Whistler; Graham Sutherland. There are hundreds more.

- Then google *Landscape Art* on Wikpedia, and you will get lots more, as well as learning what landscapes are all about.

- Having found landscapes on Google, it's time to go out and find some for ourselves. Some people do it armed with an artist's palette; others do it with a camera. But we don't need either: our two eyes and the beginnings of Mindfulness are all we need. We can find landscapes simply by wandering the countryside to find what is beautiful there.

- Some people make a rectangle with their fingers while looking at landscapes. It's a way of seeing how all the elements fit together, and can be remarkably satisfying. See how Ernst Haas does it, in the next chapter.

- Touring wooded regions like the Cotswolds is marvellously enhanced by driving in a cabriolet. Open-topped touring is not just for having wind in the hair: the real joy is that you can look upwards at the canopy of trees when the road plunges into a forest. Or at the sky when you emerge. There is no experience quite like it. And rag-tops can be surprisingly inexpensive when bought second hand.

- Re those little boreens in Ireland: they are far better explored on foot or bike than by car. It's not much fun meeting another car head-on on a lane with grass up the middle. And don't in heaven's name bring a bus. (There's the story of a French bus driver who brought his charges all the way up Ireland's most terrifying boreen – the one that goes to the top of Donegal's

Slieve League – one of Europe's highest cliffs. He couldn't turn at the top and had to back the bus the whole way down, with sheer vertical drops of hundreds of feet from the edge of the road to the hungry waiting ocean.)

22: Click or contemplate?

Not everybody trusts paintings, but people believe photographs

~ Ansel Adams

*I am no longer concerned with photography as an art form.
I believe it is potentially the best medium for explaining man
to himself and his fellow man*

~ Edward Steichen

*Photographs have been used as illustrations, but the camera no longer
illustrates. The camera tells. The camera shall take its place as the greatest
and by all measurements the most convincing reporter of contemporary life*

~ Archibald MacLeish

*Our father Adam sat under the Tree and scratched with a stick in the mould;
And the first crude sketch that the world had seen was joy to his mighty heart,
Till the Devil whispered behind the leaves, 'It's pretty, but is it Art?'*

~ Rudyard Kipling

AN article in the American Methodist magazine *Together* tells how photographer Ernst Haas took its author on a trip around New York carrying, not his camera, but a piece of black cardboard with a rectangular opening cut out of it – a frame, as he called it. 'No matter where you go, you are surrounded by pictures,' he told the writer. 'The trick is to recognise them. Look – '

Haas crumpled a sheet of wrapping paper and threw it on the floor. Viewed through the frame it revealed 'interesting patterns of light and shade that had escaped me before.'

They stepped out into the street. 'At first I saw nothing of note,' the writer says. 'But when I used the cardboard frame, pictures seemed to leap to the eye. A dribble of paint on the pavement made a striking free-form design. I framed another picture, one that resembled an ancient cave drawing, on the wall of an old building where children had been busy with chalk... To enjoy such mental snapshots requires no camera, nothing more than the will to look, observe and appreciate.'

I myself often use the framing technique. I don't carry a card frame, but make a rectangle with my fingers, and it has the extraordinary effect of helping me see a picture where before there were only things.

Of course I do get The Look. Whereas when I have a camera up to my eye, no one seems to mind. However that's not quite why I carry one. I've been carrying a camera since I was sixteen, and it has long since become an addiction. It was nearly as costly as gambling in the old days of film but, with the arrival of digital, it costs practically nothing save the price of charging the battery.

However there's a downside to that as well, namely that instead of taking three shots I now cheerfully take thirty. Or three hundred. And that indeed makes people feel for my partner Kathleen if she is with me. I and my camera have become a singular bore.

But I've got some pretty neat pictures.

Camera or not?

So, in this little book on looking to grow mindful, am I recommending the reader to carry a camera? Well, yes and no. You don't actually need it to appreciate the scene around you, but assiduous use of a camera certainly can help to train the eye and discipline it to see pictures that one might otherwise miss. It increases visual awareness.

The camera does so in a number of ways. Just looking for pictures makes us mindful of light and its magical effects – how sunlight can put a golden rim around a head of fair hair; how it can transform a field or a hillside when the morning sun caresses it.

The camera makes us conscious of visual limits – the limits enforced by the need to fit the picture into a rectangle. From that comes an awareness of balance and of composition – that that tower should be away from the centre of the picture, better to one side (perhaps about a third way in from the margin); or that it doesn't always feel right when a horizon runs right across the middle of the picture, but is more pleasing closer to the top or the bottom (about a third way up or down).

And then one realises that taking a couple of steps to left or right can completely change a picture – in other words we become aware of the critical importance of viewpoint.

Familiarity with a camera makes us better enjoy the works of the great landscape painters – because we now understand why that cottage was placed exactly there, or how those two tiny figures by the stream are a focal point that draws the eye.

Japanese woodcuts

From out of 19th century Japan have come some of the loveliest artworks I know – those colour woodcuts of Hokusai and Hiroshige (see page 67). They also happen to be models for any landscape photographer. What could 180-year-old prints teach someone armed with today's digital camera? A great deal.

Above all else, these two artists position a picture's components with what almost amounts to inerrancy: geese fly across the moon exactly where they most gladden the eye; that boat with its tiny figure appears in the frame at precisely the point where it has adequate space to travel across the picture; that cherry blossom superbly frames the distant Mt Fuji; that pine tree perfectly balances the visual weight of that distant hill.

Over the years I go back again and again to these prints, and always I learn something more about how to create a picture. They have taught me that you do not 'take' a picture – you 'make' it, perhaps by moving slightly to left or right to better position that pagoda as a focal point; or by moving back underneath a willow tree so its branches will frame the picture.

As celebrated photographer Ansel Adams once said, 'A great photograph is knowing where to stand.' The items in front of your lens are only ingredients: it's how you put them together that makes the picture. All this Hokusai and Hiroshige have taught me. (An aside, however: I thought I had invented that idea of 'making' rather than 'taking' a photograph. Until I discovered that the same Ansel Adams had said it years before. I'm not sure whether to be cross at being pipped at the post, or to be gratified that I was right all along.)

In 1820s Japan there was little respect for these prints – they were regularly used as wrapping paper. It wasn't until James McNeill Whistler discovered them, and was inspired by them to create his own celebrated *Nocturnes*, that they came into their own in Britain and France, as some of the great works of all time, helping to create the revolution we call Impressionism.

A fascinating and delightful development is the recent work of British artist Emily Allchurch, who has succeeded in fusing the vision of Hiroshige with present-day views from her digital camera. She went to Tokyo to seek out and photograph some of the very scenes immortalised by Hiroshige. Then, using a combination of her photos and watercolours, fused in the computer through Photoshop, she has succeeded in producing modern views of Japan that are eerily like the original woodcuts.

To see a Hiroshige temple scene with a red lantern in the foreground, and that print mounted side by side with the same temple and similar lantern as photographed by Allchurch, is astonishing. Or a river with a Shinto *torii* archway framed by real live cherry blossom, juxtaposed with an almost identical hand-drawn blossom by Hiroshige, makes one wonder if that blossom has remained on those boughs from that day till this.

Showing us

Even if we decide never to use a camera ourselves, the work of others, particularly the really great photographers, can do us the signal service of pointing out to us things, scenes, pictures that we might otherwise have missed. Thus we too can learn to look – to look and grow mindful.

French photographers Henri Cartier-Bresson and Robert Doisneau taught the people of Paris to see their fellow citizens as they had never before seen them – a gendarme frowning at a nude picture in a shop window; a family picnicking on the banks of the Marne; a little boy on roller skates carrying flowers to Mama; another youngster carrying home a bottle of wine to Papa. (They used to say Cartier-Bresson became invisible just before he took a photo, since everyone in his pictures is so natural and unaware.)

Father Francis Browne did the same in his stunning collection of photos from the early 20th century – negatives that were almost dumped until one of his brethren, long after his death, discovered them in a metal trunk in a Jesuit-house basement. So now we have pictures from Ireland, Britain, Australia, World-War-One France, that preserve scenes we thought were long gone. Above all, he has saved for us scenes from the doomed *Titanic*, on which he was a passenger from Southampton as far as Cobh, where his Jesuit superiors ordered him to disembark. (Did they know something?)

Many years ago, when I was starting off as editor of a pictorial magazine, I called into the Magnum Photographic Agency in Paris ('home' to Cartier-Bresson, Robert Capa and many of the greats of photography). I was young and dumb, and totally out of my depth, but I can never forget the kindness and interest with which I was received.

As I was leaving they gave me the gift of a book of pictures called *The Family of Man*. For days afterwards I was mesmerised by the photos it contained: two little toddlers, boy and girl, hold hands as they walk away into a forest – a tiny Hänsel and Gretel; the bleak face of an Oklahoma migrant stares straight from *The Grapes of Wrath*. But the picture that moved me most, and the memory still does, is of a soldier in the Korean War hugging a weeping comrade to comfort him.

I later learned, of course, that the volume was based on what is considered the greatest photographic exhibition of all time. What that book taught me was how the camera can make us mindful, not just of the beauty of this world, but of its pathos.

In the years since, the camera has done that service to a point where it has raised consciousness around the world. A little girl running from napalm made people look anew at the Vietnam War. Those gothic pictures of Ethiopia's 1984 famine shocked the world and prompted Bob Geldof to create Band Aid.

So a camera can bring us not only the Joy of Looking, but also its Sadness. There is a surely a place for both in our looking: the sadness can prompt us to empathy, and thus, one hopes, to action – while the Joy of Looking, and the beauty it unveils, can give us the strength and hope to endure that same sadness. As it did in Auschwitz.

Shadow side?

Finally, back to the question – could the use of a camera lessen our Mindfulness or spoil the Joy of Looking? It could, although it need not. I now believe my incessant and fanatical use of a camera has to some extent lessened both Mindfulness and Joy for me, and I'm going to have to do something about it. I see a marvellous sunset; I race for the camera to capture it; by the time I have finished clicking, the sunset has faded. Sure, I can look at the pictures later but I have missed the *Now* of the event, and no mere image can ever replace that.

The trouble is that photography can sometimes become a denial of that Now – and the Now is all we really have. While I'm shooting the picture, I'm thinking of how it is going to turn out, and how I'll enjoy showing it, so I'm living in the future (which doesn't yet exist). When I look at the picture later, I'm seeing what existed in the past (which no longer exists). All I really have is a memory, and some electronic impulses on a hard disk.

Alfred Stieglitz, one of the world's great photographers, said something like that, many years ago:

> I have always been a great believer in today. Most people live either in the past or in the future, so that they really never live at all... Utopia is in the moment. Not in some future time, some other place, but in the here and now, or else it is nowhere.'

I guess I should have listened. On the other hand, I wonder how Stieglitz managed to take all those marvellous photos yet stay in the here and now. Fair point, eh?

For a while I tried leaving the camera at home. But it was a miserable experience – without it I was guaranteed to see some marvellous picture just screeching to be taken. And nothing to take it with. That way lies neurosis. So my compromise now is, carry the camera, take some pictures, but then put it aside and simply contemplate that cloud, smiling meadow or sunset (if it's considerate enough to wait). A matter of timing, I suppose. But I think it's beginning to work. Time will tell.

This is something we're all going to have to make up our minds about, for nowadays we are all potential photographers, ever since our mobile phones have morphed into cameras. To click or to contemplate? The jury's still out.

Why not some of both?

Suggestions

- So, to the question, does use of a camera lessen Mindfulness? And need it always do so? Why not post your views on our website? (See back cover). Meanwhile, below are some thoughts about cameras.

- Smart phones nowadays have evolved into quite splendid cameras, which can get really good results with both stills and movies. We could use them a lot more than we do – it's just that the picture function of our phone is not always part of our awareness.

- By the way, you can now get tiny extra lenses for your smart phone – wide-angle, tele and macro. They just clip on over the lens opening at the back of the phone, and cost very little. You can also get an adaptor to fit your smart phone to a tripod -- ideal for landscapes. You can even get an app that will cut camera shake without a tripod.

- However if you want to take up photography as a serious hobby, get yourself a DSLR (digital single-lens reflex), with a zoom lens - because of the range of what such cameras can achieve, such as photos against the light. Go for the best camera you can afford – always. There are good ones now for under £400 (€500). If it's serious photography, avoid those little briquette things – they may come in pretty colours, but they are really no better than your smart phone. Of course they too are getting better by the day.

- The magazine *What Camera?* gives monthly lists and details of all cameras available, under the various price ranges.

- Before choosing, get advice from a photographer. Explain what your needs are, and follow that advice. If you want advice from a camera shop, pick a reputable one, as certain outlets may try to sell you a model that is just about to be superseded. (It happened to me once.)

- For landscapes you need at least two accessories – a lens hood and a polarizing filter. A tripod is also helpful to avoid

244

camera shake. Any guidebook will explain why you need them and how to use them.

- Obviously it's not within the scope of this book to present a course in photography, but there are many straightforward guides on how to use your digital camera. There are lots of wonderful introductory manuals, especially those by Tom Ang and John Hedgecoe. See Bibliography at the back of this book.

- At some point consider software like Adobe *Photoshop or Elements,* which can transform your photos on the computer. It's not at all essential, but can work magic on your pictures. Also Adobe *Lightroom* can help you organise them.

- But don't let that camera take you over completely or you might end up like me. *Quod Deus avertat.*

23: Foes of Mindfulness

*Life can be found only in the present moment. The past is gone, the future is
not here, and if we do not go back to ourselves in the present moment, we
cannot be in touch with life*

~ Thich Nhat Hanh

*Without the ability to be present
we are missing much of what the adventure has to offer*

~ Allan Lokos

*The world is too much with us; late and soon,
Getting and spending, we lay waste our powers;
Little we see in Nature that is ours;
We have given our hearts away, a sordid boon!*

~ William Wordsworth

*Longing for the future and nostalgia for the past
are the two great enemies of a rewarding life*

~ Desmond Morris

*All great and beautiful work has come
of first gazing without shrinking into the darkness*

~ John Ruskin

THERE are obstacles to growing mindful. And some can
be formidable. Chapter One touched on things like the
Tower-of-London Syndrome, but there are others along
the way. Perhaps the principal ones are the following – future
fixation, nostalgia, regret, resentment, familiarity, indifference,

procrastination, priorities, hurry, fear, glancing, greed, arrogance, television (addiction to), electronic screens (addiction to), anoracks, twitching, and theme parks. Not necessarily in that order. That's a pretty long list. Let's go through it anyhow.

Future fixation is a denial of the Now: If my mind is constantly running off into the future – worrying, making plans, getting uptight about what hasn't yet happened, then I am not living in the here and now, which is where Mindfulness is found. Thich Nhat Hanh puts it succinctly:

> Carried away by our worries, we're unable to live fully and happily in the present. Deep down, we believe we can't really be happy just yet—that we still have a few more boxes to be checked off before we can really enjoy life. We speculate, dream, strategize, and plan for these 'conditions of happiness' we want to have in the future; and we continually chase after that future, even while we sleep. We may have fears about the future because we don't know how it's going to turn out, and these worries and anxieties keep us from enjoying being here now.[46]

Nostalgia, regret and *resentment* are fixations on the past. If we are hung up on grieving for 'the good old days', then we are hung up on things that simply don't exist any more. Likewise, if we fritter away our energies on regretting past mistakes. Likewise again if we continue brooding over hurts from the past. They don't exist, and we are missing the only thing that does – the Now.

Familiarity: It's not for nothing that the old proverb came to be uttered – 'familiarity breeds contempt'. However it is more often indifference rather than contempt that is bred. We see something wonderful and we wonder. We see it again and we wonder less. And less again the next time. And so on until we reach *indifference.*

Yet a wonderful thing is still wonderful: it has not changed. But *we* have. We have grown indifferent – whether it be to the waves that crash upon our shores, the clouds that cavort above us, the fields and the forests that flash by our hurrying windscreen, the stars up there twinkling unheeded.

The remedy, I think, lies in our will – a deliberate decision to stop and gaze upon those waves, until we begin to contemplate their wonder. A decision to lie back and watch that cloud disappear. A decision to pull in the car and saunter down that woodland path. A decision, in short, to be mindful.

So we say, 'Must think about that. Yeah, fairly soon.' That's the next obstacle – *procrastination.* For there really is only the Now.

I have found that in my own life 'fairly soon' never actually comes. And that has often been my undoing. So now that I spend my days writing, I have a strict rule: whenever a day of brilliant sunshine comes (which, God knows, is rare enough), I simply drop everything and take to the hills with my camera. There are lots of hills around here.

'It's OK for you – a writer can do as he pleases,' I hear the response. Point taken. Well, granted I'm free to assign my time (I wasn't always), yet I still feel the pressure common to all workaholics. Actually this chapter should have been finished yesterday, and I really felt I ought to stay at the computer. But in the end my real priorities won the contest – those blue skies and dancing sunbeams might not be around again for a while, whereas the keyboard will.

PS: I nearly didn't go.

PPS: But I did.

Priorities

Priorities are there for all of us, whether they be household chores or office jobs or children. Sometimes however they can be rearranged, if only momentarily. A decision might be something as simple as pausing while taking in the washing so as to watch a rainbow grow, or stopping a car at a forest entrance and walking a little distance in. It's the will to do so that counts and, if we have that will, the wonder and the beauty will find us. And so will Mindfulness.

But even when the will is there, the *hurry* of everyday life can prevent us from pausing. And yet, in all our gallop through a day, there are still moments when we could pause. Like looking up at the sky above a parking lot before climbing into the car. Looking out over the city skyline from the office window. Watching a raindrop on that same window.

So we can pause at a window even on a busy day; or on a weekend we can take off to hike through woodlands; or we can get up from the TV to go out to the yard and watch the snowflakes fall. But we will do none of these unless we are convinced it is worthwhile – that doing so is more important than not pausing at a window, not woodland hiking, not going out to the yard.

Or if not more important, at least more immediate. Which all depends on our priorities. And we only get those right by pondering them, and perhaps deciding to rearrange them. Again, a matter of the will.

Fear

Fear is surely another obstacle to the Mindfulness of the eye. It's twofold: There's the fear of wasting time – 'wasting' it on just looking at something instead of *doing* something. And then the fear of being 'different' – of getting The Look.

The first fear is endemic in our clock-time society. It is a modern version of the puritan fear of waste – waste not, want not. And in this Type-A helter-skelter culture of ours, time is the one precious thing we dare not waste. Unfortunately we assume that the time we might give to stop and look and wonder would be time 'wasted'. There's no money in it, see.

The remedy surely must be, again, priorities. In other words convincing ourselves that mindful looking, gazing in wonder, will enrich our lives so much that it makes it one of the most important things in life. It puts us into what sociologist Bernard Levine calls 'event time' as opposed to 'clock time'.[47]

The second fear holds back many people: the fear that stopping too often to gaze might seem a bit peculiar. Young people often tell me they fear seeming a bit different. And of course for youngsters especially, being different is anathema.

For men the fear can be of seeming slightly, well, too gentle, too sensitive. We like to see ourselves as hard men, well endowed, with strong beards or five-o'clock shadow, firm chins, broad shoulders, hairy chests, rippling muscles, flat bellies, riveting gaze – able to take on the big things of life. Whereas appreciating little things, like an insect, a buttercup, a violet by a mossy stone – stuff like that might be better left to poets and suchlike. That riveting gaze might soften a bit too much if focused too long on anything delicate or beautiful.

The remedy here comes in two words – *grow up*. Which some would-be machos don't, ever.

To glance or to gaze?

Glancing: If in any one day we were to make a tally of how many times we glanced at things, and how many times we gazed, what would that tally be? Bet is there would be hardly enough gazes and perhaps too many glances. I just hope those gazes would be mindful ones.

However it is surely the proportion that counts. Too few gazes, or none at all, would betoken a life without much Joy of Looking, and thus without much wonder or Mindfulness. But if we can increase the proportion to any extent, then we become more open to all of these.

The Oxford Dictionary defines *to glance* as 'to take a brief or hurried look'. Whereas *to gaze* is 'to look steadily and intently, especially in admiration, surprise, or thought'. As usual, good old OED says it all. For if I look steadily and intently at a starry sky or a bumble bee, not only will I be lost in surprise and admiration, but I may even find myself deep in thought. And that cannot but lead to wonder.

Greed. Remember 'greed is good'? The drive to own rather than enjoy? I knew one couple where the wife genuinely seemed to have achieved a measure of Mindfulness. However her husband was constantly asking, 'Does all this looking make money? If not, what's the bloody point?'

The quest for money or power seems by its very nature to demand total commitment, with neither time nor energy for looking beyond such things. If that truly be the case, then the seeker must make a choice – power or wonder. Money or Mindfulness. It's a dismal choice, recalling the proverb, 'We spend our health to get wealth, then our wealth to get health.' I hope it's not so – that one could manage both. But I know very few who have achieved it.

The fellow who kept asking 'Does it make money?' has lost most of it in the downturn, and now has all the time in the world to look at things, especially his unfinished construction sites. But does he look? Has he lost the knack? Has he lost his vision? Well, if not his vision, he'll still have his television.

Then there is *arrogance*, that hideous outward face of pride, which leads us to despise the earth and try to conquer it. Arrogance means we can never learn from the earth. According to Meister Eckhart, humility – the opposite of arrogance – comes from the word *humus*, or earth. Philosopher and theologian Matthew Fox puts is beautifully:

> The opposite of arrogance is indeed humility – but
> not the decadent humility of denying one's gifts and
> uniqueness. Rather the healthy humility of
> remaining true and close to the earth and the
> things of the earth. Simple living. Simplicity is
> today's very accurate synonym for humility. For the
> earth and its simple creatures – the vine and the
> water, the dogs and the flowers, the birds and the
> fishes – do not tolerate arrogance for long.[48]

Fox illustrates this by describing how, after the nuclear accident at Three Mile Island, a resident with tears in his eyes said, 'The birds have all gone.'

Television

Plato has this startling image of people chained up all their lives in a cave so that they cannot turn around. Only thing the poor wretches can see are shadows projected on the wall before them – shadows of people and things passing in front of a fire, and of course they think those shadows are reality, since they have never seen anything else. [49]

If I am addicted to *television*, I am not unlike those cave dwellers. All I am really seeing are flickering shadows. Yet it is too easy to mistake them for reality, especially if I see little else during my day. If I watch soaps for several hours daily I am watching events that do not really happen, and people pretending to be what they are not, for that's what acting is. Even 'reality' TV shows people in contrived situations, trying to be what they are not – not much reality there either. Thus much of my life is devoted to the unreal.

Mumford and Sons have a wonderful song about Plato's cave. And they have a line that says it all:

> So come out of your cave, walking on your hands
> And see the world hanging upside down...

I have a theory that the old division of society into patricians and plebs, or aristocrats and commoners, is out of date. We have a new division now – the creators and the consumers.

There is now a new elite – that relatively small number of people who have an absolute ball being creative – making programmes for TV which the rest of us passively just gape at; directing and acting in films; writing songs and performing on world tours; writing novels; designing clothes and modelling them; being celebrity chefs; scoring goals for Man U.

These elite get to create those mini series we are hooked on; they get to roam the jungles seeing wildlife close up; they travel the world making documentaries; they get to cook up gorgeous things which leave us drooling at the screen (and get to eat them afterwards, presumably – well, someone must); they invent the stories and write the music and strut the parts that win the Oscars; and get paid huge sums of money just for having a good time.

These creator elite are the aristocrats of today. We commoners no longer create, but merely consume things like TV programmes that the elite choose to hand down to us – the old Roman *panes et circenses* – bread and circuses – updated for the plebs of today. And most of it shadows in the end.

At least the gladiators were for real.

Of course TV can be a blessing when it brings us great sporting events, world news, those brilliant documentaries or enlightening discussions, but when it dominates all of our evenings we could perhaps be looking at too many shadows and failing to see the reality and wonder around us.

In other words, moderation is surely the key.

(A brief aside on moderation, which has just occurred to me as I write this. I've been trying for years to apply in my life that old adage, 'moderation in all things'. So I've become moderately honest, moderately truthful, moderately trustworthy, moderately pure, moderately reliable, moderately responsible, moderately decent, moderately dependable, moderately likeable, moderately mindful, moderately OK. So this book should be considered just moderately believable! Just a thought. Or maybe we should go back to Petronius: 'Moderation in all things, *including moderation.*')

Computers

The *computer* is undoubtedly one of the greatest blessings of today's world. Especially for the access it gives to the Internet. It has been a godsend in researching this book. And throughout it I have given references to websites that I have found helpful, indeed sometimes magical.

The only caution is not to get totally hooked on the websites, and fail to go out and find those starlings for ourselves. Again a matter of moderation versus addiction.

In fact, while the computer is a blessing, addiction can be a curse. Indeed all sorts of rectangular screens have taken over our lives. Not just monitors and laptops, but smart phones, notebooks, netbooks, tablets, TVs, airport arrivals boards, and even sat-navs while we're driving.

If we were to estimate just how much time we spend gazing into screens instead of at the world around us, we might be astonished. And maybe just a little concerned.

Perhaps the greatest curse of all must be addiction to those electronic games, from which little can be learned. Recently I heard two adults talking about hiding in the bathroom to continue one such game, and staying up long after bedtime to finish one.

At least they are adults and know what they are doing. But what about the children who spend literally every waking hour tapping the screen of some electronic tablet? Will they ever emerge from those games to notice the world around them? I have even seen a three-year-old impatiently tapping at a picture book, and quite angry that it would not respond electronically.

Twitchers

I was a teenage *twitcher*, which was at least slightly better than a teenage vampire – a twitcher being defined in the dictionary as 'a birdwatcher whose main aim is to collect sightings of rare birds'. However I didn't twitch over birds: I twitched over aeroplanes. Actually I started at about seven – whenever an unfamiliar plane passed overhead I would scurry into the house to one of my many spotter books, find the plane and mark a big red ✔ against it. That was it: no further interest in that plane – been there and done that (except that I went on to build models of these planes, which I'm still doing, and is ridiculous at my age).

Twitching is just another form of collecting: instead of stamps, one gathers lists of sightings. It hardly differs from what I call *anorak-sia* – the activity of writing down train numbers while wearing an anorak. Both activities may be fun for the twitchers and the anoraks, but they are as far from the Joy of Looking or Mindfulness or as glancing is from gazing. Their practitioners are the Gradgrinds of Looking (see next chapter).

The main downside of such activities is that they can so easily eliminate gazing and wondering. Spot that bird; twitch; jot it down; move on to the next one. No time to ponder. Less time to wonder. Indeed photography can have a similar effect – need not, but can – as I have lately been finding out to my dismay. See that scene; click; move on to the next shot.

And lastly, *theme parks*. Fine and noble enterprises, I am sure. However they could be symbolic of an unhealthy trend in modern life. The danger of an over-emphasis on the whole theme-park phenomenon is surely this: those wonderful rides, those incredible illusions and experiences they offer, *are all human constructs*.

They can easily lead (especially in the eyes of young people) to a downgrading of the far more wondrous constructs of nature – the sky, the ocean, the forest, and all those things that live and move and have their being. The things we can be truly mindful about.

Rachel Carson takes this even further:

> I believe that whenever we substitute something
> human-made and artificial for a natural feature of
> the earth, we have retarded some part of
> humanity's spiritual growth.[50]

Suggestions

The suggestions are all embedded in the above chapter. Perhaps we should —

- live in the Now rather than in the future;
- forget nostalgia;
- dump our regrets and resentments;
- look once more with wonder at familiar things;
- not postpone, but grab opportunities when they come;
- slow down;
- gaze more and glance less;
- get priorities right;
- cut out the hurry;
- not be afraid to 'waste' time;
- remember greed as the enemy of Mindfulness;
- avoid *addiction* to electronic screens of whatever sort;
- see nature as the greatest theme park of all;
- remember, if we're too busy to look, we're too busy.

24: The need to know

Master Gradgrind: 'Now, what I want is, Facts. Teach these boys and girls nothing but Facts. Facts alone are wanted in life. Plant nothing else, and root out everything else. You can only form the minds of reasoning animals upon Facts: nothing else will ever be of any service to them. This is the principle on which I bring up my own children, and this is the principle on which I bring up these children. Stick to Facts, sir!'

~ Charles Dickens (*Hard Times*)

We lay and looked up at the sky and the millions of stars that blazed in darkness.... An experience like that, when one's thoughts are released to roam through the lonely spaces of the Universe, can be shared with a child even if you don't know the name of a single star

~ Rachel Carson

*Beauty is truth, and truth beauty.
That is all ye know on earth, and all ye need to know*

~ John Keats

ONE of life's great griefs is to be utterly without talent in some particular sphere of human achievement. And even greater grief is being required to study the thing for which one has no talent. A greater grief than either of these is to be a disappointment to one's parents.

I have managed all three. In my case all three griefs are intertwined. So how was I a disappointment? Let me count the ways. For the moment, however, let me discuss just one.

My mother played the piano. Now it seems that she had long dreamt of having a graceful, musically-gifted son, able to take his place in any society and bring gasps of admiration with his virtuosity at piano.

Instead, she had *me*.

The reverse of the infant Mozart, from my tenderest years I clearly manifested, in matters musical, a quite oafish lack of both talent and interest.

This lack caused grief to my mother.

It caused none to me. What did cause me grief, however, was the necessity of learning piano. From the age of eight I trudged like a snail unwilling to my Saturday morning piano lesson, to one or other of a succession of music teachers, none of whom survived for long. Theirs were the first hearts I ever broke.

'No, No, NO. Eff *sharp*. Can't you read?'

'Sorry, Miss Fitt.'

The funereal polonaise would start again. The eff would be sharp, but the left hand would crash down in some hideous arpeggio – whatever an arpeggio is.

Then would come what, in my mind, I referred to as The Long Silence. It usually followed an especially awful bit of fumbling at the keyboard. During The Long Silence one hung one's head.

'Did you practise this?' Uttered in steely tones, mingling menace with despair.

'Yes, Miss Fitt.' Uttered in humble tones, with hanging head.

'How many times?' Steely; menacing.

'Lots of times, Miss. Every day, Miss. Well, once, Miss.'

As I look back on it now, I suppose Miss Fitt had her own private griefs, one of which undoubtedly was her face. But my existence must have augmented those griefs considerably. I could discern it in her eyes as she opened her front door for me to slink out.

However I now know the source of my own grief (apart from my utter lack of talent). It was Miss Fitt's inability or unwillingness to explain things like – what a key really means; what exactly are treble and bass; what are thirds and fifths;

what the dickens is an E Flat Major, for heaven's sake. And as for *andante quasi allegretto*, forget it. To Miss Fitt, they were all just there. Just do as you're told and get on with it. Maybe Miss F didn't understand them herself.

In the years that followed it gradually dawned on me that I could love music (once I realised I didn't have to play any). Nowadays Wagner's *Parsifal* takes me halfway to the heaven Amfortas was longing to get to. I've been to Bayreuth and it's been almost a pilgrimage.

But this only happened after I slowly began to realise I didn't need all that technical know-how about intermezzos and adagios and *andantino un poco agitato*. All I had to do was listen to lovely sounds. (I actually discovered that if you leave an unfamiliar classical piece playing in the background for several days, it becomes part of you, and that's what I've been doing for years.)

We can enjoy a novel without knowing anything about stasis or resolution. It's the same for poetry. What exactly is an Iambic Pentameter? Who cares? What I do know about it is that for years in school it ruined poetry for me. As did its nasty siblings – the Spondees, the Anceps, the Dactylic Hexameters and all those other dinosaurs that stalked the classroom. Yet today I love poetry, and bards from Philip Larkin to Seamus Heaney to Tennyson inspire me every day.

Know enough?

So what has all this about music and poetry to do with looking? This – that far too many people are put off from enjoying the finest experiences in life simply by the fear that they don't know enough – don't understand enough technical jargon. As happened to me in the above instances, and indeed in several others.

How many of us are put off visiting art galleries by the fear that we don't know enough about art? And how much of this is due to the cant of critics? How many are even scared away from concert halls by words like *Opus* and *Köchel*, or titles like *No 4 in E Flat Major?*

Actually every human endeavour, but especially the arts, has its elite, the keepers of the knowledge, so to speak. It is in their interest literally to *keep* that knowledge – to themselves, to foster the exclusiveness and the mystery. For if we mere common folk knew it all, the elite wouldn't be an elite any more. Yet, as broadcaster Paul Herriot never tires of insisting, everyone has an entitlement to everything which artists or musicians create. We are just not aware of that entitlement.

We also have an entitlement to the night sky, in as much as it is there for all of us to gaze at. Yet how many of us are scared off by those maps of the stars, with their Pegasus and Cassiopea and Bears great and little? How many of us ignore trees because we can't tell the difference between an alder leaf and an elm leaf? Or how many don't even bother looking at birds, because we don't know a finch from a tit? Yet what we are missing. (Thank heaven for Christmas cards, for at least we all know a robin.)

It is sad that diffidence, which, in my experience is widespread, deters so many people from so many aspects of the Joy of Looking, as, indeed, of listening, reading, and so much else.

A military man I know gave me the answer, in the blunt terms I would expect from him – JFDI. Which, to put it politely, are the initials for *Just Effin Do It*. It's as simple as that. Get out there and simply look. Let the scene wash over you. Only I wish I had known it years ago. The fact is, we do not need to know a great deal to experience the Joy of Looking. All we need to do is look. JFDI.

The Joy of Knowing

Am I therefore saying that knowledge is of no consequence? Far from it. To begin with, knowledge is never a burden. And even the slightest knowledge, since it brings understanding, can enhance our joy out of all proportion.

I have always been fascinated by skies, and I knew a few things about clouds from my parents and from the *Children's Encyclopedia* of years ago. But Gavin Pretor-Pinney's *Cloudspotter's Guide* has enriched my enjoyment exponentially. That gorgeous little book goes everywhere with me. I check my clouds against its descriptions and pictures. The diagrams explain to me the why and how as well as the what – why a cloud can take the shape of an anvil; how clouds form in the first place; even how clouds can predict earthquakes. The *Guide* has convinced me more than ever of Emerson's words, which it quotes, 'The sky is the daily bread of the eyes... the ultimate art gallery above.'

Right now I am enthralled by Martin Walters's stunningly illustrated *Encyclopedia of Insects*, which has taught me how these tiny critters are the dominant and most successful group of all living things. I have learnt how beetles manage without heart or lungs, yet breathe air and pump blood. I have learnt how glow-worms create light without heat; how many different kinds of filament a spider spins to create its web; how wasps have their own caste system with elites as arrogant and silly as our own; how a larva becomes a butterfly in one of the most extraordinary transformations in all of nature. Now when I look at that miniature world I look with more respect and mindfulness than ever. A little knowledge has opened my eyes so wonderfully wide.[51]

A TV programme on birds showed me how most finches have the same kind of powerful rounded beak, evolved for cracking seeds and nuts. Stephen Dalton's beautiful book, *The Miracle of Flight*,[52] showed me how the shape of a bird's wing is perpetually changing in flight – 'a more intricate wing arrangement than anything created by man or any other beast.' I now watch the first swooping swallow of summer with more wonder and joy than ever. That book has also taught me more again about the incredible flight of insects. Indeed a lot of what I have written here has been learnt from books like these.

My partner Kathleen studied geology, and has for years given a new dimension to our travels together. She has shown me how rocks once folded and how the folds are now revealed, after billions of years, at the side of a new motorway cutting; how a cliff far in from the Ayrshire shoreline was once washed by the sea, which then receded to reveal the raised beach on which we now stood.

It's all part of that Joy of Looking which leads to Mindfulness.

In sum, we do not really need much or indeed any knowledge to experience that Joy, and its lack should never deter us. However even a small amount of knowledge can multiply the joy beyond measure. And it makes us want more knowledge, and then more, then more again. There is no end to it.

Suggestions

- There are guide books galore on all aspects of looking – on insects, birds, trees, clouds. At the end of this book I will list some of the ones that have helped me most. Any one of them will almost certainly transform the reader's potential for seeing. And to access a list of the *Observer* books on various subjects, turn to 142.

- Nature documentaries are among TV's most valuable offerings, and there are lots of free DVDs on the Internet. Just google *Best nature films* on You Tube, or try *http://topdocumentaryfilms.com/category/nature-wildlife/* . Particularly helpful are documentaries on the nature around us in the British Isles, which we can go out and look at later for ourselves (which we can't really do when it comes to tigers). David Attenborough can wonderfully raise our our Joy of Looking and our Mindfulness – *provided we do go out afterwards and see for ourselves.*

- As already mentioned in another context, joining a club is an effective way to broaden our looking experiences. There are clubs for just about everything, and invariably there are people in them who are willing to share insights, and vision – to show us the things they see which we do not (as yet).

- However, in hiking and hill-walking clubs there is one caveat – beware people who bring the cares of the valley with them up into the mountains. I mean the ones who talk and talk about back-down-there and see nothing beyond the rocks they are clambering around. Such people haunt many hiking clubs and are best avoided.

- Why not join The Cloud Appreciation Society? I just did. It was founded by Gavin Pretor-Pinney, whose book is mentioned above. Just google *cloudappreciationsociety.org*

25: To look with wonder

This sudden plash into wilderness – baptism in Nature's warm heart, how utterly happy it made us! Nature streaming into us, wooingly teaching her wonderful glowing lessons

~ John Muir

There are worlds of experience beyond the world of the aggressive man, beyond history, and beyond science. The moods and qualities of nature and the revelations of great art are equally difficult to define; we can grasp them only in the depth of our perceptive spirit

~ Ansel Adams

It was through the feeling of wonder that men now and at first began to philosophize

~ Aristotle

That is the essence of contemplation: the sense of wonder.... contemplation produces wonder no matter what it observes, a sunset or a stone

~ Anthony de Mello

SACAGAWEA at the Big Water is the title of a painting by U.S. artist John Clymer. That picture contains for me the quintessence of wonder. The story it tells is this. In 1804, U.S. President Jefferson sent what is now known as the Lewis and Clark Expedition to explore the uncharted Northwestern Territories of the United States. On their way the explorers invited a young Shoshone woman, a native American called Sacagawea, to join them and be their interpreter with local tribes. Finally, after many months, they sailed down the Columbia River to reach the Pacific Ocean. Meriwether Lewis's journal recounts Sacagawea's longing to see what she called 'The Big Water':

> January 6, 1806. Last evening [the] Indian woman was very impatient to be permitted to go with me, and was therefore indulged; she observed that she had traveled a long way with us to see the great waters... She had never been to the Ocian [sic]. [53]

Clymer's painting depicts that meeting of water and woman. Seagulls wheel above a young girl clad in deerskin, moccasins in her hand, who wades through the surf in a kind of ecstasy. The uplifted hands, the thrown-back shoulders, the head tilted back as she breathes in the ocean air, the wide-open eyes and mouth – all speak of speechless wonder.

What happened the second time Sacagawea saw the ocean? Or any subsequent time? Did she feel the same emotion? I hope she did, but even the asking of the question kind of spoils the loveliness of that marvellous first image. Yet it needs to be asked. In other words, is it possible to keep wonder in our lives – to live lives of wonder? I believe it is, and I hope to show how, later in this chapter.

The second question that needs to be asked is – why bother? Is wonder any use in our lives? What is its function?

What exactly *is* wonder anyhow? Darwin writes of 'surprise, astonishment and amazement', but not wonder. Psychologists disagree on whether to include it in their varying lists of human emotions. The Oxford Dictionary defines wonder as 'a feeling of amazement and admiration, caused by something beautiful, remarkable or unfamiliar'.

Wonder seems to exist on two levels – the first being akin to curiosity, asking why and how ('I wonder why a magnet attracts'); but then there is another kind of wonder that is closer to *awe* ('Omigod!'). The latter asks no questions, but just mindfully gazes and contemplates.

Many psychologists and evolutionary biologists see the level-one wonder (curiosity?) as crucial to our adaptation to the environment. As Richard Dawkins puts it: 'We have an appetite for wonder... It is my thesis that the spirit of wonder... is the very same spirit that moves great scientists.'

Without such wonder William Harvey might never have discovered the circulation of the blood; Marconi might never have explored radio waves; nor might Thomas Edison have experimented with incandescence and given us the light bulb. Indeed one could argue that the modern world is the result of much such wonder.

However the other level of wonder (akin to awe) also adapts us to our environment. Nowhere is this more clear than in the life of John Muir, whose whole being was shaped by wonder.

A native of Dunbar, Scotland, he emigrated as a child to the United States. As a farm boy in the fields and forests of Wisconsin, Muir early found wonder. He would marvel at how mosquitoes could unerringly select their targets and would 'wonder more and more at the extent of their knowledge'; or 'how the woodpeckers could bore holes so perfectly round, true mathematical circles'.

It was when he moved to the Sierra Mountains in California that his wonder grew to become awe – the beauty of those mountain peaks, their sheer vastness, led him gradually to an awareness of the Universe as one great whole, so that he found himself just letting go and being filled 'with rejoicing and wondering.' [54]

It was for Muir a new way of perceiving the world. At level-one wonder (related to curiosity), scientists break reality into smaller, more understandable fragments, and indeed do so to our benefit. However Muir went in the opposite direction, beginning to see reality as one vast unity: 'The freshness of perception [allows us to] lose consciousness of our separate existence; you blend with the landscape and become part and parcel of Nature.'

Effects of wonder

Muir's Mindfulness of being a part of the whole of nature led him to protect it instead of conquering it. This brought him to found the Sierra Club, which revolutionised attitudes to conservation throughout the United States, and later throughout the world. Indeed Muir's sense of wonder before Nature, as a whole of which we are but a tiny part, is a key source of the environmental movement of today – a movement which adapts us to our world in a way that may save its very existence – and ours.

So in a way it all goes back to Muir's sense of wonder. As psychologist Robert C. Fuller puts it: 'Muir's lasting contribution to the world was not just what to see in nature, but *how* to see it. Muir taught us that learning to behold nature in a manner permeated by "rejoicing and wonder" is the important first step toward becoming a citizen of an ecologically healthy Universe.' [55]

It seems then that looking with wonder can in the long run save our lives. But even in the short run, it can change our lives and enrich them immeasurably, especially if we can learn how to keep wonder always in our lives. When alone with nature, 'all mean egotism vanishes,' Emerson says. 'I become a transparent eyeball; I am nothing; I see all; the currents of the Universal Being circulate through me.' [56]

This is especially true if we can make wonder a permanent feature of our lives. But how can we make it so? How can I become someone who forever looks on things with wonder? Or is it even possible, especially in this hectic world? I believe it is, through a life of Mindfulness.

I walked once with a colleague along a road in Glencree in the Wicklow Hills. Let's call him Muggins. Anyhow Muggins yakked on and on and on about happenings back in the workplace. It was a superbly lovely day, and the dark woods

270

massed in the valley below us, while the heather-clad mountainside rose on either side, with Sugar Loaf mountain filling the end of the valley like Hokusai's Mount Fuji. I was thinking of Robert Frost's 'The woods are lovely, dark and deep', and I wished Muggins would shut up.

Every now and then I would interrupt with – 'Wow, would you just look at those pines against the sky?' Or 'D'y'see that cloud just capping the Sugar Loaf?'

'Uh huh, yeah. Nice. Now, as I was telling you...' And off he'd go again, yakety-yak, yakety-yak, dragging me right back to the doings down in the plain we had left behind. Yakety-yak. Yackety-yak. He just went on and on. And on.

I could have wrung his neck. I wish I had. But then I realised that Muggins had every right to be like that if he so chose.

Except he hadn't chosen. He just didn't know he was missing anything. He was blind. Not physically, of course. 'To have eyes and not to see,' as Helen Keller said.

Furthermore Muggins had no escape from his workplace doings and problems, not even among the mountains, for he brought those problems right up there with him. So even while in the mountains he was living down on the plain.

At that moment I felt profound sadness for Muggins – for all that he was missing. Was he sad too? Not in the least. Irritated, probably – with this idiot beside him who kept interrupting with stuff about trees and clouds.

Learning to wonder

So is it possible to become a person of wonder? Of constant wonder? I believe it is. There are a number of things we need.

The first is awareness, that there surely must really be wondrous things out there, even if I don't yet perceive them – no, not out there, but right under my nose. (I keep hoping a little book like this might just spark some such awareness.) The second thing is to wish to see them – I must want to grow in wonder.

The next is to learn to gaze instead of glance – I must be willing to stop everything for a moment so as to watch that shark's fin of a crescent moon slice through those scudding clouds; or to turn away from the TV so as to wait for that sunset to develop beyond the window; or to catch the feathers of snow on my sleeve* and try to see a crystal before it melts; or to have my eye follow that flock of starlings as it undulates and weaves through the darkening winter sky.

In other words, leisure is what is needed. The leisure to gaze. And if anyone says we have no leisure, I reply, yes we do, except we choose to use it for sleep (get up earlier); or for television (cut back on the box); or for yakking like my friend Muggins (shut up and look); or for shopping (pass by that mall and take to the hills).

So it all comes down to choice. I must choose to wonder. Choose to take the steps needed to become a wondering person. Choose to let go, at least for a while, of this world that is 'too much with us'. Choose to encounter the mystery of being. In sum, choose to be Mindful.

'It is our capacity for wonder at the mystery of being that makes us human and separates us from the rest of creation,' says Argentinean philosopher Juan de Pascuale:

> The experience of wonder brings the world into relief and makes a person take life seriously. In wonder you realise that this is it. You have the opportunity to swim through the river of life rather than just float on it, to own you life rather than be owned by it.[57]

So what exactly am I to wonder at? *Everything* is the short answer. As Confucius says, 'Everything has beauty, but not everyone sees it.' Wonder is simply the way to see it.

---

* Don't try to catch a snowflake on your hand, as the heat of you hand will melt it before you have time to look at it. Your sleeve is colder and will hold the flake longer.

It is a particular way of seeing things – of seeing anything – perceiving in that thing some meed of beauty, or of order, or vitality, or design or of chance pattern, which provokes in us that amazement and admiration of which the dictionary speaks. It's a way of seeing that can occasionally make us conscious of some all-encompassing reality out there, whether we call it Existence, or the Great Spirit, or a Higher Power, or God, or Allah, or just simply Nature – whatever we're comfortable with.

Such seeing and wondering can be cultivated and can grow in us with practice, just as our skill at tennis grows with practice. A sense of wonder can gradually blossom within us, until our whole outlook on life is altered and enhanced.

I have never seen this process of wonder growth expressed better than by writer, broadcaster, teacher and painter Hervey Adams, who wrote, more than 60 years ago:

> Gradually, by the deliberate and persistent observation of things which we feel to be lovely, we develop the muscles of our perceptive anatomy, till we begin to discover a host of treasures in the most unexpected places. Simple things which we have taken as a matter of course gain the power to quicken us. We find that we are increasingly watchful and aware. The process is cumulative and a habit is formed which soon dissolves that calloused skin of indifference by which we protect ourselves from so much that is ugly in our man-made environment.[58]

Useless beauty

A word on beauty. The dictionary mentions it as one of the principal triggers of wonder. I used to be frightened of the word beauty, a fear that goes back to my macho boarding school. Only feminine beauty was acknowledged there – not that we

273

saw any, but we fantasised about it constantly. Which goes without saying.

But any other sort of beauty would have been, well, a bit suspect, perhaps ever-so-slightly sissy. Like, could a real red-blooded he-man stop to pick up a violet and admire it? Or stand gawking at a cloud or a sunset? Or get up close up and personal with some old spider's web? (Well Robert Bruce did, didn't he?)

The attitude even followed me into early adulthood, where I thought it rather ridiculous to bring flowers to a young woman. You can't eat the bloody things was my attitude. All you do is shove them in water and gape at them. So I would bring chocolates (which I happened to like). That went on until a certain young woman explained that a gift should be selected to meet the preferences of the recipient, and that she liked flowers.

It may have been my first lesson in empathy.

I still find hints of this attitude among some of my male acquaintances. There's even one who regularly challenges me: 'C'm'ere, you. What's all this fuss about beauty anyway? You can't eat it [remember?]. You can't use it for anything. It doesn't feed the hungry. It doesn't make the world better. It's good for nothing, except to provoke a few sighs and groans. It's useless.'

Not his exact words, but near enough.

In fairness, my friend makes a point that needs answering. Beauty doesn't feed anyone. So why bother with it? Elvis Costello expressed it succinctly when he sang, 'What shall we do, what shall we do with all this useless beauty?'

Useless Beauty is also the title of a short story by Guy de Maupassant. The Comtesse de Mascaret, still stunningly beautiful after seven children, tells her husband that one of the children is not his. Result: hubbie stops making her useful (as in brood mare), and she returns useless to society where she is worshipped as a wondrous beauty. Indeed she is more beautiful by being utterly useless.

So to the question – is beauty really useless? Well, whatever of that, it is inescapable: just as anything that exists is good and true (unless we corrupt it), so all existence is intrinsically beautiful unless we mess with its completeness. So we encounter beauty whenever we encounter existence. There is no getting away from it.

But is it any use? I think the answer is fivefold.

Firstly, beauty is a principal trigger of wonder, and wonder is far from useless. It gives us an awareness of something greater than ourselves – a reality far beyond what we can conceive – that which 'rolls through all things', as Wordsworth put it. And in that awareness, that Mindfulness, lies the beginnings of spirituality, in whatever way we understand that word.

Secondly, by being taken beyond ourselves we are enabled to see the world as something greater than our own individual selfish needs. Then, by moving beyond those needs, we become at least open to compassion and empathy. Which empathy and compassion can extend far beyond people, even to embrace the earth, its forests, its ice-caps and its ozone layer. All this is a part of Mindfulness. And as Thich Nhat Hanh says, 'Once there is seeing, there must be acting. With Mindfulness, we know what to do and what not to do to help.'

Thirdly, beauty anchors us in the Now. It only functions there, for the contemplation of immediate loveliness cuts out future and past and has only present awareness. But it is in the Now that our spiritual being is nourished. It is in the Now that Mindfulness is encountered.

Fourthly, the sight of beauty triggers joy as well as wonder. Psychologist Carroll Izard points out that joy is contagious, creates empathy, and thus contributes to the well-being of the social group. 'Joy heightens an openness to experience,' Izard explains, '[which] can contribute to affiliative behaviour and the strengthening of social bonds. No other emotion serves this function so effectively, providing significant benefits at little or no cost.' [59]

In other words, surely, a life in which there is enjoyment of beauty changes not just us but those around us.

And lastly, beauty can also be a crucial source of hope, and as such can help to make life bearable. A life deprived of it is grim indeed. Even the miniscule encounters with beauty in Auschwitz, in the guise of a glimpsed sunset or a tiny bird, gave some souls hope and the ultimate strength to endure, as Viktor Frankl testifies.

Suggestions

- Get and read Rachel Carson's book, *The Sense of Wonder*, which is perhaps the most wonder-full book I have ever read. Details in Bibliography at end of this book.

- To see that picture of of Sacagawea, just google (Images) *Sacagawea at the Big Water*. There you'll see real wonder.

- Let a child lead you. Spending time with young children, and heeding them when they wonder at something, is one of the best ways to develop wonder in ourselves. A child is naturally mindful and sees things we no longer notice, and wonders at them. If we follow the child's lead, we will wonder too. However if we tut-tut and hurry the child on, we lose that chance to learn, and the child eventually loses its sense of wonder.

- Let's not be scared of beauty. If we see something beautiful let's point it out to others. The Joy of Looking is contagious.

26: From wonder to Awe

IF we are mindful enough and gaze enough and contemplate nature enough, and wonder enough, we can occasionally in our lives break through a kind of membrane and encounter sheer, downright *awe*. It can come in a dark, whispering forest, or when gazing at a luminous night sky, or watching a storm from cliffs, or simply contemplating a new moon.

It can come to parents when a newborn babe is placed in their arms. It can come while holding the hand of someone dying. It can happen after reaching a mountain peak. It can come from gazing at a dinosaur footprint from 65 million years ago. It can come when contemplating a spider's web, or a wildflower in spring. It can come during meditation.

Nature writer Michael McCarthy touches on it when he describes the blue flash of a kingfisher: 'This is not on any colour chart in a paint shop, and I would feel that most people, seeing it for the first time, have a curious, elated experience, which is that their sense of what the world can contain is actually enlarged.' [60]

What is this awe? I am aware that I have used the word loosely in previous chapters. But here I want to use it in its purest meaning. Like so many other words it has been devalued by the childish use of 'awesome' for anything novel or impressive. The Oxford Dictionary defines awe as 'a feeling of reverential respect mixed with fear or wonder'.

But the awe of which I speak is far more than that, and perhaps we need a new word for it. The Hawaiians call it *ihihia* – it is a stepping out of oneself, out of time, out of space, out of what we thought was reality, and sensing that one is nothing more than, nothing less than, an integral part of the Universe.

This awe seems to be far more common than we realise. Europeans seem often reticent about admitting to such experiences, but they are an intrinsic part of most Eastern philosophies, and were very much part of the experience of our great 12th- and 14th-century mystics such as Hildegard of Bingen, Julian of Norwich and Meister Eckhart.

Even today some people in private will admit to having experienced moments like these, when the conscious mind seems to shut down and you find yourself intuiting the environment – with extraordinary awareness, you feel, both physically and spiritually, at one with the world around you.

The Eastern philosophers made this the aim of meditation, but it can happen to any of us, often when least expecting it.

278

American psychologist Paul Pearsall has spent more than 40 years collecting hundreds of such experiences through interviews. I will quote briefly from just one such:

> I was afraid I would get lost in the woods today, but instead I found myself there, or maybe God found me. I was in awe not just of the beauty of where I was, but the sense of what it meant and what it would mean to me later. It was as if my heart had eyes...
>
> Then I began to feel afraid... but it was a good kind of fear that you feel when you're excited about something big that's going to happen... It was like – for that timeless moment – I actually became the forest and there was no more me...[61]

I have asked a number of my friends if they have ever had such awe, and I am astonished at how many admit to it. My friend Michael Lewis encountered it simply from looking into the eyes of a beloved dog. He told me he suddenly felt he was in touch with the whole animal kingdom. 'Don't ask me to explain,' he said. 'It just *was*.'

Maybe that's not so farfetched at all. After all, it was the great Jewish theologian Martin Buber who once said: 'An animal's eyes have the power to speak a great language.'

Another friend told me it could happen simply while looking at a beautiful woman. It was something quite apart from sexuality, he said. You were for one glorious moment in touch with the Creator of such Beauty. And he said it had nothing to do with looking at youth – beauty can be encountered in any age. Which I know to be true.

I think Scott Masson must have experienced this awe when he saw that flock of starlings (page 138) which he said had 'the most profound spiritual effect' on him, and gave him 'renewed hope about life and the world in general'.

Eleventh emotion

Awe has been called the eleventh emotion (although there seems to be no great agreement among psychologists about the other ten). Pearsall describes it as 'a sacred hunch, an overwhelming emotion that indicates that something within us is sensing something about the world that our brain has yet to discover.' [62] It's a realisation, as Hamlet put it, that 'there are more things in heaven and earth, Horatio, than are dreamt of in your philosophy'.

But it's a *realisation* – not just an intellectual assent. Something becomes *real* to you that wasn't real before – usually about the world and your relation to it. Even more than a realisation, it is an experience, in which one momentarily ceases to be an individual and finds oneself an integral part of the Universe.

Most of the great thinkers of the East, from Siddhartha to Lao Tzu, say that all things in the world are but manifestations of one single ultimate reality. Some call that reality *Tao*, others *Dharmakaya*, others *Brahman*, others *Suchness*. Whatever its name, it is the Totality of All Things.

As a result, all things are inseparable, irrevocably interlocked, forever dependent on one another. And that includes us. As it includes our neighbours, friends, enemies, animals, the forests, the atmosphere, the oceans, the Third World, the planets, space, the Universe – and, for believers, the Great Spirit, or Allah, or God.

The aim of most Eastern philosophies and religions is to help people permanently live this as a reality, through Mindfulness, meditation, exercises, prayer and awe. As indeed do Christian mystics. As indeed do all who truly love their neighbour as themselves.

So then awe, if we are fortunate enough to experience it, gives us at least a glimpse of this interdependence of all things, including ourselves.

Scientific basis

Is there, however, any basis for accepting such interdependence – any scientific basis? There seems to be now, since the advent of quantum physics, and the findings are almost frightening.

The most extraordinary is that when certain sub-atomic particles are observed or measured, *the very fact of being observed actually changes them*. This can only mean, says world-renowned physicist Fritjof Capra, that we, the observers, and they, the particles, are inextricably linked. We are no longer just observers, but *participants*.[63]

'This is a participatory Universe,' as the late John Archibald Wheeler wrote in 1990.[64] It is but a short step to the conclusion that we are all part of One Great Thing.

It is one thing to reach this conclusion intellectually, as physicists do. But the great joy of awe is to encounter it experientially, when our awe reaches a point that takes us out of ourselves so that, as Wordsworth put it, 'we fall asleep in body and become a living soul.' I think perhaps what I experienced at that tree in Ayrshire was a minor instance of this (page 34).

The philosopher William James was a pioneer in making us aware of awe. Once when on a solitary hiking trip in the Adirondacks in 1898, he stopped to rest:

> I spent a good deal of the night in the woods where
> the streaming moonlight lit up things in a magical
> checkered play, and it seemed as if the gods of all
> the nature-mythologies were holding an
> indescribable meeting in my breast with the moral
> gods of the inner life. The two kinds of gods have
> nothing in common... [This had an] intense
> significance of some sort, of the whole scene, if one
> could only tell the significance.... I can't find a
> single word for all that significance, and don't know

what it was significant of, so there it remains a
boulder of impression.[65]

Later James wrote, about that experience, 'It was one of the
happiest lonesome nights of my existence, and I understand
now what a poet is.' Pondering on this and other experiences,
he gradually reached the conclusion that the visible world is
part of a more spiritual Universe from which it draws its chief
significance. From this he concluded that union with that
higher Universe is our true end.

One conclusion was forced upon his mind at that time: 'It is
that our normal waking consciousness, rational consciousness
as we call it, is but one special type of consciousness, whilst all
about it, parted from it by the flimsiest of screens, there lie
potential forms of consciousness entirely different.' [66]

Spirituality

According to psychologist Robert C. Fuller, William James
believed that these other forms of consciousness hold the key
to understanding how one might steer a middle course between
scientific materialism and conventional religiosity. And in that
middle way, he says, lies genuine spirituality – something
fraught with wonder that produces a different kind of
happiness and power. Surely this is Mindfulness.

'Spirituality exists,' Fuller writes, 'wherever we struggle with
the issue of how our lives fit into the greater cosmic scheme of
things. This is true even when our questions never give way to
specific answers or give rise to specific practices such as prayer
or meditation. We encounter spiritual issues every time we
wonder where the Universe comes from, why we are here, or
what happens when we die.

'We also become spiritual when we become moved by values
such as beauty, love, or creativity that seem to reveal a
meaning or power beyond our visible world. An idea or practice
is "spiritual" when it reveals our personal desire to establish a

felt relationship with the deepest meanings or powers governing life.' [67]

Not alone

All this takes us a long way from merely looking or even gazing. But it mostly has its beginnings there, where gazing leads to Mindfulness, Mindfulness to contemplation, contemplation to wonder, wonder leads to awe, and awe shows us we are not alone.

Nor is it just for poets or contemplatives. Scientists, particularly those involved in quantum theory, are coming more and more around to such views. In the words of one such physicist, Fritjof Capra, 'mysticism is being taken seriously even within the scientific community.' [68] In his seminal book, *The Tao of Physics*, he points up how the revelations of quantum physics eerily parallel the perennial concepts of eastern philosophies and religions – that we are indeed all part of a single unity.[69] He tells us that modern physics has opened up a drastic choice for scientists: 'They may lead us – to put it in extreme terms – to the Buddha or to the Bomb.' [70] Mercifully many are opting for the former.

Let me conclude, with Capra's permission, with a description this scientist wrote about an experience he once had, which led to his writing *The Tao of Physics*:

> I was sitting by the ocean one late summer afternoon, watching the waves rolling in and feeling the rhythm of my breathing, when I suddenly became aware of my whole environment as being engaged in a gigantic cosmic dance. Being a physicist, I knew that the sand, rocks, water and air around me were made of vibrating molecules and atoms, and that these consisted of particles which interacted with one another by creating and destroying other particles. I knew also that the Earth's atmosphere was continually bombarded by

showers of 'cosmic rays', particles of high energy undergoing multiple collisions as they penetrated the air. All this was familiar to me from my research in high-energy physics, but until that moment I had only experienced it through graphs, diagrams and mathematical theories. As I sat on that beach my former experiences came to life; I 'saw' cascades of energy coming down from outer space, in which particles were created and destroyed in rhythmic pulses; I 'saw' the atoms of the elements and those of my body participating in this cosmic dance of energy; I felt its rhythm and I 'heard' its sound, and at that moment I knew that this was the Dance of Shiva, the Lord of Dancers, worshipped by the Hindus.[71]

Let us remember that these are the words of one of the world's most eminent physicists.

Suggestions

- Awe seems a little like happiness – if you pursue it it eludes you. Whereas Mindfulness is always to hand, if we continually practise it. So perhaps we should just do our ordinary looking, gazing and wondering. If awe creeps in unbidden, it will be an added bonus. But what a bonus.

- Almost all the experiences of awe seem to come when someone is alone. So try some solitary gazing, and make sure to find time alone in nature. You may be alone but you will never be lonely.

- Read Fritjof Capra's *The Tao of Physics*. It is quite literally a life-changing book. Details in Bibliography at back of this book.

- Many people practise meditation as a way to encountering awe. And awe can bring the stillness that we all so badly need in our lives. There are many different forms of meditation from both East and West – most of which partake of Mindfulness to some extent - Transcendental, Zen, Buddhist, Taoist, Christian Prayer, Yoga. Just google *Forms of meditation* to find out more.

- One of the most helpful books on meditation is Thich Nhat Hanh's *The Miracle of Mindfulness.* Details in the Bibliography.

27: Mindful of the young

The Earth belongs to our children.
We have already borrowed too much from it, from them;
and the way things have been going, we're not sure we'll be able
to give it back to them in decent shape

~ Thich Nhat Hanh

Our children need to learn not only how to read books composed by human
genius but also how to read the Great Book of the World.
Reading this Great Book is natural to children

~ Thomas Berry

Teaching a child not to step on a caterpillar
is as valuable to the child as it is to the caterpillar

~ Bradley Millar

Accept the children with reverence, educate them with love,
send them forth in freedom

~ Rudolf Steiner

To contemplate, and to give to others
the fruits of our contemplation

~ Motto of the Dominicans

ONE of my vivid early memories is of being out for a walk with my parents and my older brother Dermot, in the countryside near our home. I was about four. We came upon a rounded, oval stone on the grassy margin of the lane, which my father gently lifted away. Beneath it was an ants' nest. We were looking into a miniature city. I can still see those little creatures scuttling in and out of myriad tiny tunnel entrances, some of them carrying minute white balls that might have been eggs. Their speed was astonishing.

'Do you realise,' my father said, 'that that little fellow would be going as fast as a racing car, if he were the size of one? And all without wheels – just six legs!' He then gently replaced the stone, explaining that, having seen them, we must now leave the little creatures in peace to run their tiny city.

My mother often told us stories about her own father, who used to take her and her siblings out on similar walks.

She remembered him showing them a tiny woven sphere which was a wren's nest; pointing out the first frail thread of a new moon; he taught them where to wait to see a kingfisher; he had them watch a spider weave its web; he helped them feel the thrill of being the very first to see the inside of a freshly-cut apple.

He used take them to the railway embankment at night, to watch a late express train thunder past in its glory of sparks and steam – which the children called 'the Midnight Express'.

I never knew this Grandfather Stokes. He died many years before I was born, in a car crash while exploring the World War One battlefields where his son had died. But I feel I do know him. For he taught my mother the Joy of Looking, and she taught it to us. (For that alone I forgive her those piano lessons.)

Give me the child

The ability to look and see is really only one aspect of a far wider mental or spiritual attitude which perhaps we should call awareness. Or, in its most evolved form, Mindfulness.

This awareness has been insightfully expressed in a blog by one Sue Knight which I found on the Internet: 'Everything you teach a child, every value you instil in a child, is so important in forming the person they become. Teach them manners, respect, understanding of handicap/differences, love of books, awe of nature, friendship to animals, anything, early in their lives – before they are seven – and they are the values that they will take through life with them, forever.' [72]

For me every word of that rings true. With the following proviso, that the child is not seen as an empty bank account which parents or teachers fill with their ideas. Rather the understanding that little ones are already filled with wonder, and that parents gently direct that wonder towards nature, animals, people, books, anything, so that it segues into respect and love.

It is this wider Mindfulness, to which the Joy of Looking leads, that I want to talk about with in this final chapter.

The following was lately written down for me, during a conversation, by Marie Parker-Jenkyns, Professor of Education at the University of Limerick:

> I can never remember, in the whole of my educational experience, being asked to look at a cobweb – or any other potential object of beauty or wonderment. Instead my education has been a process of absorbing facts to be regurgitated at appropriate junctures, usually exams, and then forgotten or discarded. Indeed, the annual programme of memory retention or grinds is the very opposite of what education should be about.

Grinds. What a hideous word – take the youngsters, ram the facts into their heads, or their heads into the facts, and grind them down. I wonder did they get the word from Dickens? Certainly it's apt: Master Gradgrind still rules OK (page 259).

Yet how can we do without him? We are told day in, day out, of our desperate need of science graduates, technicians, computer experts, maths graduates, if we are at all to remain competitive. There is no time in education for anything else.

Or so we are told.

Yet the results so far are dismal – incompetent and dishonest bankers, venal politicians, an embittered underclass, unemployment, anomie, boredom, frustration, a dearth of initiative, lack of creativity, growing suicide stats – with pubs, bookies and sport among the few things that keep so many of us from losing our grip.

What is the answer? Wiser people than I have tried and failed to find one. I can only tell of something from my time as an educator.

In my work as a journalist on three continents, I often had the duty of supervising both interns and young journalism graduates at the organizations where I worked. I was regularly appalled by their lack of spontaneous interest in things around them, their lack of excitement, their lack of imagination.

They were often superb technicians of the word: they could report on an accident or a crime far and away better than I ever could; they could construct a news story in the classic inverted-pyramid format, with the five Ws and H* all present and correct, Sir.

Now, granted that accurate and dispassionate reporting is the essence of hard-news reporting, there is also a place in journalism for a wider awareness, for creativity, particularly in feature writing. But few of these youngsters could stir the reader to joy or euphoria or enthusiasm or excitement, perhaps because they never seemed to feel it themselves.

Years later, towards the end of my years as head of the Rathmines School of Journalism (later part of the Dublin Institute of Technology) – I was there for 18 years – I decided to try an experiment. I arranged that every Wednesday morning would be devoted to developing our sense of wonder. If I had known then, I'd have called it our sense of Mindfulness.

How? Well, all I could think of was this: each week seven of the young people would undertake each to read a book of choice – any book, fiction or non-fiction – and on the

*What; when; where; who; why; & how.

Wednesday all seven would read brief reports on the various books they had selected.

It was the discussions that followed that were magic. These were extremely gifted young people (at the time it was the second hardest course in the country to get into), and one idea would trigger another in a flurry of insights and imagination.

Discussions ranged from philosophy to poetry to art, from truth to beauty, especially the beauty around us daily; imaginations ran riot, and I learned more from those young men and women in those sessions than they ever learned from me. The magic was theirs, not mine.

We were invariably on a high when a session ended. I will never forget overhearing young Tom Felle, as he came out at the end of one of these sessions, whisper to someone, 'Best course in the world!' I wish it were true, but this much is – that once imaginations are let loose, like the genie out of the bottle, they are not easily put back.

Many of the participants have gone on to become household names in the media of these islands. I shall always remember them as the most gifted young people I have ever had the privilege of encountering, and am honoured and proud to have known them.

And I remain convinced that those Wednesday mornings, filched from the curriculum, were the least wasted of all the hours of our journalism training.

Decisions

When Finland had its financial crisis, 20 years before the rest of us, the Finns were faced with problems similar to ours of today. But the government there made one crucial decision, based broadly on the teaching of Ivan Illich – *cut everything but education.*

Moreover, create an education system that would stress the development of the individual, rather than simply create a compliant labour force – mere cogs to fit the industrial machine. Such individual development would involve the ability and the will to question the status quo – which is an intrinsic part of Mindfulness.

Twenty years later Finland is up there with Singapore as one of the truly successful societies and economies in the world.

More than 60 years ago an art master at Tonbridge School in Kent published a book that is as relevant today as it was then. Relevant because so little has changed.

In *The Adventure of Looking*, Hervey Adams utters a warning that might have been uttered this very day: 'We are all endowed with creative energy whose power is not diminished because it lacks outlet. Deny it an adequate outlet and it will manifest in the form of some destructive activity, distressing inhibition or smouldering discontent.' [73]

Adams laments how young people's development is ignored 'by the method of examinations that exalts brain capacity at the expense of sensibility and imagination.' Sounds eerily familiar? There is more, equally familiar:

> Even though educationalists are aware of this limitation they are still shackled by it, and are compelled to serve a system in which the making of a living makes larger claims than the leading of a full life. The profit motive still exacts its tribute at the cost of individual liberty of mind and spirit, and success in life is too often measured in terms of hard cash and social preferment... How far are the claims of Performance, in the form of examination successes, reconciled with the needs of Personality? [74]

Anything new there? We are familiar with the results – public servants lacking empathy; insensitive health services; doctors without a bedside manner; developers whose own lack of development leads to the outrages now so familiar; lager louts; football hooligans; gangs; depression.

Even if we take as given that the stress on numeracy, science and technology is essential for a nation's survival in the modern world, nevertheless the making of time for looking, for awareness of our Universe, for Mindfulness, for the wonder and awe that can follow, and for the questioning of the status quo which must follow that, is equally essential for that modern world to be worth surviving in.

Without all of this there is a grave danger of creating what Ortega y Gasset called 'the learned ignoramus' – one who is ignorant of all that does not enter into his or her specialty.[75] In our harsh educational world of points, Pisa-ranking, and league tables, is there a danger of creating a whole nation of such creatures?

Aleksandr Solzhenitsyn remembered being one such, when he worked head down at technology and never questioned the ideology of the Soviet Union. It was only in labour camp, when he had time both to look and to think, and thus grow, that he became the writer and philosopher we now know.

The 'father' of the nuclear bomb, J Robert Oppenheimer, worked equally head down as director of the Los Alamos project. But when that first atomic explosion took place, he raised his head and looked for the first time. As he later described it:

> We knew the world would not be the same. A few
> people laughed, a few people cried. Most people
> were silent. I remembered the line from the Hindu
> scripture, the Bhagavad-Gita... 'Now I am become
> Death, the destroyer of worlds.' I suppose we all
> thought that, one way or another.

(You can actually hear and watch him saying those words on *http://www.atomicarchive.com/Movies/Movie8.shtm.*)

Oppenheimer devoted much of the rest of his life trying to convince the world of the scale of the unleashed horror, and of the absolute necessity to come together to control it. Which the world is still trying to do.

Sociologist Donaldo Macedo explains it thus: 'Because the "learned ignoramus" is mainly concerned with his or her tiny portion of the world, disconnected from other bodies of knowledge, he or she is never able to relate the flux of information so as to gain a critical reading of the world.' [76]

Such people he calls 'semi-literate': one who 'reads the word but is unable to read the world.' It can result in a plethora of 'experts' who, for example, have no Mindfulness of, or understanding of, inequality or genuine democracy.

Macedo for example refers to the brilliant technological advances in the American medical world, yet the concurrent facts that 30 million Americans are too poor to avail of them, and that the US has the highest infant mortality among the developed nations.

Educationalist Paulo Freire saw much of our schooling as simply preparing us to accept uncritically the status quo of rich and poor, educated and ignorant, the powerful and the powerless, to accept it as a given, and to conform to the world as it is. Thus of course perpetuating the status quo.

There's nothing new here – in 1804 the poet William Blake was tried for treason for questioning the status quo of the time. According to Christopher Rowland, Professor of Theology at Oxford University, 'Blake wanted to stir people from their intellectual slumbers, and the daily grind of their toil, to see that they were captivated in the grip of a culture which kept them thinking in ways which served the interests of the powerful.' [77]

Two centuries later sociologist Peter McLaren is attempting to take up where Blake left off, and he too has suffered considerably for doing just that. His concept of *critical pedagogy* proposes an education that would expose permanent conditions of exploitation and oppression, that would foster true Mindfulness, and challenge all those dominant myths that we mistake for real democracy and equality. In sum, he wants the coming generation critically to question the world around them, and argues for an education system that would make that happen (which is precisely what certain people in power would like to prevent).[78]

However no such education is possible if we simply tie young people down to points and assessment and league tables, and to looking mindlessly into rectangles – the electronic rectangles of computer monitors, laptops, notebooks and smart phones.

No matter how brilliant those youngsters may later emerge as computer wizards or technical achievers, there is simply no time for them to look, to see, to wonder, to grow, to become mindful, and finally to question the world around them. For one of the effects of Mindfulness is precisely such questioning. And, by the time they mature, the inclination to question may have withered.

Yet without such Mindfulness in the coming generation, who is to call a halt to pollution, inequality, damage to the planet, nuclear proliferation, unbridled capitalism, debt crises, war mongering?

According to Hervey Adams, writing 60 years ago, 'the habits of looking are at present largely formed in relation to book and ball.' Has much changed since then? Is learning to look beyond book and ball the cure? Hardly.

But it would be a beginning. For, if we learn to look, we may learn to rejoice in the beauty around us; we may grow more mindful; we may learn to feel; our powers of imagination may grow; imagination may lead to insights and understanding of the unity of all things, both the earth and its people, and thus lead to empathy with that same earth and people.

Thence we may learn to reject the ugliness foisted on us from all sides – environmental ugliness as well as the ugliness of inequality and injustice – and then to work to change it; creativity may be sparked within us, so that we become doers and creators instead of mere consumers. To repeat the words of Thich Nhat Hanh: 'Once there is seeing, there must be acting. With Mindfulness, we know what to do and what not to do to help.'

If educators tell us there is not enough time, *then let us make time*. Take some from the curriculum, even a little, as I once did, for the aware and fulfilled individual will be a better scientist or technician, whereas the unaware or unfulfilled one could be dangerous.

And if they still say there is not enough time due to the pressure of modern life, one could reply, as Adams once did, that the life of a cave man, a hunter-gatherer scrabbling for the next meal, must have been very pressured indeed. Yet he found time to paint reindeers on the walls of his cave.

Worldwide movement

This little book, however, is not just about showing the beauty of this world to young people. We *all* need to find the Joy of Looking and the Mindfulness to which it leads. It is a theme that is really part of a worldwide phenomenon, and ties in with the parallel *Heimat* (Homeland) movement in Europe, which is a a return-to-nature drive spreading from its beginnings in Germany, triggered by uncertainty about globalisation and the persistent euro-zone crisis.

The whole *Heimat* movement has spawned a plethora of magazines devoted to looking with Mindfulness, to rural living and to nature. *Hör Zu Heimat* stresses 'the smell of grandma's apple pie, the rattle of autumn leaves, family, childhood, security'. It is a theme to which Europe is awakening.

So please don't let this book end as an interesting philosophy to be put back on the shelf, but as something that can grow into a joyful way of life, learning and Mindfulness. I hope and pray that you will be inspired to make this happen, and that, by so doing, you will be enriched, inspired, indeed empowered, beyond anything you can now imagine. Remember the words of Thich Nhat Hanh: 'One Buddha is not enough. All of us have to become Buddhas in order for our planet to have a chance. Fortunately we have the power to wake up, to touch enlightenment from moment to moment, in our very own ordinary and, yes, busy lives. So let's start now.' [79]

I should like to finish with words from a poem written by a teenage girl dying of cancer in New York. It came to me over the eMail as one of those anonymous things that people forward to one another, begging the recipient to forward it on to as many as possible. Apparently it was originally sent by a medical doctor, probably the one who attended the dying girl. The poem is called *Slow Dance*:

Have you ever
watched
kids

On a merry-go-round?

Or listened to
the
rain

Slapping on the ground?

Ever followed a
butterfly's erratic flight?

Or gazed at the sun into the
fading
light?

You better slow down.

Don't
dance so
fast.

Time is short.

The music
won't
last.

Do you run through each day

On
the
fly?

When you ask How are you?

Do you hear
the
reply?

Ever told your
child,

We'll do it
tomorrow?

And in your
haste,

Not see
his
sorrow?

You'd
better slow down.

Don't dance
so fast.

Time
is short.

The music won't
last...

When you run
so fast to get somewhere

You
miss half the fun of getting
there.

When you worry and hurry
through your
day,

It is like an unopened
gift...

Thrown
away.

Life is not a race.

Do take it
slower.

Hear the
music

Before the song is
over

At the end of the poem, the following words appear:

'Dear All: Please pass this mail on to everyone you know – even those you don't know. It is the request of a special girl who will soon leave this world due to cancer. This young girl has six months left to live and, as her dying wish, she wanted to send a letter telling everyone to live their life to the fullest, since she never will. She'll never make it to a prom, graduate from high school, or get married and have a family of her own.'

That young girl is surely gone by now. May she rest in peace. But what better way to conclude this book than with her dying words?

And may you have Mindfulness in your life and Joy in your Looking.

Suggestions

- If you want learn more about Mindfulness, the two most helpful introductions are *Wherever You Go, There You Are*, by Jon Kabat-Zinn, and *The Miracle of Mindfulness*, by Thich Nhat Hanh. Full details in the Bibliography below.

- Hervey Adams's *Adventure of Looking* is long out of print, but get it if you can. I can only describe it as life changing. It opened my eyes at the age of 17, when I borrowed it from the local library. Recently I went looking for it again, and got it through ABE Books (*www.abebooks.co.uk*).

- For me 'the Four Masters' of the Joy of Looking are Rachel Carson, John Muir, William James and the above-mentioned Hervey Adams. And four modern thinkers whose Mindfulness underpins all they say, are – Thich Nhat Hanh, Jon Kabat-Zinn, Matthew Fox and Fritjof Capra. Read anything by any of them. And if anyone can add to that list of masters, please let me know.

    If you would like to share your experiences of Look and Grow Mindful with our readers, why not do so on our blog and website? Address on back cover.

- By the way, I know this invitation and the website have been mentioned in previous chapters – the reason I have repeated it several times is that people like to dip into chapters at random, and thus might miss the invitation.

- An excellent UK source of information on Mindfulness is The Community of Interbeing. Telephone 0870-041-1242 (*www.interbeing.org.uk*)

- For Ireland there is a group called Mindfulness Ireland. Website: *www.mindfulnessireland.org*. Contacts: – Josephine Lynch, Dublin (eMail: *josephinemarylynch@gmail.com*). Tel: (087) 237 2130. In Northern Ireland, Bridgeen Rea (eMail: *bridjeen@hotmail.com*). Tel: 0044 (0) 7981 623 566.

- There is a centre for Mindfulness in France at the monastery where Thich Nhat Hanh lives. You can go there for a retreat. Address is: Plum Village, 13 Martineau, 33580 Dieulvol, France. Website: *www.plumvillage.org*

- Best known in the United States is the Center for Mindfulness at the University of Massachusetts. Address: Chang Building, 222 Maple Avenue, Shrewsbury, MA 01545. Phone: +508-856-2656 (eMail: *mindfulness@umassmed.edu*)
    Website: *http://www.umassmed.edu/cfm/contact/index.aspx*

Reader: A final word to you

I WROTE this little book to share with you my Joy of Looking, and in the hope that we would *all* get more Mindfulness, beauty, wonder and joy into our lives — lives which naturally can be difficult enough at times. (*I'm* still only learning as I go along.)

So, if you feel it has been in any way useful, would you consider letting others know about it?

If you were simply to tell three friends about the book and its blog and website, and if each were to tell three more, there's no knowing where it would all end. You could even do it through Facebook or Twitter. And wouldn't it be great if it brought Mindfulness to lots more people?

Goodbye for now. Why don't we meet on our website and blog – *www.LookAndGrowMindful.com*

Best wishes, and thank you for reading this book.

—*David Rice*

References

[1] Wilde, Oscar. *Complete Works*. London: Collins, 2003

[2] Mitchell, Gordon. *R.J. Mitchell: Schooldays to Spitfire*. London: The History Press, 2006. (As cited in *Aeroplane Monthly*, September 2011, page 19)

[3] Einstein, Albert: 'The World As I See It'. Essay originally published in *Forum and Century*, Vol. 84, pp. 193-194 – 13th in the Forum series, *Living Philosophies*

[4] Plato. *Timaeus*. Translated from Stallbaum Text by Henry Davis, MA. London: Henry G. Bohn, 1854. Page 353

[5] Frankl, Viktor E. *Man's Search for Meaning*. London: Rider, 2004

[6] Carson, Rachel & Kelsh, Nick. *The Sense of Wonder*. New York: HarperCollins, 1998. Page 67

[7] De Mello, Anthony. *The Song of the Bird*. New York: Doubleday, 1984. Page 15

[8] Lagermann. John Kord. 'Stop, Look, and See!' Article in *Together* magazine, July 1963. Park Ridge, Illinois: Methodist Publishing House

[9] Pretor-Pinney, Gavin. *The Cloudspotter's Guide*. London: Septre, 2007. Page 23

[10] Ibid.

[11] Lagermann. Op cit.

[12] Dugan, Emily: 'Are we losing the fight to save our hedgerows?' *The Independent*, 29 August, 2010

[13] Adams, Hervey. *The Adventure of Looking.* London: G. Bell & Sons, 1949. Page 34

[14] Eastoe, Jane. *Hedgerow and Wildlife: Guide to Animals and Plants of the Hedgerow.* London: The National Trust/ Anova Books, 2008

[15] Hickie, David, & Dwyer, Rosaleen B. *Irish Hedgerows: Networks for Nature.* Dublin: Networks for Nature, 2004

[16] O'Faolain, Sean. *Vive Moi.* London: Sinclair-Stevenson, 1993

[17] Belloc, Hilaire. *The Path to Rome.* London: Longmans, Green & Co, 1902

[18] Stevenson, Robert Louis. *Essays of Travel* (1905). Forest Notes.

[19] Ó Duinn, Seán, OSB. *Where Three Streams Meet: Celtic Spirituality.* Dublin: Columba Press, 2002. Page 86

[20] Thoreau, Henry David. *Walden or, Life in the Woods.* London: Everyman's Library,1992. 'Where I Lived & What I Lived For.' Page 80

[21] Blackwell, Lewis. *The Life & Love of Trees.* San Francisco: Chronicle Books, 2009. Page 77

[22] Wilde, Oscar. *Complete Works.* London: Collins, 2003

[23] Thich Nhat Hanh, *The Miracle of Mindfulness.* London: Rider/Ebury/Random House, 2008. Page12
.

[24] O'Donohue, John. *Anam Cara.* London: Bantam Press, 1997. Page 88

[25] Homer. *The Iliad.* Translated by Martin Hammond. London: Penguin Classics, 1987. Book 20. Page 333

[26] Whistler, James McNeill. 'Letter to a sitter who asked how it was possible to paint when it was so dark.' Quoted in Eddy, *Recollections,* 1903. Page 214

[27] Rilke, Ranier Maria. *Rodin.* Translated by Lemont & Trausil. Billericay, Essex: Grey Walls Press. c. 1940

[28] Muir, John. *The Story of my Boyhood & Youth.* Project Gutenberg, 2006. eBook # 18359. Chapter 1

[29] Camões, Luis Vas. *Os Lusiadas.* Canto V

[30] Levine, Robert. *A Geography of Time.* New York: Basic Books, 1997. Page 75

[31] Sheldrake, Rupert. *The Presence of the Past.* London: HarperColllins, 1994. Page 236

[32] Thoreau, Henry David. *Journal:* 5 January, 1856

[33] Carson & Kelsh. Op cit. Pages 76-77

[34] Dalton, Stephen. *The Miracle of Flight.* London: Merrell Publishers Ltd, 2001. Page 55

[35] Op cit.

[36] Hogarth, William. *The Analysis of Beauty.* First published 1753

[37] Holtom, Gerard. Letter to Hugh Brock, editor of *Peace News.* Information is from the CND website – *http://www.cnduk.org/information/info-sheets/item/435-the-cnd-symbol*

[38] Carson & Kelsh. Op cit. Page 68

[39] Gerald of Wales. *The History and Topography of Ireland.*

[40] Lagermann. Op cit.

[41] Quoted in Bishop Hassan Dchqani Tafti: *Christ & Christianity in Persian Poetry. (www.farsinet.com/ChristInPersianPoetry//index.)*

[42] Dyson, Einstein & Calaprice. *The New Quotable Einstein.* New Jersey: Princeton University Press, 2005. Page 206

[43] Kabat-Zinn, Jon. *Arriving at Your Own Door: 108 Lessons in Mindfulness..* London: Piatkus Books, 2008.

44 Suzuki, David & Hehner, Barbara. *Looking at the Body*. New York: John Wiley & Son, 1981

45 Lagermann. Op cit.

46 Thich Nhat Hanh. *Peace Is Every Breath: A Practice for Our Busy Lives*. London: Rider/Ebury/Random House, 2011.

47 Levine, Bernard. Op Cit. Page 85 ff.

48 Fox, Matthew. *Original Blessing*. Santa Fe: Bear and Co, 1983. Page 61

49 Plato. *The Republic*. Book 7. Translated by Benjamin Jowett. Project Gutenburg, 2008. eBook #1497

50 Lear, Linda, (Ed.). *Lost Woods: The Discovered Writing of Rachel Carson*. Boston: Beacon Press, 1998. Page 160 ff. An address presented by Carson in 1954.

51 Walters, Martin. *The Complete Illustrated World Encyclopedia of Insects*. London: Hermes House, 2010

52 Dalton, Stephen. *The Miracle of Flight*. London: Merrell Publishers, 2001

53 Lewis, Meriwether. *Journal*. Entry of 6 January, 1806. *LewisAndClarkTrail.com*

54 Muir, John. Op cit.

55 Fuller, Robert C. *Wonder: From Emotion to Spirituality*. University of North Carolina Press, 2006. Page 53

56 Emerson, Ralph Waldo. *Complete Works*. New York: AMS Press, 1968. Vol. I; Page 62

57 De Pascuale, Juan. 'A Wonder Full Life'. Essay in *Notre Dame Magazine*, September 2002. Page 49

58 Adams, Hervey. Op cit. Page 3

59 Izard, Caroll, & Ackerman, Brian. 'Motivational, Organizational, & Regulatory Functions of Discrete Emotions'. Essay in Lewis,

Haviland-Jones & Barrett. *Handbook of Emotions*. New York: The Guildford Press, 2008. Page 258 ff.

[60] McCarthy, Michael. Article in *The Independent*, 05 November, 2010.

[61] Pearsall, Paul, PhD. *Awe: The Delights and Dangers of Our Eleventh Emotion*. Florida: Health Communications, Inc, 2007. Page 37

[62] Ibid. Page 93

[63] Capra, Fritjof. *The Tao of Physics*. London: Flamingo, 1991. Page 153 ff.

[64] Wheeler, John Archibald. *Complexity, Entropy, and the Physics of Information*. Redwood City, California: Addison-Wesley, 1990 (as cited in Capra, op. cit.)

[65] James, William. Cited in Fuller, op. cit. Page 75

[66] Ibid. Page 76

[67] Fuller, Robert C. *Spiritual but not Religious: Understanding Unchurched America*. Oxford University Press, 2001. Page 8

[68] Capra, Fritjof. *The Turning Point*. London: Flamingo, 1985. Page 66

[69] Capra, Fritjof. *The Tao of Physics*. London: Flamingo,1991. Page 141 ff

[70] Capra, Fritjof. *The Turning Point*. London: Flamingo, 1985. Page 77

[71] Capra, Fritjof. *The Tao of Physics*. London: Flamingo,1991. Page 11

[72] Sue Knight's blog is on *http://arjendu.wordpress.com*

[73] Adams, Hervey. Op. cit. Page 127

[74] Ibid. Page 121

[75] Ortega y Gasset, Jose. Essay: 'The Barbarism of Specialization'. Chapter 12, *The Revolt of the Masses*. New York: WW Norton, 1993. Page 107

[76] McLaren, Peter L., & Lankshear, Colin, editors. *The Politics of Liberation: Paths from Freire*. London: Routledge/ Taylor & Francis *e-Library*, 2003. Preface by Donaldo Macedo

[77] Rowland, Christopher. Essay: 'William Blake: a Visionary for our Time.' 2007. *www.openDemocracy.net*

[78] McLaren. Op cit.

[79] Thich Nhat Hanh,. Op cit.

Bibliography

Adams, Hervey. *The Adventure of Looking*. London: G. Bell & Sons, Ltd, 1940

Ang, Tom. Digital *Photographer's Handbook*. London: Dorling Kindersley, 2002

Ang, Tom. *Fundamentals of Modern Photography*. London: Mitchell Beazley, 2008

Berger, John. *Ways of Seeing*. London: Penguin & BBC, 1982

Blackwell, Lewis. *The Life and Love of Trees*. San Francisco: PQ Blackwell; Chronicle Books, 2009

Bradley, Ian. *The Celtic Way*. London: Darton, Longman & Todd, 1993

Capra, Fritjof. *The Tao of Physics: An Exploration of the Parallels between Modern Physics and Eastern Mysticism*. London: Flamingo, 1991

Capra, Fritjof. *The Web of Life: A New Synthesis of Mind and Matter*. London: Flamingo, 1996

Capra, Steindl-Rast, & Matus. *Belonging to the Universe: New Thinkng about God & Nature*. London: Penguin, 1992

Carson, Rachel & Kelsh, Nick. *The Sense of Wonder*. New York: HarperCollins, 1998

Cumming, Robert, & Porter, Tom. *The Colour Eye*. London: BBC Books, 1990

Dalton, Stephen. *The Miracle of Flight*. Ontario: Firefly Books, 1999

Eastoe, Jane. *Hedgerow and Wildlife: Guide to Animals and Plants of the Hedgerow.* London: National Trust & Anova Books, 2008

Eisler, Riana. *The Real Wealth of Nations.* San Francisco: Berrett-Koehler, 2007

Fox, Matthew. *Original Blessing.* Santa Fe: Bear & Co, 1983

Fox, Matthew. *One River, Many Wells: Wisdom Springing from Global Faiths.* Dublin: Gill & Macmillan, 2001

Frankl, Viktor E. *Man's Search for Meaning.* London: Rider, 2004

Fuller, Robert C. *Wonder: From Emotion to Spirituality.* Chapel Hill: University of North Carolina Press, 2006

Harman, Doug. *The Digital Photography Handbook.* London: Quercus Publishing, 2010

Hedgecoe, John. *The Art of Digital Photography.* London: Dorling Kindersley, 2009.

Hickie, David, & Dwyer, Rosaleen B. *Irish Hedgerows: Networks for Nature.* Dublin: Networks for Nature, 2004

Hoole Gavin, & Smith, Cheryl. *Digital Photography for Absolute Beginners of All Ages.* London: New Holland, 2006

Hume, Rob. *Observer Book of Birds.* London: Penguin, 1992.

Johnson, Owen & Moore, David. *Collins Tree Guide.* London: HarperCollins, 2009

Kabat-Zinn, Jon. *Arriving at Your Own Door: 108 Lessons in Mindfulness..* London: Piatkus Books, 2008

Kabat-Zinn, Jon. *Wherever You Go, There You Are: Meditations for Everyday Life.* London: Piatkus Books, 2004

Kabat-Zinn, Jon. *Full Catastrophe Living: How to Cope with Stress, Pain and Illness using Mindfulness Meditation.* London: Piatkus Books, 2010

Kabat-Zinn, Jon. *Mindfulness for Beginners: Reclaiming the Present Moment – and Your Life.* Boulder, CO: Sounds True, 2012

Kilbracken, John. *The Easy Way to Tree Recognition.* London: Larousse, 1995

King, Julie Adair. *Digital Photography for Dummies.* IDG Books Worldwide

Kuhnke, Elizabeth. *Body Language for Dummies.* Chichester: John Wiley, 2007

Levine, Robert. *A Geography of Time.* New York: Basic Books, 1997

McLaren, Peter & Lankshear, Colin. *Politics of Liberation: Paths from Freire.* London: Routledge 1994; 2003

McLaren, Peter. *Life in Schools: An Introduction to Critical Pedagogy in the Foundations of Education.* New York: Allyn & Bacon, 2005

Morris, Desmond. *Peoplewatching.* London: Vintage/ Random House, 2002

Moynihan, Anselm, OP. *The Presence of God.* Dublin: Dominican Publications, 2001

O'Sullivan & Wilson. *Ireland's Garden Birds: How to Attract, Identify, & Care for Garden Birds.* Cork: Collins Press, 2008

Parker, Andrew. *Seven Deadly Colours: the Genius of Nature's Palette and how it Eluded Darwin.* London: Free Press, 2005

Pearsall, Paul. *Awe: the Delights and Dangers of our Eleventh Emotion.* Deerfield Beach: Health Communications Inc, 2007

Pretor-Pinney, Gavin. *The Cloudspotter's Guide.* London: Sceptre, 2006

Russell, Tony. *Nature Guide to Trees.* London: Dorling Kindersley, 2013

Sheldrake, Rupert. *The Presence of the Past.* London: HarperColllins, 1994.

Sterry, Paul. *Collins Complete Guide to British Birds.* London: HarperCollins, 2004

Sterry, Paul. *Collins Complete Guide to British Trees.* London: HarperCollins, 2008

Svensson, Mullarney Zetterström & Grant. *Collins Bird Guide.* London: HarperCollins

Taylor, Barbara Brown. *The Luminous Web.* Manham, Md: Rowman & Littlefield, 2000

Thich Nhat Hanh. *Peace Is Every Breath: A Practice for Our Busy Lives*. London: Rider/Ebury/Random House, 2011.

Thich Nhat Hanh. *Peace Is Every Step: The Path of Mindfulness in Everyday Life*. London: Rider/Ebury/Random House, 1995

Thich Nhat Hanh, *The Miracle of Mindfulness*. London: Rider/Ebury/Random House, 2008

Thich Nhat Hanh, *Good Citizens: Creating Enlightened Society*. Berkeley, Ca: Parallax Press, 2012

Thich Nhat Hanh, *Beyond the Self*. Berkeley, Ca: Parallax Press, 2010

Tolle, Eckhart. *The Power of Now: A Guide to Spiritual Enlightenment*. London: Hodder & Stoughton, 2005

Acknowledgements

This little book is about looking at the ordinary things of the world around us, but looking with wonder, so that we see for the first time how miraculous they really are. Thus we grow into Mindfulness. Yet it is inevitable that I must at times touch on things best understood by experts – be they scientists, artists, educators, medics, theologians, mathematicians, sociologists, critics. However I have been fortunate to be able at times to turn to experts in person, and at other times to access their writings when I could not meet them. Among those who have helped me immeasurably, in person or through their writings or artistic work, or simply through their insights, are my partner Catherine Thorne; my editor, Isobel Creed, of The Writers' Consultancy; Dr Jon Kabat-Zinn; *Dharmacharya* Thich Nhat Hanh; Fiona Clark-Echlin; Roger Marsh; Dr Dan Minchin; Pippa Newcomb; Paul Herriot; Prof Marie Parker-Jenkyns, Professor of Education at the University of Limerick; Eugene McDonough; Deidre McDonough; Dr Brendan Thornton; Dr Fritjof Capra; Gavin Pretor-Pinney; David Courtney; Gerard McGrath; Erin McGrath; my brother, Dermot Rice; Noellvie Watson, my sister; my engineer brothers-in-law Dr Christopher Bruce and Mike Watson; Tom McCarthy OP; the late Fergal O'Connor, OP; Thomas Ryan RHA, former president of the Royal Hibernian Academy; John Berger; Hong Kennedy-Bell; Matthew Fox; Dr Robert C. Fuller; Dr Paul Pearsall; the members of our Killaloe Writers' Group, who have patiently listened to bits of this book over months and years, and have given me such helpful feedback. And of course those long departed this life, whose writings have so inspired me – those whom I call 'the Four Masters of the Joy of Looking' – John Muir, William James, Rachel Carson and Hervey Adams. Indeed it was Hervey Adams's book, *The Adventure of Looking*, that changed my life at the age of seventeen. Indeed if it were still in print there might be no need for this present book.